Runaway Kids and Teenage Prostitution

America's Lost, Abandoned, and Sexually Exploited Children

R. BARRI FLOWERS

Contributions in Criminology and Penology, Number 54

GREENWOOD PRESS
Westport, Connecticut • London

Library of Congress Cataloging-in-Publication Data

Flowers, Ronald B.
Runaway kids and teenage prostitution : America's lost, abandoned, and sexually exploited children / R. Barri Flowers.
p. cm.—(Contributions in criminology and penology, ISSN 0732–4464 ; no. 54)
Includes bibliographical references and index.
ISBN 0–313–31492–6 (alk. paper)
1. Runaway teenagers—United States. 2. Teenage prostitution—United States.
I. Title. II. Series.
HV1431.F58 2001
362.74—dc21 00–069131

British Library Cataloging in Publication Data is available.

A paperback edition of *Runaway Kids and Teenage Prostitution* is available from Praeger Publishers, an imprint of Greenwood Publishing Group, Inc. (ISBN 0–275–97342–5).

Library of Congress Catalog Card Number: 00–069131
ISBN: 0–313–31492–6
ISSN: 0732–4464

First published in 2001

Greenwood Press, 88 Post Road West, Westport, CT 06881
An imprint of Greenwood Publishing Group, Inc.
www.greenwood.com

Printed in the United States of America

The paper used in this book complies with the Permanent Paper Standard issued by the National Information Standards Organization (Z39.48–1984).

10 9 8 7 6 5 4 3 2 1

Runaway Kids and Teenage Prostitution

Recent Titles in
Contributions in Criminology and Penology

In Defense of Prisons
Richard A. Wright

Police in Contradiction: The Evolution of the Police Function in Society
Cyril D. Robinson, Richard Scaglion, with J. Michael Olivero

Drug Abuse Treatment: The Implementation of Innovative Approaches
Bennett W. Fletcher, James A. Inciardi, and Arthur M. Horton

State Police in the United States: A Socio-Historical Analysis
H. Kenneth Bechtel

Academic Politics and the History of Criminal Justice Education
Frank Morn

Crime History and Histories of Crime: Studies in the Historiography of Crime and Criminal Justice in Modern History
Clive Emsley and Louis A. Knafla, editors

The Effectiveness of Innovative Approaches in the Treatment of Drug Abuse
Frank M. Tims, James A. Inciardi, Bennett W. Fletcher, and Arthur MacNeill Horton, Jr., editors

Tradition of the Law and Law of the Tradition: Law, State, and Social Control in China
Xin Ren

Evaluating Criminology and Criminal Justice
Ellen G. Cohn, David P. Farrington, and Richard A. Wright

Shakespeare's Criminals: Criminology, Fiction, and Drama
Victoria M. Time

Crime and Social Control in a Changing China
Jianhong Liu, Lening Zhang, and Steven F. Messner, editors

To the one who keeps the sun shining in my life and times even during rainy days. Love you, S.S.

And to those dedicated to preventing child abuse and getting runaway and prostituted youth off the streets and into a safe, responsible environment.

Contents

Figures and Tables

FIGURES

TABLES

Preface

At the dawn of the twenty-first century, we are confronted with a number of serious social issues that have carried over from the past century. One of these relates to the growing phenomenon of runaway prostitution involved children and the implications. Each year in the United States, as many as 2 million children leave home for whereabouts unknown by the parents or caretakers. Tens of thousands of other children are pushed out of the house or abandoned by parents or guardians. These caretakers may be aware of where these youths are located, but do not want to find them and bring them back home. This only exacerbates the problem of homeless street kids who must not only search for survival but also search for love in all the wrong places. However, not all runaways leave home due to intolerable conditions or family dysfunction. Some find they prefer to be on their own for various reasons including independence, sex, problems at school, rebellion, drug addiction, and adventure. Rarely do they find a better life away from home.

The correlation between running away from home and harsh street life such as exposure to prostitution, substance abuse, AIDS, sexually transmitted diseases, violence, criminality, and victimization has been well documented, as have findings that many children who run away from home were victims of child sexual abuse, neglect, family violence, broken homes, impoverishment, mental illness, and other familial and personal conflicts. Given the convergence of past, present, and future abuses and traumas the runaway is typically exposed to, it is obvious that most are caught up in a horrible cycle for which there seems no escape. Of course, there is a way out, but only if we as a society come to better understand how and why children leave home in the first place, and how their needs can most effectively be addressed and acted upon.

Runaway Kids and Teenage Prostitution: America's Lost, Abandoned, and Sexually Exploited Children was written to shed greater light on the dual problem of running from home or institutional care and teen prostitution, which often emerges as a consequence. Through comprehensive examination of this correlation, the book's goal is to add new perspectives to the body of literature on the subject. It is written for undergraduate and graduate level studies in the areas of criminology, child abuse and neglect, child sexual abuse and exploitation, juvenile delinquency, criminal justice, psychology, social science, social work, sociology, law, and related disciplines. Further, it is intended for reading and education by academians, social scientists, psychologists, medical personnel, law enforcement, legislators, and the layperson with an interest in the plight of runaway youth and teen prostitution.

I would like to thank Greenwood Publishing Group for recognizing the importance of publishing this book as a contribution to studies in criminology and sociology, adding to my previous Greenwood titles.

In conclusion, I am forever indebted to my longtime assistant, best friend, kindred spirit, and soul mate, H. Loraine, for her tireless work on my behalf in helping to bring this project and others to fruition.

Introduction

Runaway youth have become, if not an epidemic, a major concern in American society in the 2000s. Since the 1970s, much attention has been shed on the issue of homeless and sexually exploited street kids through public outcry, the media, and legislative and social policy initiatives. According to the National Center for Missing or Exploited Children, there are at least 1 million children who are classified as "missing" in the United States annually. Of these, more than half are runaways from home or institutional care or children who have been thrown away or abandoned by parents or caretakers. Although most runaways eventually return home, there are still hundreds of thousands who end up permanently living on the streets each year. Many of these kids have been sexually, physically, or emotionally abused or neglected at home; have problems with substance abuse, school attendance, or mental disorders; or are otherwise seriously disadvantaged in their displacement to street life.

Runaway children typically encounter a number of troubling situations when away from home for an extended time, beginning with the lack of food, shelter, and other basic necessities. Most must turn to prostitution or other forms of sexual exploitation just to survive and, in many cases, become addicted to or abuse drugs and alcohol. The risks of HIV infection, sexually transmitted diseases, sexual assaults, and other forms of victimization are high among runaway teens caught at the crossroads of high-risk activities and dangerous street life. Many of these runaways graduate into drug dealing, petty theft, and violent criminal activities in order to support drug habits and make ends meet.

Runaway Kids and Teenage Prostitution will explore the correlation between runaways and prostitution and its implications for children and society. Part I will examine the dynamics of running away. This includes the scope and characteristics of runaway youth; the extent and dimensions of throwaway kids; runaways, arrest, and police contact; why teens run away; the perils of running away from home for many teenagers; theories on delinquency and prostitution; and responding to the issues of runaway and prostitution engaged youth.

Part II will study the dynamics of teenage prostitution. This includes the nature of teenage prostitution; teen prostitutes, arrest, and the criminal justice system; girl prostitution; the pimp's role in teen prostitution; and boy prostitution.

Part III will study correlates of runaways and teenage prostitution, including child sexual abuse, child pornography, and child sex rings.

Part IV will address laws related to runaways, child prostitution, and child sexual exploitation.

Part V will explore the problem of runaways and teenage prostitution in other countries.

Tables and figures are incorporated in the text to supplement the reading where relevant.

This examination of the multifaceted dimensions and characteristics of runaways and prostitution involved teens should give weight to its significance as one of the more tragic issues of our time that needs to be further addressed and resolved.

Part I

The Dynamics of Running Away

Chapter 1

The Scope of Runaway Youth

Each year untold numbers of teenagers run away from home in the United States. Most have been victims of child physical or sexual abuse, neglect, or other forms of familial dysfunction, stress, or trauma. Some have been literally forced out of their homes and onto the streets. Others have run away from juvenile facilities, shelters, or other types of accommodations. What these teens have in common is they usually live on the streets and their lives are typically fraught with high-risk activities, exposures, and hazards at every turn. These include prostitution, substance abuse, AIDS, and death. Many will never find their way back home.

WHAT IS A RUNAWAY?

Typically a runaway is defined as a person under the age of eighteen who voluntarily leaves home or another residence, and thereby the custody and control of parents or guardians. Some of these runaways are, in fact, throwaways—children who have been forced by parents or guardians to leave home or are not actively sought after (see Chapter 2). Definitions of what constitutes a runaway youth are not always clear or uniform. They are often dependent upon the duration of time absent from the home, the nature of the running way, and parental knowledge of the missing youth's whereabouts, among other criteria.

According to the Office of Juvenile Justice and Delinquency Prevention (OJJDP), a runaway is a "child/youth who has left (or not returned to) a parent's or caretaker's supervision without permission." A subset of these young people are throwaway children/youth who have been forced to leave their parents' or guardians' homes or are not allowed to return.[1] The

OJJDP further defines the runaway as a subgroup of missing persons under the age of eighteen who have been reported as such to local law enforcement agencies.[2]

In the U.S. Department of Justice's *Juvenile Offenders and Victims: 1999 National Report*, the runaway is defined as "a child who left home without permission and stayed away at least overnight or who was already away and refused to return home."[3]

Runaways are also defined in legal terms. Running away from home or institutional care is considered a status offense applicable only to minors (usually age seventeen and under). The Department of Justice's Uniform Crime Reporting Program defines arrests of runaways as "juveniles taken into protective custody under provisions of local statutes."[4]

C. J. English broke runaways into four types, based on the commitment to stay away from home and the circumstances involved in running away, as follows:

- *Floaters*—youth who leave home for a short time, usually returning after things "cool off."
- *Runaways*—youth who stay away from home for a long period of time (often weeks or months), often due to an unstable family environment or a serious personal problem.
- *Splitters*—youth who are pleasure seekers and also seek to gain status among their peer group.
- *Hard-Rock Freaks*—youth who leave home permanently having chosen a life on their own, often due to severe family troubles.[5]

These types can overlap, depending upon the runaway, circumstances of leaving home, and experiences away from home. An example of such can be seen in the following account of a runaway youth:

> With only a Swiss Army knife and the clothes on his back, 14-year-old Jascha Ephraim made a . . . "spur of the moment" decision—a hasty, impulsive beginning to the days of "total debauchery and mayhem" that would follow. Fueled by a flare for rebellion, Ephraim, a freshman at the time, decided to run away from home in the fleeting moments before an Amtrak train would begin its journey to New York City, more than 200 miles away.
>
> "I had to make a conscious effort to put low the concerns of friends and family to do it," [he recalled]. "That sounds very selfish, but I wouldn't have been able to do it otherwise." Ephraim maintains that certain disagreements between him and his parents provoked him to run away. [He] was not allowed to attend a four day party in New York because his parents felt that the group associated with the party

> was involved with various illegal drugs. However, Ephraim . . . decided to hop onto [the] Amtrak train to New York despite [his] parents' wishes.[6]

Perhaps the most comprehensive definition of runaways was established by the National Incidence Studies report, *Missing, Abducted, Runaway, and Thrownaway Children in America* (NISMART).[7] It identified three types of "runaway phenomena," defining runaways as (1) Broad Scope Runaways, (2) Policy Focal Runaways, and (3) Runaway Gestures.

Broad Scope Runaways are defined as juveniles who leave or stay away from home without permission for at least one night.[8] An exception to this is teenagers age fifteen or older who have permission to be out, but do not return home at the agreed-upon time. This reflects typical patterns of older teens who violate curfews when out on dates or at parties. Two nights away from home are necessary for these teens to be considered Broad Scope Runaways.

Policy Focal Runaways are defined as minors who, along with fitting the broad scope definition of runaways, are also endangered due to not having a familiar, safe place to stay.[9] An example of a Policy Focal Runaway is a youth who leaves home and spends some time on the street, in a car, or a shelter. Police and policymakers are most concerned about this high-risk category of runaways.

Runaway Gestures are defined as children who leave home for only a matter of hours, but do not stay away overnight. This also refers to runaways who leave a "runaway note." Runaway Gestures include some older teens whose overnight stay without permission was not considered a serious concern. Though runaway youth in this category are seen as indicative of family problems, they are not included in national figures on the incidence of runaways.[10]

According to the National Runaway Switchboard (NRS), many runaways are away from home for only a short while, but still long enough to be considered a runaway by family if not law enforcement authorities. It estimated that 40 percent of teens who leave home remain away for anywhere from one to three days.[11] However, the NRS found that more than half of runaway youth believed that their home crisis could not be resolved by social service agencies.

The NISMART report differentiated non-household runaways from runaways from household settings. Non-household runaways refer to children who ran away from juvenile facilities such as detention centers, summer camps, group foster homes, boarding schools, hospitals, and mental health institutions.[12] This type of runaway can be seen in the following recent report from the *San Diego Union-Tribune*:

> Six girls and one boy jumped a wall at the Polinsky Children's Center yesterday afternoon. . . . The seven youths, whose ages range from 11

to 17, bolted at 2:45 P.M. after school let out at the county-run center in Kearny Mesa. . . . The center is the county's home for children who are homeless, neglected, abandoned, or abused. . . . Children ran away from the center 185 times last year, with many of the incidents involving the same group of kids, officials said. . . . All but one [of the runaway youth] was located within the hour.[13]

THE INCIDENCE OF RUNAWAY YOUTH

It is virtually impossible to know precisely how many runaways there are at any given time in this country. Estimates range from hundreds of thousands to as many as 2 million children who run away from home annually.[14] A child runs or is thrown away from home every twenty-six seconds in the United States.[15] A national survey found that more than half a million families were affected by children running away every year.[16] A recent report estimated that more than half of runaways had run away from home at least three times.[17] Approximately 300,000 runaways are believed to be "hard core" street kids who run away repeatedly.[18]

The NISMART estimated that there are 446,700 Broad Scope Runaways from households each year in the United States.[19] Of these, 129,500 are Policy Focal Runaways, or runaways without a secure, familiar place to stay outside of the household. An estimated 12,800 youths run away from juvenile facilities annually.[20] Many of these also ran away from households during the same year. Approximately 4,000 children run away from juvenile facilities only. The report estimated that there are 450,700 total Broad Scope Runaways every year. Additionally, some 173,700 children are defined as Runaway Gestures annually.[21]

Other pertinent details on the nature of runaways from households based on NISMART surveys include the following:

- One in ten Broad Scope Runaways travel a distance of more than 100 miles from home.
- Three in ten runaways travel eleven to fifty miles from home.
- Seven percent of runaways from households leave the state.
- More than one in four runaways stay away from home overnight, though for twenty-four hours or less.
- Nearly one in four runaways are gone for one to two days.
- One in ten runaways never return home.
- More than one in three runaways run away more than once over a twelve-month period.
- Six in ten Broad Scope Runaways initially go to a friend's house.
- Eight in ten runaways run to a friend's house at any time.

- More than one in ten runaways are without a place to sleep any night.
- Only 2 percent of runaways go to runaway shelters.
- Nearly eight in ten runaways are accompanied by others.
- One-third of runaways were involved in an argument prior to leaving home.
- Nearly seven in ten children run away during a weekday.
- Almost four in ten caretakers know the whereabouts of the runaway youth most of the time.
- More than one in four caretakers do not know the whereabouts of runaways.[22]

Additional NISMART findings on the nature of juvenile facility runaway episodes are as follows:

- Nearly four in ten runaways travel between fifty and ninety-nine miles from home.
- Almost half the runaways leave the state.
- Juvenile facility runaways are most likely to run away from group foster homes, mental health facilities, and residential treatment centers.
- About four in ten ran away more than once from the same facility within the previous twelve months.
- Nearly half the runaways' initial destination is a friend's house.
- More than nine in ten juvenile facility runaways are found or return.
- In nearly half the runaway cases, the institution does not know the whereabouts of the juvenile facility runaway.
- Almost half the runaways are in the company of others when running away.
- Three in ten runaways are absent for twenty-four hours or less.
- Approximately 30 percent of runaways are missing for three to six days.
- Eight percent of juvenile facility runaways remain absent.[23]

A recent example of juvenile facility runaways occurred at a wilderness camp for troubled teens. Eight youths, ages fourteen to seventeen, ran away after overpowering counselors. They remained on the run for four days.[24]

Self-report studies can also yield important data on the incidence of runaways. After interviewing a nationally representative group of youths age twelve to sixteen, the 1997 National Longitudinal Survey of Youth (NLSY97) reported that more than one in ten youths had ever run away from home.[25]

Arrest statistics further illustrate the problem of runaways. Approximately 117,000 juveniles were arrested as runaways in the United States in 1998.[26] (See Chapter 3 for greater detail on runaway arrests.)

CHARACTERIZING THE RUNAWAY

Sex of Runaways

Girls are more likely to run away from home than boys, according to studies, surveys, and arrest data. The OJJDP reported that 58 percent of runaways were female, while 42 percent were male.[27] Similarly, around 60 percent of the juveniles arrested for running away are female.[28] Other studies have steadily supported this contention, finding that there are approximately six girl runaways for every four boy runaways.[29] The numbers are closer among juvenile facility runaways, with an estimated 53 percent of the runaways female, compared to 47 percent male.[30] The NLSY97 found that 11 percent of the girl respondents had ever run away from home compared to 10 percent of the boy respondents.[31]

Female runaways are disproportionate relative to their population figures in the United States. Sociologists believe the disparity between female and male runaways may be the result of greater tendency by female teenagers to look for help in dealing with problems than a greater inclination to run away, per se.[32] There is also an indication that the higher numbers of runaway girls may be a reflection of a general increase in delinquent behavior among girls.[33]

A typical girl runaway is illustrated by "Honey," a sixteen-year-old chronic runaway who has left an abusive, unstable home on a number of occasions, only to return:

> "She's thrown me up against walls," [Honey says of her mother,] "and once she threw me up against the radiator when it was on. I never hit her back. She doesn't know how to deal with her feelings, and she has low self-esteem. I just took it because that's the way it was supposed to be."
>
> Many San Diego area runaway girls Honey's age leave home because of conflicts with their mothers and stay away for days or weeks at a time before returning. . . . Honey says the counselors didn't offer constructive solutions. But she partly blames herself for the troubles she and her mother have had. "I didn't know who was boss," [she] says.[34]

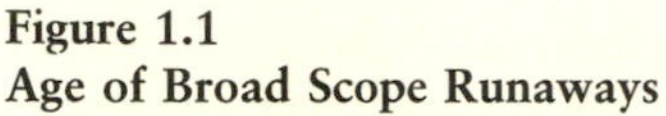

Figure 1.1
Age of Broad Scope Runaways

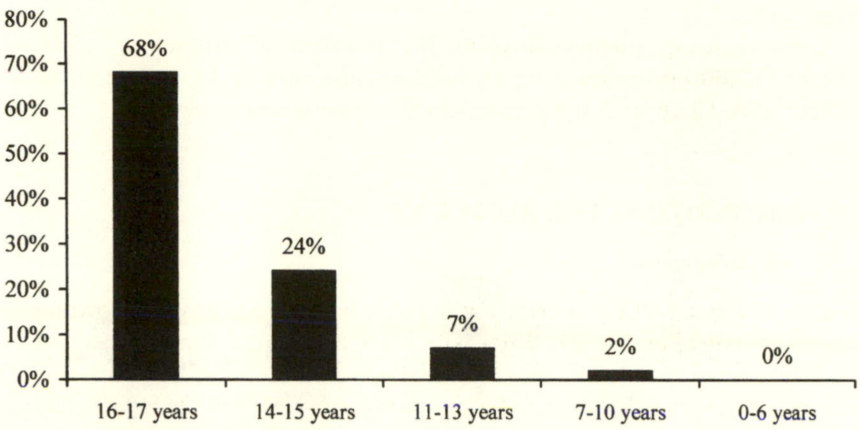

Note: Percentages do not equal 100 due to rounding.
Source: Derived from U.S. Department of Justice, Office of Juvenile Justice and Delinquency Prevention, *Missing, Abducted, Runaway, and Thrownaway Children in America, First Report: Numbers and Characteristics, National Incidence Studies* (Washington, D.C.: Government Printing Office, 1990), p. 107.

Age of Runaways

The majority of runaway youth are teenagers. Eighty-six percent of runaways are between fourteen and seventeen years of age, as reported by the NRS.[35] Older teens tend to run away much more often than younger teens. According to the NISMART, sixteen- and seventeen-year-olds account for more than two-thirds of Broad Scope runaway children, with nearly another one-fourth fourteen to fifteen years of age (see Figure 1.1). Other studies have yielded similar results.[36] The NLSY97 reported that 17 percent of the sixteen-year-old respondents had ever run away, compared to 12 percent of those age fourteen to fifteen, and 6 percent age twelve to thirteen.[37]

The National Incidence Studies found that more than half the runaways from juvenile facilities are age sixteen and seventeen, while more than 40 percent are between fourteen and fifteen years old.[38] These figures show less older runaways and more younger ones in comparison to runaways from households.

When examining age and sex of runaways, studies have indicated that this tends to vary depending upon the age, sex, and motivation for running away. In J. A. Betchel's study, females were found to run away more often than males in general, while thirteen- to fourteen-year-olds constituted more than one-third of total runaways.[39] However, for runaways age four-

Figure 1.2
Race and Ethnicity of Broad Scope Runaways

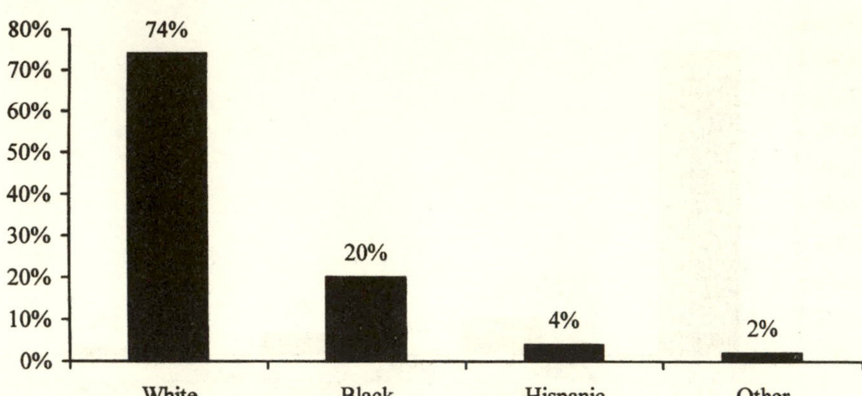

Source: Derived from U.S. Department of Justice, Office of Juvenile Justice and Delinquency Prevention, *Missing, Abducted, Runaway, and Thrownaway Children in America, First Report: Numbers and Characteristics, National Incidence Studies* (Washington, D.C.: Government Printing Office, 1990), p. 109.

teen and under, males ran away at a higher rate than females. Starting at age fifteen, female runaways outnumbered male runaways with the actual numbers for both sexes decreasing with age. This is attributed to parents loosening restrictions as the child gets older.

Younger runaways have been characterized as junior adventurers in search of action of some kind, whereas older runaways are seen as seeking to establish themselves as grownups. The greater number of female runaways age thirteen and up reflects their greater tendency to "look for action" during those years, prompting them to leave home.[40] Also many older female teens tend to run away due to more severe problems in the home—such as sexual abuse—than older male teens.[41]

Race and Ethnicity of Runaways

The vast majority of runaways are white, non-Hispanic youths. The NISMART reveals that nearly three out of every four Broad Scope Runaways in the United States are white (see Figure 1.2). Blacks constitute approximately two in every ten runaways. About 4 percent of runaways are Hispanic, and 2 percent other races. White and black runaways are over represented in relation to their overall population figures.[42] In terms of having ever run away, slightly more non-whites (11 percent) than whites (10 percent) ran away from home, according to self-report findings.[43]

The percentage of white runaways is even higher among juvenile facility runaways (see Figure 1.3). More than eight out of every ten children who

Figure 1.3
Race and Ethnicity of Juvenile Facility Runaways

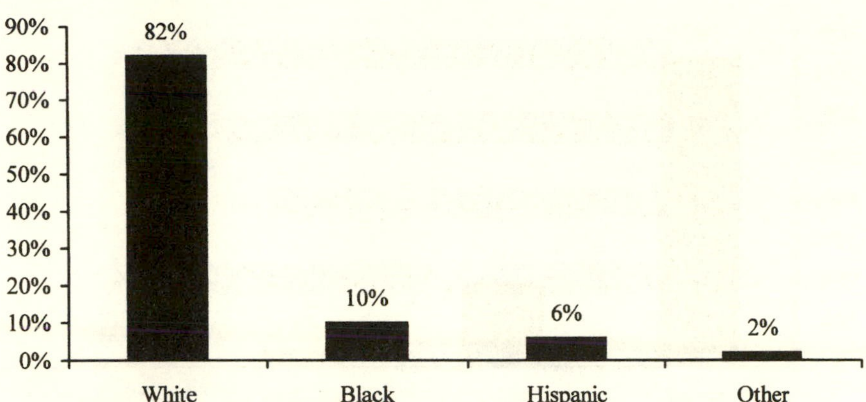

Source: Derived from U.S. Department of Justice, Office of Juvenile Justice and Delinquency Prevention, *Missing, Abducted, Runaway, and Thrownaway Children in America, First Report: Numbers and Characteristics, National Incidence Studies* (Washington, D.C.: Government Printing Office, 1990), p. 124.

run away from juvenile facilities are white, compared to just one in ten black. Hispanic youths are more likely to run away from juvenile facilities than households, while the rate of running away for other races and ethnic minorities is roughly equal for household and juvenile facility runaways.

With respect to runaway and homeless girls—who constituted the greater percentage of runaway youth—it is estimated that 70 percent are white, 20 percent black, and 10 percent Hispanic or other racial or ethnic groups.[44] The following narrative of a white female teenage runaway shows sexual exploitation and perils typically experienced away from home:

> I was homeless and staying with a friend. While I was there, I met a woman who seemed really nice. She said she knew a way I could make a lot of money. She owned an escort service. After I turned two tricks, I decided that I couldn't do it anymore. I told my female pimp I wanted to stop. She held a gun to my head and threatened to hurt me if I stopped.[45]

Socioeconomics and Runaways

Socioeconomics play an important role in the familial characteristics of the runaway, though findings on social class and runaways have been inconsistent. Most research indicates that there is a strong correlation between runaways and poverty. According to the Family and Youth Services Bureau (FYSB), an estimated 40 percent of runaway youth in shelters and

Figure 1.4
Household Income and Broad Scope Runaways

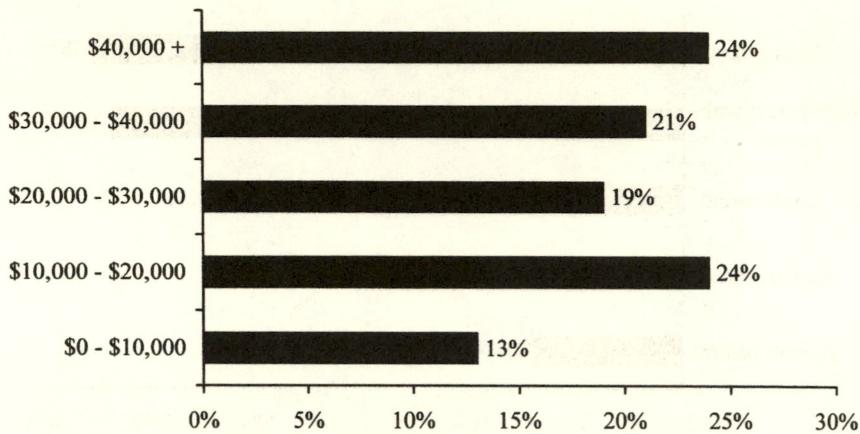

Note: Percentages do not total 100 due to rounding.
Source: Derived from U.S. Department of Justice, Office of Juvenile Justice and Delinquency Prevention, *Missing, Abducted, Runaway, and Thrownaway Children in America, First Report: Numbers and Characteristics, National Incidence Studies* (Washington, D.C.: Government Printing Office, 1990), p. 109.

homeless came from families receiving public assistance.[46] This is nearly twice the percent of youth in poverty in the population at large, as reported by the U.S. Census Bureau.[47] In Louise Homer's study of runaway girls, most were from the lower and lower middle classes, with 70 percent of the families living on welfare.[48]

Other studies indicate that runaways are more likely to come from middle-class families than lower-class ones. James Hildebrand found that the "vast majority" of the runaways in his study were from the middle class.[49] Similarly, in Robert Shellow's study of suburban runaways, over half were middle-class and working-class teens.[50] Fifteen percent of the runaways ran from upper-middle-class families.

The NISMART findings suggest that there is no significant relationship between running away and income. As shown in Figure 1.4, the household income of Broad Scope Runaways tends to be more middle and upper class than lower class. Only 13 percent of the runaways come from families with an income of $10,000 or less, and 24 percent with a household income of $10,000 to $20,000. This compares to 24 percent of runaways who come from families with a household income of $40,000 or more, and 40 percent with family incomes between $20,000 and $40,000. These figures are fairly proportionate relative to income levels in the general population.[51] Other studies support the relative distribution of runaway youth across income levels.[52]

Figure 1.5
Family Structure of Broad Scope Runaways

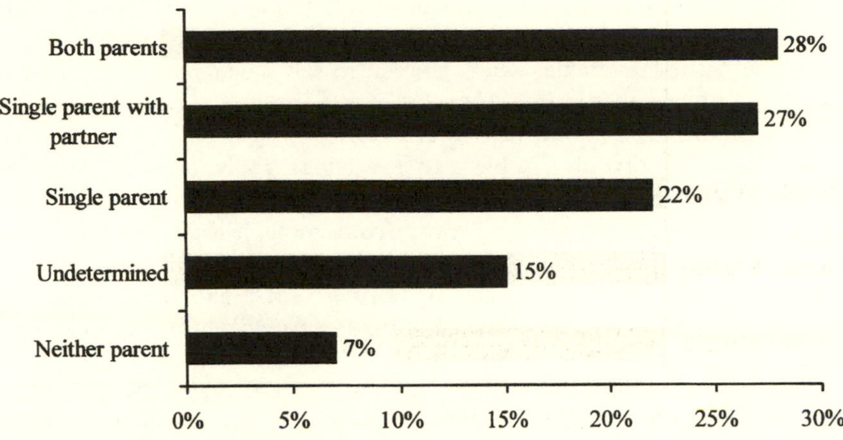

Note: Percentages do not total 100 due to rounding.
Source: Derived from U.S. Department of Justice, Office of Juvenile Justice and Delinquency Prevention, *Missing, Abducted, Runaway, and Thrownaway Children in America, First Report: Numbers and Characteristics, National Incidence Studies* (Washington, D.C.: Government Printing Office, 1990), p. 108.

Family Structure and Runaways

Most runaways run from broken homes, where at least one parent is absent. Only 28 percent of the Broad Scope Runaways studied by NISMART lived with both parents (natural or adoptive) at the time of departure (see Figure 1.5). This compares to nearly 50 percent of runaways who lived with a single parent with no partner or a single parent with a partner. Seven percent of the runaways left homes where neither parent was present, while for 15 percent of the runaways, the nature of their family structure was undetermined.

Studies indicate that children are less likely to run away from households with both natural or adoptive parents present.[53] Running away from home is disproportionately more likely in families with stepparents or live-in partners.[54]

Runaways from juvenile facilities tend to most often come from homes with a single parent or one natural parent and partner before their institutional stay. More than half the runaways in the NISMART studies fit into this category.[55] Only slightly more than one-quarter of the runaways had both parents present in the household before they were institutionalized.

SUMMARY

Runaway refers to children who have left home or a juvenile facility voluntarily. Every year as many as 2 million youths in the United States run away. Most are female, white, sixteen to seventeen years old, and ran away from homes absent at least one parent. Family income level does not appear significantly relevant for children who run away. Legally, the runaway is a status offender, subject to laws that apply only to juveniles. Runaway children from households are broken down into three categories: Broad Scope Runaways who stay away from home at least overnight, Policy Focal Runaways without a secure place to stay, and Runaway Gestures who leave home for only a matter of hours. Nearly half of all runaways return home within two days. Most end up at a friend's house upon leaving home.

Runaways from juvenile facilities are most often white, female, older teens from broken homes. Most run away from group foster homes and residential treatment centers. Nearly half the runaways leave the state, and around 40 percent ran away from the juvenile facility at least once before.

NOTES

1. U.S. Department of Justice, Office of Juvenile Justice and Delinquency Prevention, *Law Enforcement Policies and Practices Regarding Missing Children and Homeless Youth: Research Project* (Washington, D.C.: Government Printing Office, 1993), p. 3.
2. Ibid.
3. U.S. Department of Justice, Office of Juvenile Justice and Delinquency Prevention, *Juvenile Offenders and Victims: 1999 National Report* (Washington, D.C.: Government Printing Office, 1999), p. 38.
4. U.S. Department of Justice, Federal Bureau of Investigation, *Crime in the United States: Uniform Crime Reports 1998* (Washington, D.C.: Government Printing Office, 1999), p. 403.
5. C. J. English, "Leaving Home: A Typology of Runaways," *Society* 10 (1973): 22–24.
6. Lindsay Crawford, "Troubled Teens Take to the Streets: Rebellious Youths with Nowhere to Run Away from Their Problems and Their Homes," *Silver Chips Online* (April 13, 2000), p. 1.
7. U.S. Department of Justice, Office of Juvenile Justice and Delinquency Prevention, *Missing, Abducted, Runaway, and Thrownaway Children in America, First Report: Numbers and Characteristics, National Incidence Studies* (Washington, D.C.: Government Printing Office, 1990).
8. Ibid., p. 98.
9. Ibid., pp. 98–99.
10. Ibid.
11. Ibid.
12. Ibid., pp. 121–22.

13. Caitlin Rother, "7 More Youths Flee from County Children's Centre," *San Diego Union-Tribune* (February 18, 1998), p. B1.

14. *Missing, Abducted, Runaway, and Thrownaway Children*, p. 98; R. Barri Flowers, *The Victimization and Exploitation of Women and Children: A Study of Physical, Mental and Sexual Maltreatment in the United States* (Jefferson, N.C.: McFarland, 1994), p. 36; R. Barri Flowers, *The Prostitution of Women and Girls* (Jefferson, N.C.: McFarland, 1998), p. 89.

15. Crawford, "Troubled Teens Take to the Streets," p. 1.

16. Tim Brennan, *The Social Psychology of Runaways* (Toronto: Lexington Books, 1978), p. 5.

17. Cited in Flowers, *The Victimization and Exploitation of Women and Children*, p. 36.

18. Patricia Hersch, "Coming of Age on City Streets," *Psychology Today* (January 1998), p. 34.

19. *Missing, Abducted, Runaway, and Thrownaway Children*, p. 103.

20. Ibid.

21. Ibid. Runaway Gestures are not included in figures for Broad Scope and Policy Focal Runaways.

22. Ibid., pp. 107–18.

23. Ibid., pp. 121–28.

24. Cited by the Associated Press news report (January 12, 2000).

25. *Juvenile Offenders and Victims*, p. 58.

26. *Uniform Crime Reports 1998*, p. 220.

27. *Juvenile Offenders and Victims*, p. 38.

28. *Uniform Crime Reports 1998*, p. 227.

29. Flowers, *The Victimization and Exploitation of Women and Children*, p. 37; S. Jorgenson, H. Thornburg, and J. Williams, "The Experience of Running Away: Perceptions of Adolescents Seeking Help in a Shelter Case Facility," *High School Journal* 12 (1980): 87–96.

30. *Missing, Abducted, Runaway, and Thrownaway Children*, p. 123.

31. *Juvenile Offenders and Victims*, p. 58.

32. R. C. Kessler, R. L. Brown, and C. L. Broman, "Sex Differences in Psychiatric Help-Seeking: Evidence from Four Large-Scale Surveys," *Journal of Health and Social Behavior* 22 (1981): 49–64.

33. Freda Adler, *The Incidence of Female Criminology in the Contemporary World* (New York: New York University Press, 1981); R. Barri Flowers, *The Adolescent Criminal: An Examination of Today's Juvenile Offender* (Jefferson, N.C.: McFarland, 1990), pp. 16–17.

34. Gil Griffin, "Running on Empty: Kids Take to the Streets When They Don't Feel Loved at Home," *San Diego Union-Tribune* (July 26, 1997), p. E1.

35. Cited in Crawford, "Troubled Teens Take to the Streets," p. 1.

36. Flowers, *The Victimization and Exploitation of Women and Children*, pp. 37–38; Flowers, *The Adolescent Criminal*, pp. 49–50.

37. *Juvenile Offenders and Victims*, p. 58.

38. *Missing, Abducted, Runaway, and Thrownaway Children*, p. 123.

39. J. A. Betchel, "Statement before the Senate Subcommittee to Investigate Juvenile Delinquency," Washington, D.C., January 14, 1973.

40. R. Barri Flowers, *Children and Criminality: The Child as Victim and Perpetrator* (Westport, Conn.: Greenwood Press, 1986), p. 133.

41. Flowers, *The Victimization and Exploitation of Women and Children*, pp. 41–42.

42. *Missing, Abducted, Runaway, and Thrownaway Children*, p. 109.

43. *Juvenile Offenders and Victims*, p. 58.

44. Flowers, *The Prostitution of Women and Girls*, pp. 91–93.

45. Minnesota Attorney General's Office, *The Hofstede Committee Report: Juvenile Prostitution in Minnesota*, http://www.ag.state.mn.us/home/files/news/hofstede.htm, August 23, 2000, p. 6.

46. U.S. Department of Health and Human Services, Family Youth and Services Bureau, *Youth with Runaway, Throwaway, and Homeless Experiences: Prevalence, Drug Use, and Other At-Risk Behaviors* (Silver Springs, Md.: National Clearinghouse on Families & Youth, October 1995), p. 5.

47. Ibid.

48. Louise Homer, "Criminality Based Resource for Runaway Girls," *Social Casework* 10 (1973): 474.

49. James A. Hildebrand, "Why Runaways Leave Home," *Police Science* 54 (1963): 211–16.

50. Robert Shellow, "Suburban Runaways of the 60s," *Monographs of the Society for Research in Child Development* 32 (1967): 17.

51. *Missing, Abducted, Runaway, and Thrownaway Children*, p. 109.

52. R. Barri Flowers, *Female Crime, Criminals, and Cellmates: An Exploration of Female Criminality* (Jefferson, N.C.: McFarland, 1995), p. 144.

53. *Missing, Abducted, Runaway, and Thrownaway Children*, p. 108.

54. Ibid.

55. Ibid., p. 124.

Chapter 2

The Extent of Throwaway Kids

Along with traditional runaways, there are a growing number of missing children who are forced out of the home or unreported as missing by parents. Many struggle with sexual identity issues, rebellion, and other problems in the family, hastening their departure. These throwaway kids are showing up across America and, until recently, were bunched together with other runaways in most statistical and survey data. As a result, they have often become lost in the shuffle of the plight of runaways, misdiagnosed by authorities or others they come into contact with, and find themselves in circumstances they have little to no control over.

WHAT CONSTITUTES A THROWAWAY YOUTH?

Within the categories of missing children and runaway children falls a subclassification of homeless youth. These children—mostly teenagers—are often referred to as "throwaways," "thrownaways," "pushouts," "castouts," and "castaways." Unlike the runaway who leaves home of his or her own accord, the throwaway typically is put out of the house either directly or indirectly, usually against the child's wishes. In *Juvenile Offenders and Victims 1999 National Report*, throwaway children are divided into four types:

- Children who were directly told to leave home.
- Children whose parents or other caretakers refused to allow them to return home after being away.

- Children whose parents or guardians made no effort to recover them after the child ran away.
- Children who were abandoned or deserted.[1]

The National Incidence Study's *Missing, Abducted, Runaway, and Thrownaway Children in America* (NISMART) used the term "thrownaway" in describing this group of runaways, which "unambiguously conveys what has been done to the child."[2]

Thrownaways are further broken down as Broad Scope Thrownaways and Policy Focal Thrownaways as follows:

- *Broad Scope Thrownaways*—children thrown out of the household for at least overnight. They usually arrange to stay with a friend.
- *Policy Focal Thrownaways*—children thrown out of the home without a safe place to stay while absent.[3]

In both instances, the missing children are seen as thrownaways because of lack of parental supervision or custody.

The notion of throwaway children began in the 1970s as researchers and child welfare professionals recognized that many "runaways" did not voluntary leave home as the term implies, but rather were manipulated into leaving, compelled to leave due to intolerable conditions at home, or outright forced onto the street by parents or guardians. Other so-called missing children are abandoned by parents who either moved and left them behind or failed to report the child missing to authorities. These disturbing realities of a significant percentage of homeless youth made it necessary to include them in runaway studies, while distinguishing throwaway children from other missing children.

K. C. Brown sought to differentiate the throwaway from the runaway or other missing children, noting the particular susceptibility and vulnerability throwaways face as homeless youths. "These are the children most preyed upon and exploited, the children most likely to be lying in John and Jane Doe graves all over the United States, unidentified because no one has reported them missing."[4]

Teenage homosexuals are especially at risk to be thrownaways as "children whose parents or guardians evict them from their homes, most often because they are gay or lesbian . . . or otherwise considered . . . as just too much trouble to deal with."[5] A classic example of a thrownaway can be seen in the following excerpt from an article on homeless youth:

> Six years ago, Daniel left home. At age 12. His mom and dad . . . verbally abused him and his brother. Sometimes the ugly confrontations got physical. Daniel is gay, which he says his mother had a hard

time accepting. So . . . like thousands of children who feel unwanted, unloved and unsafe at home, [he] took his chances elsewhere, staying at friends' houses or sleeping on San Diego's streets. Daniel describes himself not as a runaway but as a "refugee fighting for his stability."[6]

THE INCIDENCE OF THROWAWAY CHILDREN

How many runaways or missing children are actually throwaways? Most experts agree that this category of runaway youth is mostly underreported and, therefore, hard to ascertain. A number of surveys of youth at runaway shelters have reported that throwaway children make up anywhere from 10 percent,[7] to one-third,[8] to as many as half the homes and street kids population.[9] The Youth Development Bureau estimated that 30 to 35 percent of the runaway children in the United States were actually thrown out of their homes.[10] Similarly, the National Network of Runaway and Youth Services estimated that 40 percent of the country's 1.5 million homeless youth were throwaways.[11]

In a study funded by the Family and Youth Services Bureau (FYSB)—*Youth with Runaway, Throwaway and Homeless Experiences: Prevalence, Drug Use, and Other At-Risk Behaviors*—the term "runaway" was described as misleading with respect to homeless youth. The study found that about half of those in shelters and on the streets had either been forced to leave the household by a caretaker or the caretaker did not care if they left home.[12] One study suggested that the difference between runaways and throwaways depended to a large degree on who returned home, finding that runaway children were more than twice as likely to return home as throwaways.[13] Carolyn Males and Julie Raskin noted that throwaway kids "crash" wherever they can, putting into perspective the difficulty in placing accurate figures on the magnitude of throwaways in this country.[14]

Perhaps the study most widely regarded on the number of throwaway children comes from the NISMART report (see Figure 2.1). It estimated that there are 127,100 Broad Scope Thrownaways annually in the United States. Among these, some 59,200 are Policy Focal Thrownaways without a secure, familiar environment (see also Chapter 1). Nearly 15,000 of the thrownaways each year are estimated to be the result of abandonment, or children "whose parents or caretakers had gone off and left them (rather than kicking them out)."[15]

The NISMART also cross-classified Broad Scope Thrownaways and Runaways, as shown in Figure 2.2. It estimated that there is a combined group of 513,400 runaways and thrownaways every year. Of these, 400,800 are runaways only, while 66,700 are thrownaways only, and 45,900 are classified as runaways and thrownaways.

The NISMART research also revealed the following characteristics on the nature of thrownaway incidents:

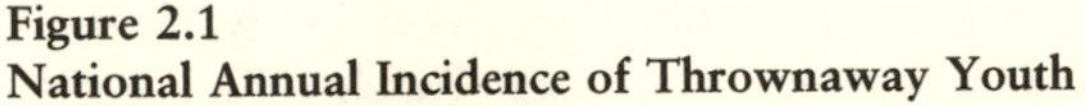

Figure 2.1
National Annual Incidence of Thrownaway Youth

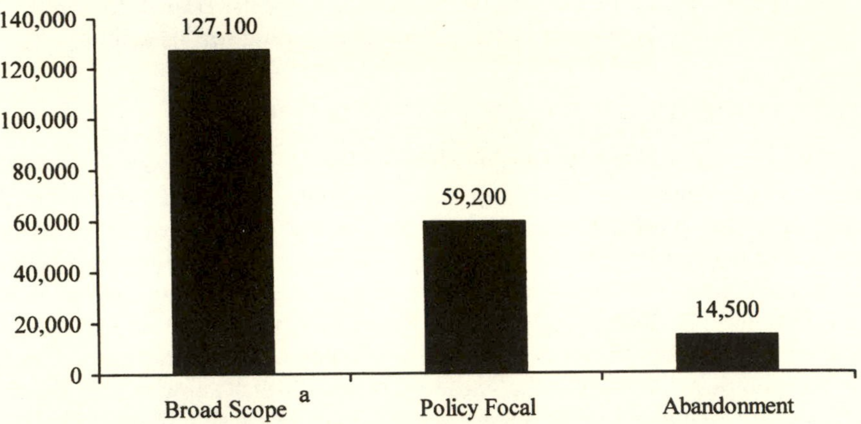

[a]The Broad Scope figures included the Policy Focal and Abandonment numbers.
Source: Derived from U.S. Department of Justice, Office of Juvenile Justice and Delinquency Prevention, *Missing, Abducted, Runaway, and Thrownaway Children in America, First Report: Numbers and Characteristics, National Incidence Studies* (Washington, D.C.: Government Printing Office, 1990), p. 141.

- More than eight in ten Broad Scope Thrownaways lived at home prior to being put out.
- Over four in ten thrownaways are asked to leave home.
- One in four run away and parents or caretakers don't care.
- Nearly three in ten run away and no effort is made by parents or guardians to recover them.
- More than one in five thrownaways are away from home one day or less.
- One in five are gone from home less than two weeks.
- One in five thrownaways never return home.
- More than half of thrownaway youth travel one to nine miles from home.
- Only 1 percent of thrownaways leave the state.
- Nearly half of abandonment cases occur in the West.
- Over three in ten cases of abandonment occur in the Northeast.
- Mothers are more likely to throw away children than fathers.
- Half of thrownaways are thrown away on weekdays.
- Nearly six in ten thrownaways had an argument prior to being pushed out of the home.

Figure 2.2
Cross-Classification of Broad Scope Runaway and Thrownaway Children

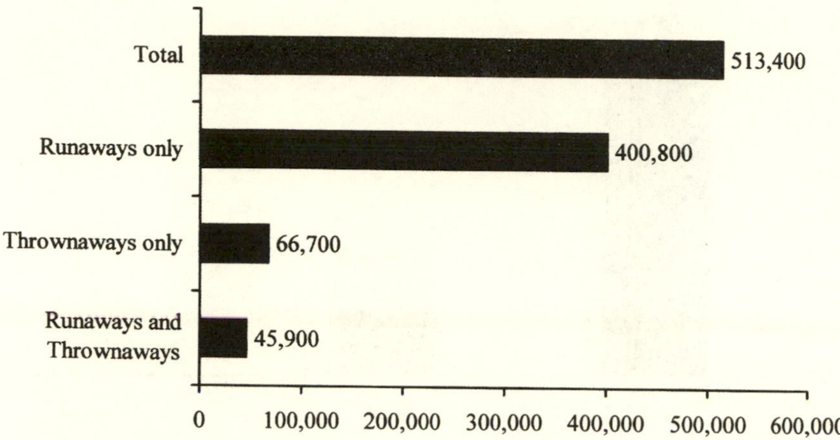

Source: Derived from U.S. Department of Justice, Office of Juvenile Justice and Delinquency Prevention, *Missing, Abducted, Runaway, and Thrownaway Children in America, First Report: Numbers and Characteristics, National Incidence Studies* (Washington, D.C.: Government Printing Office, 1990), p. 143.

- Almost three in ten thrownaway incidences involved physical violence in the household.
- Six in ten thrownaways' initial destination is a friend's house.
- More than one in ten children thrown away are without a place to sleep.
- More than eight in ten thrownaways are accompanied by others when leaving home.[16]

CHARACTERIZING THE THROWNAWAY

Sex of Thrownaways

Girls are generally more likely to be thrown away than boys. In its household survey, the NISMART estimated that 53 percent of Broad Scope Thrownaways are female, and 47 percent are male.[17] Female runaways are slightly disproportionate to their population figures.

Girl thrownaways are most often put out of home because of disputes with their mothers and related behavior problems. In one example, a sixteen year old runaway named "Honey" recalled that

> The fights with her mother started two years ago. When her mother [asked her] to help . . . with household chores, she would refuse.

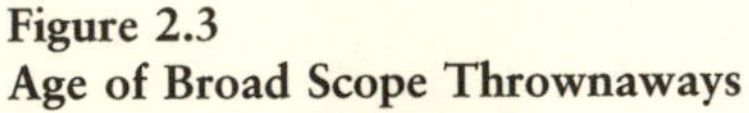

Figure 2.3
Age of Broad Scope Thrownaways

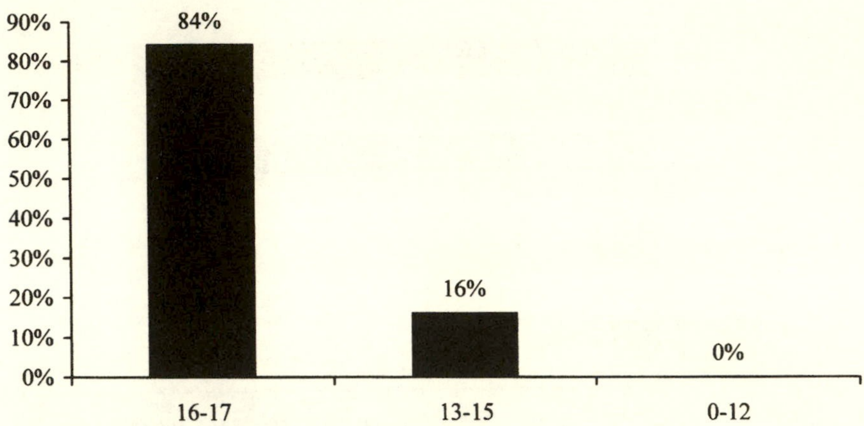

Source: Derived from U.S. Department of Justice, Office of Juvenile Justice and Delinquency Prevention, *Missing, Abducted, Runaway, and Thrownaway Children in America, First Report: Numbers and Characteristics, National Incidence Studies* (Washington, D.C.: Government Printing Office, 1990), p. 145.

> "Then she'd go into a tizzy and throw trash bags at me and tell me to pack up and get out," Honey recalls. So she did. "Once [my mother] put me on a bus to El Centro with $300 and told me to get a job and not come back. . . . I've been kicked out about six times."[18]

Abandoned children tend to be male more than female. In the National Incidence Study's Community Professionals Study of Abandoned Children, 52 percent of the thrownaways were boys and 48 percent were girls. This was fairly representative of the general population.[19] Abandonment is considered a form of child abuse and neglect, along with "many other types of throwing away behaviors."[20] Because of the nature of abandonment and lack of knowledge by professionals of many children who fall into this area of thrownaway youth, estimates of abandoned children are generally considered to be conservative at best.

Age of Thrownaways

Thrownaway children are predominantly older teens. As shown in Figure 2.3, 84 percent of Broad Scope Thrownaways are age sixteen to seventeen, with 16 percent age thirteen to fifteen. The NISMART reported no cases of thrownaway children age twelve or under, though there are some younger children who are confirmed thrownaways.[21]

Thrownaway children abandoned by their parents or caretakers tend to

Figure 2.4
Age of Abandoned Thrownaways

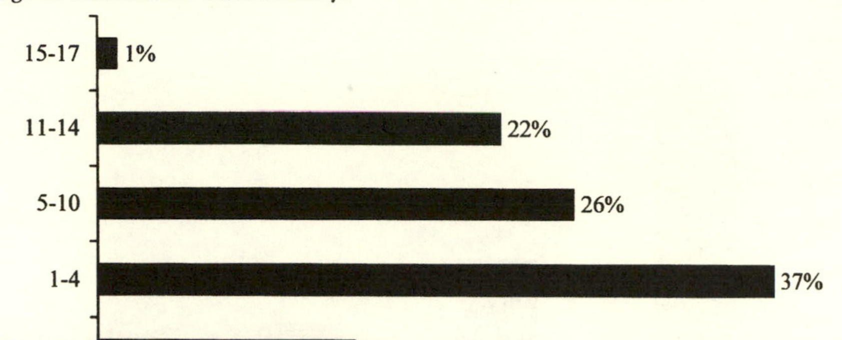

Source: Derived from U.S. Department of Justice, Office of Juvenile Justice and Delinquency Prevention, *Missing, Abducted, Runaway, and Thrownaway Children in America, First Report: Numbers and Characteristics, National Incidence Studies* (Washington, D.C.: Government Printing Office, 1990), p. 149.

be much younger than thrownaways forced out of the home (see Figure 2.4). According to the Community Professionals Study, more than half the abandoned children were age four or under. Nearly half fall between the ages of five and fourteen, while only 1 percent was age fifteen to seventeen.

Race and Ethnicity of Thrownaways

Most youths thrown away are white. As shown in Figure 2.5, more than 60 percent of the Broad Scope Thrownaways are white, with nearly 25 percent black. Black thrownaways are out of proportion to their population at large. Hispanics thrown away constitute an estimated 11 percent of the total thrownaways, with others accounting for 3 percent.

In the Community Professionals Study, approximately half the thrownaways abandoned were white, including Hispanic whites. Thirty-one percent were disproportionately non-white, while 18 percent of abandoned childrens' race was unknown.[22]

Income Level and Thrownaways

Throwaway children often tend to come from low-income families. Forty percent of Broad Scope Thrownaways' household incomes are $20,000 or less.[23] However, thrownaways are over represented in high-

Figure 2.5
Race and Ethnicity of Broad Scope Thrownaways

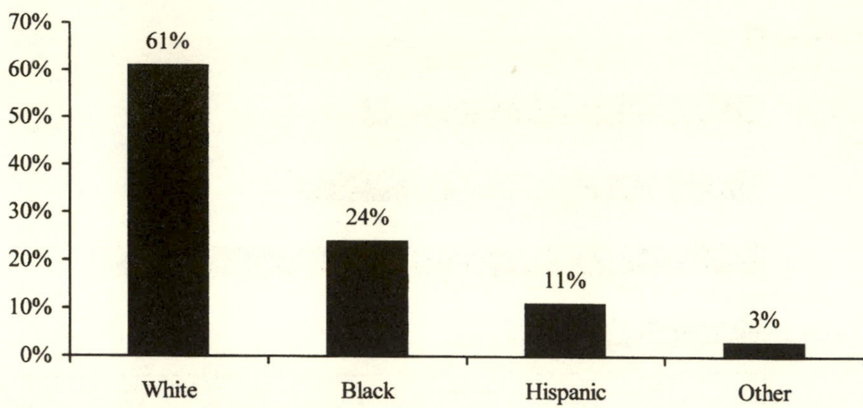

Note: Percentages do not total 100 due to rounding.
Source: Derived from U.S. Department of Justice, Office of Juvenile Justice and Delinquency Prevention, *Missing, Abducted, Runaway, and Thrownaway Children in America, First Report: Numbers and Characteristics, National Incidence Studies* (Washington, D.C.: Government Printing Office, 1990), p. 147.

income families. More than 30 percent of Broad Scope Thrownaways come from families with household incomes of $40,000 or more.[24]

Abandoned thrownaway children are more likely to be from families with low household incomes. Forty-six percent of abandoned youths had a family income of $15,000 or less.[25]

Family Structure and Thrownaways

Thrownaway children are more likely to come from broken homes than households with both parents (see Figure 2.6). Twenty-nine percent of Broad Scope Thrownaways were put out of homes with only a single parent with no partner. Twelve percent of thrownaways had neither parent present when they left home. Only 19 percent of thrownaways came from households with two parents.

Abandoned thrownaway children are more likely to come from homes where both parents were present. Thirty-seven percent of the abandoned youth in the Community Professional Study lived with both parents prior to being abandoned.[26] This group of thrownaways is underrepresented relative to population figures. Twenty-five percent of the abandoned children lived in households with a mother only, and 14 percent with a father only. The family structure was unknown for 25 percent of the thrownaways.

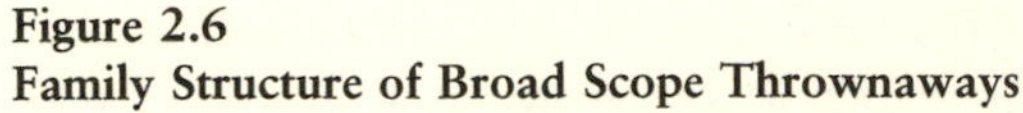

Figure 2.6
Family Structure of Broad Scope Thrownaways

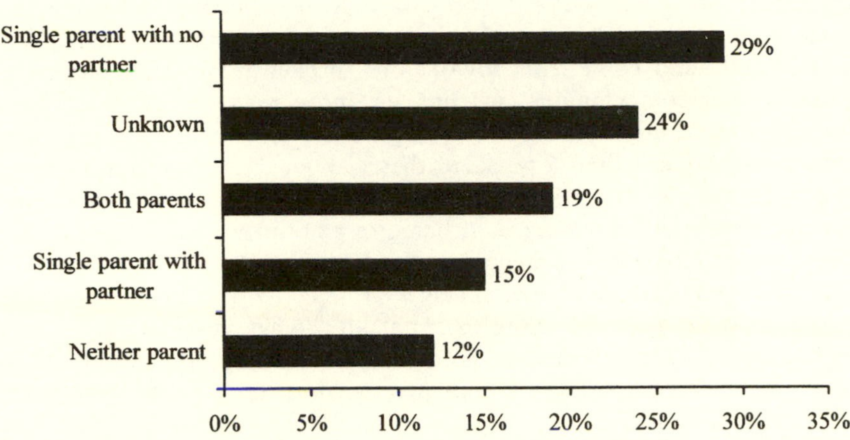

Note: Percentages do not total 100 due to rounding.
Source: Derived from U.S. Department of Justice, Office of Juvenile Justice and Delinquency Prevention, *Missing, Abducted, Runaway, and Thrownaway Children in America, First Report: Numbers and Characteristics, National Incidence Studies* (Washington, D.C.: Government Printing Office, 1990), p. 146.

RAT PACKERS

A growing number of suburban throwaway children are referred to as "rat packers."[27] These teens are often forced to leave home due to family problems, financial burdens, incorrigibility, rebelliousness, and an inability to relate to parental authority figures. Rat packers often tend to substitute peers for family and have a strong dislike for the "establishment." Some of these youths are victims of abuse, while others are abusive towards parents or other family members. Many suffer from learning disabilities, while others are highly intelligent.[28]

Rack packers often leave home for weeks or months, staying with friends, neighbors, or even other family members. It is estimated that more than 30,000 teenagers from the middle and upper class become rat packer throwaways annually in the United States.[29] One expert observed that these troubled youth "glory in anarchy and destruction," oftentimes stealing what they need to survive, engaging in alcohol and drug abuse, and committing vandalism and petty crimes.[30]

SUMMARY

Throwaway children are a branch of runaways who are forced out of the home, neglected, or abandoned by parents or caretakers. Some estimates are that as many as half the homeless and street kids are, in fact, thrown away. Broad Scope Thrownaways are away from home at least overnight, while Policy Focal Thrownaways are children without a safe place to stay outside the home. Most thrown away youth are female, older teens, white, and come from low-income, broken homes. Thrownaways from upper-income families account for more than one-third of those forced to leave home. More than 40 percent of thrownaways are away from home for less than a week; of these, about 21 percent return home in one day or less. Around 20 percent of thrownaways do not return home. Rat packers are an increasing suburban group of throwaways, often leaving home out of rebellion to parental control.

Abandoned children are more likely to be male, non-white, younger than other thrownaways, with more than half under five years of age. Nearly half of thrownaways abandoned come from low-income households. There is an under representation of both parents present in households where children are abandoned.

NOTES

1. U.S. Department of Justice, Office of Juvenile Justice and Delinquency Prevention, *Juvenile Offenders and Victims: 1999 National Report* (Washington, D.C.: Government Printing Office, 1999), p. 38.

2. U.S. Department of Justice, Office of Juvenile Justice and Delinquency Prevention, *Missing, Abducted, Runaway, and Thrownaway Children in America, First Report: Number and Characteristics, National Incidence Studies* (Washington, D.C.: Government Printing Office, 1990), p. 135.

3. Ibid., p. 136.

4. Quoted in R. Barri Flowers, *The Victimization and Exploitation of Women and Children: A Study of Physical, Mental and Sexual Maltreatment in the United States* (Jefferson, N.C.: McFarland, 1994), p. 42.

5. Gil Griffin, "Running on Empty: Kids Take to the Streets When They Don't Feel Loved at Home," *San Diego Union-Tribune* (July 26, 1997), p. E1.

6. Ibid.

7. J. K. Felsman, "Abandoned Children: A Reconsideration," *Children Today* (1984): 13–18; D. Butler, *Runaway House: A Youth-Run Project* (Washington, D.C.: Government Printing Office, 1974).

8. J. L. Powers, B. Jaklitsch, and J. Eckenrode, "Behavioral Indicators of Maltreatment among Runaway and Homeless Youth," paper presented at the National Symposium on Child Victimization, Anaheim, Calif., April 1988.

9. R. S. Levine, D. Metzendorf, and K. A. Van Boskirk, "Runaway and Throwaway Youth: A Case for Early Intervention with Truants," *Social Work in Education* 8 (1986): 93–106; G. R. Adams, T. Gulotta, and M. A. Clancy, "Homeless Adolescents: A Descriptive Study of Similarities and Differences between Runaways and Throwaways," *Adolescence* 79 (1985): 715–24.

10. Cited in Carolyn Males and Julie Raskin, "The Children Nobody Wants," *Reader's Digest* (January 1984): 63.

11. Cited in " 'Runaways,' 'Throwaways,' 'Bag Kids'—An Army of Drifter Teens," *U.S. News & World Report* (March 11, 1985): 53.

12. U.S. Department of Health and Human Services, Family Youth and Services Bureau, "FYSB Update" (Silver Springs, Md.: National Clearinghouse on Families & Youth, October 1995), p. 2.

13. Opinion Research Corporation as cited in *Missing, Abducted, Runaway, and Thrownaway Children*, p. 136.

14. Males and Raskin, "The Children Nobody Wants," p. 63.

15. *Missing, Abducted, Runaway, and Thrownaway Children*, p. 140.

16. Ibid., pp. 148–60.

17. Ibid., p. 145.

18. Griffin, "Running on Empty," p. E2.

19. *Missing, Abducted, Runaway, and Thrownaway Children*, p. 149.

20. Ibid., p. 140.

21. R. Barri Flowers, *The Prostitution of Women and Girls* (Jefferson, N.C.: McFarland, 1998), p. 96.

22. *Missing, Abducted, Runaway, and Thrownaway Children*, p. 151.

23. Ibid., p. 147.

24. Ibid.

25. Ibid., p. 151.

26. Ibid., p. 150.

27. " 'Rat Pack' Youth: Teenage Rebels in Suburbia," *U.S. News & World Report* (March 11, 1985): 51.

28. Flowers, *The Victimization and Exploitation of Women and Children*, p. 43.

29. Ibid.

30. Ibid.

Chapter 3

Runaways, Arrest, and the Police

Thousands of juveniles are arrested in the United States each year for running away from home or a juvenile facility. Other runaways are arrested and charged with other offenses such as prostitution, curfew and loitering violations, and drug- or alcohol-related offenses. Since the runaway is considered a status offender (under the age of eighteen) rather than a criminal offender, the police must walk a delicate line in making arrests, detaining runaways, and returning them to parents or caretakers. This discretion and uncertainty can be further impacted by the circumstances that may have caused the child to run away, such as physical or sexual abuse, or abandonment by parents who essentially threw the runaway out of the house or did not report the child as missing. Hence, many runaways can be considered both offenders and victims, complicating the eventual outcome of the case.

ARRESTS OF RUNAWAYS

The preeminent means for gathering arrest data on runaways and other offenders in the United States is the Federal Bureau of Investigation's annual publication, *Crime in the United States: Uniform Crime Reports* (*UCR*).[1] In 1998, there were an estimated 165,100 arrests of persons as runaways.[2] As some of the runaways were repeat offenders, the *UCR* data focuses on the number of arrests reported by law enforcement agencies rather than the number of individuals arrested. The rate of runaway arrests was sixty-three per 100,000 inhabitants—nearly twice as high as the arrest rate for prostitution and commercialized vice, commonly associated with runaway teens.[3]

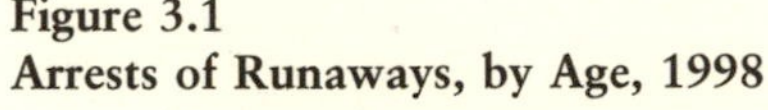

Figure 3.1
Arrests of Runaways, by Age, 1998

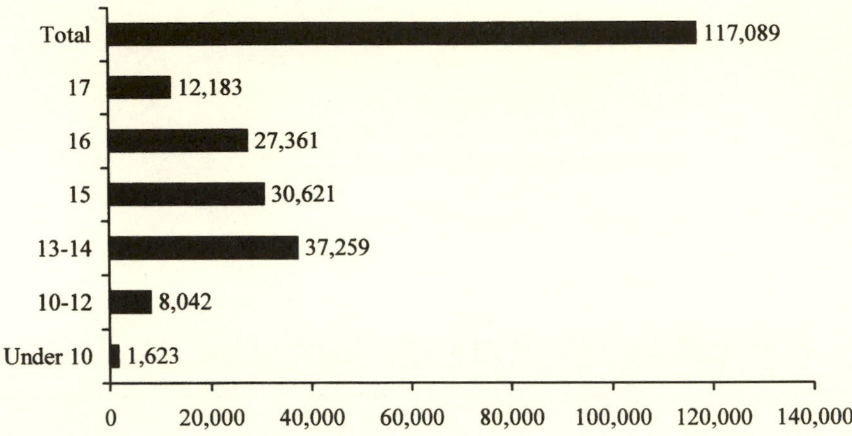

Source: Derived from U.S. Department of Justice, Federal Bureau of Investigation, *Crime in the United States: Uniform Crime Reports 1998* (Washington, D.C.: Government Printing Office, 1999), p. 220.

Sex of Runaway Arrestees

Females tend to be arrested more than males as runaways. There were 68,170 arrests of females for running away in 1998, compared to 48,919 male runaways arrested. Females constituted 58.2 percent of total arrests as runaways, while males accounted for 41.8 percent.[4] The percentage of total arrests was five times higher for females arrested as runaways than males.[5] The ratio of runaway arrests was 1.4 females for every one male arrested. Experts attribute this disparity to a number of reasons, including a greater willingness of teenage girls to run away from home than teenage boys, police discretion in arrests, and more male teen runaways arrested for other offenses.

Runaway girls not only are more likely to face arrest than their male counterparts, but also likely to have run from abusive homes. In a recent survey of girls in a runaway shelters, more than 70 percent admitted to running away from home due to sexual abuse.[6] This compares to nearly 40 percent of the boy runaways at the shelter.

Age of Runaway Arrestees

All persons arrested as runaways are under the age of eighteen. Most tend to be older teens. Of 117,089 reported arrests of runaways in 1998, 57.9 percent were between the ages of fifteen and seventeen, while 40.1 percent were under age fifteen.[7] Figure 3.1 breaks down arrests for running

Figure 3.2
Arrests of Runaways, by Age and Sex, 1998

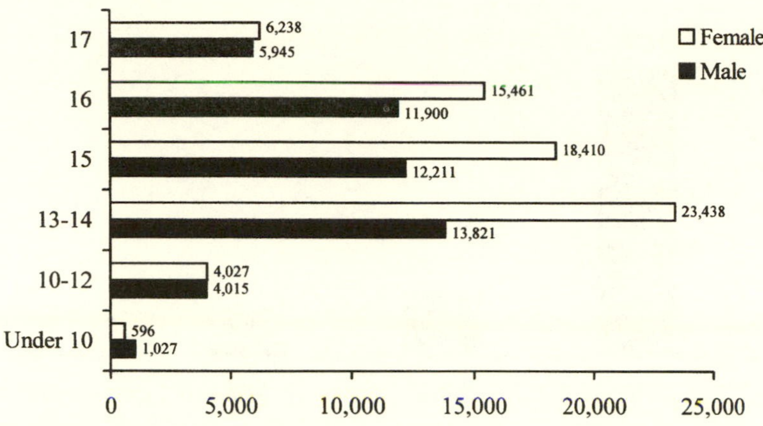

Source: Derived from U.S. Department of Justice, Federal Bureau of Investigation, *Crime in the United States: Uniform Crime Reports 1998* (Washington, D.C.: Government Printing Office, 1999), p. 222, 224.

away by age in 1998. Consistent with survey findings on runaways, arrests were lowest among younger teens and highest for fifteen and sixteen year olds, decreasing at age seventeen as adulthood approaches.

Arrests of runaways in 1998, combining age and sex, can be seen in Figure 3.2. Females were more likely to be arrested in every age bracket, except for under ten, where the male-female ratio of arrest was 1.7 to 1. Arrests for males and females peaked at age fifteen. More than 34 percent of the female arrestees for running away were thirteen to fourteen years of age.

In addition to the labeling faced by runaways who are arrested and brought into the criminal justice system, they are also at risk for suicide or other victimization while in police custody. This is illustrated by the following recent tragedy of one runaway teen:

> On a Saturday night . . . Kathy Robbins, a 15-year-old girl [runaway] from Glenn County, California, was arrested. . . . She was taken in handcuffs to a 54-year-old cell in Glenn County's adult jail. Four days after she was arrested, at a juvenile court hearing, a judge refused to release her to a juvenile detention facility. On that day, still isolated and alone in an adult jail cell, Kathy Robbins twisted a bed sheet around her neck, and hanged herself from the rail of the top bunk bed.[8]

Figure 3.3
Arrests of Runaways, by Race,[a] 1998

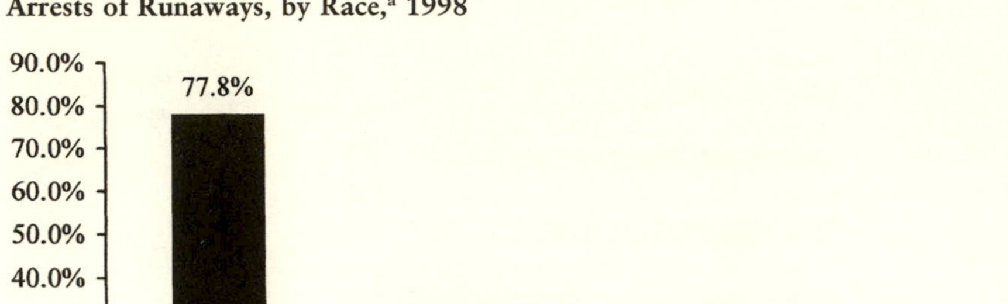

Note: Percentages do not total 100 due to rounding.

[a]Native American includes American Indians and Alaskan Natives. Asian includes Asian or Pacific Islander.

Source: Derived from U.S. Department of Justice, Federal Bureau of Investigation, *Crime in the United States: Uniform Crime Reports 1998* (Washington, D.C.: Government Printing Office, 1999), p. 229.

Race of Runaway Arrestees

Persons arrested as runaways are predominantly white. The *UCR* reported that 77.8 percent of those arrested in this country for running away in 1998 were white (see Figure 3.3). Blacks accounted for 17.9 percent of the runaway arrestees, Asians 3.4 percent, and Native Americans just 1 percent of the arrests. These proportions are not statistically significant relative to the population at large. The rate of arrest for black runaways is higher in cities than in other community types, whereas the arrest rate for white runaways tends to be higher in the suburbs and rural areas than in cities.[9]

Community Size and Arrests of Runaways

Runaway youth tend to be arrested most often in cities and suburban areas. Figure 3.4 shows that there were nearly 90,000 city arrests of runaways in 1998, compared to less than 8,000 arrests in rural counties. Suburban areas accounted for nearly 45,000 runaway arrests, including more than 20,000 in suburban counties. Older teens are more likely to be arrested as runaways in all the community sizes than younger teens. However, young runaways are well represented in arrest figures by community size. Arrests of persons under the age of fifteen as runaways constituted the

Figure 3.4
Arrests of Runaways, by Community Size,[a] 1998

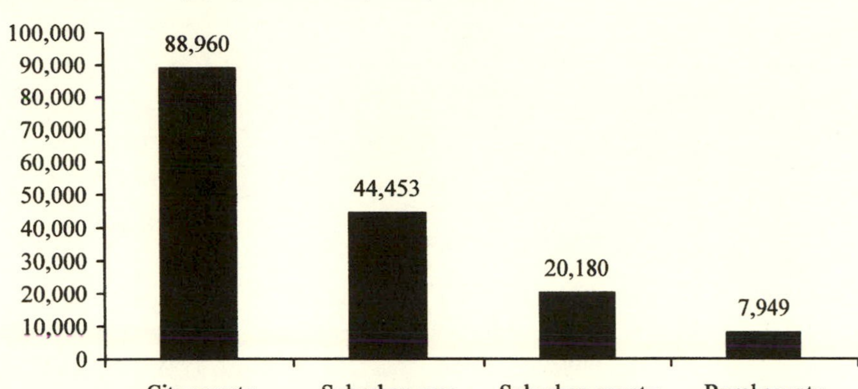

[a] Suburban area includes suburban city and county law enforcement agencies inside of metropolitan areas, while excluding central cities.

Source: Derived from U.S. Department of Justice, Federal Bureau of Investigation, *Crime in the United States: Uniform Crime Reports 1998* (Washington, D.C.: Government Printing Office, 1999), p. 233, 245, 254, 261.

following percent of overall runaway arrests: city arrests (41 percent), suburban county arrests (37.7 percent), rural county arrests (35.4 percent), and suburban area arrests (37.9 percent).[10]

Most runaways, irrespective of the community type they fled from, share a common theme of "running into a myriad of problems and illegal situations while away from home."[11] In one case of a fourteen year old suburban runaway, he notes: "We got into this group made up of runaway and homeless kids where there were a lot of hallucinogens offered. There was a lot of violence, most of it deliberate. There were a lot of drugs and just brain-numbing noise."[12] He was eventually arrested by law enforcement authorities and returned home.

Arrest Trends for Runaways

Long-term trends indicate that juvenile arrests for running away are on the decline. Figure 3.5 shows that total arrests of runaways, between 1989 and 1998, dropped nearly 5 percent. The decrease was even sharper for the five-year arrest trend between 1994 and 1998, which saw a more than 21 percent decline in runaway arrests (see Figure 3.6).

When looking at arrest trends of runaways by sex, male arrests are decreasing at a greater rate than female arrests (see Figure 3.7). From 1989 to 1998, male arrests for running away dropped by 9.5 percent, compared to only a 1.2 percent decline in female arrests.

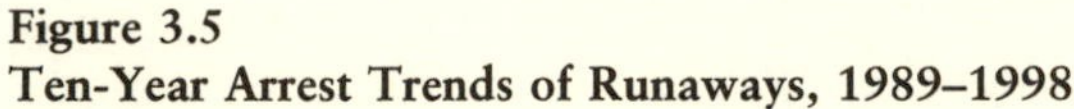

Figure 3.5
Ten-Year Arrest Trends of Runaways, 1989–1998

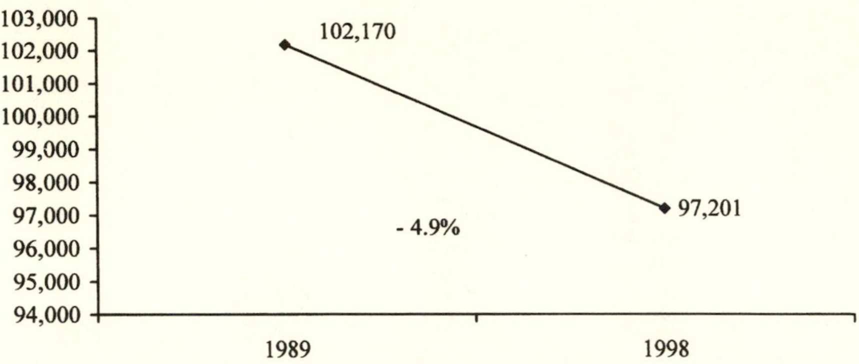

Source: Derived from U.S. Department of Justice, Federal Bureau of Investigation, *Crime in the United States: Uniform Crime Reports 1998* (Washington, D.C.: Government Printing Office, 1999), p. 214.

Figure 3.6
Five-Year Arrest Trends of Runaways, 1994–1998

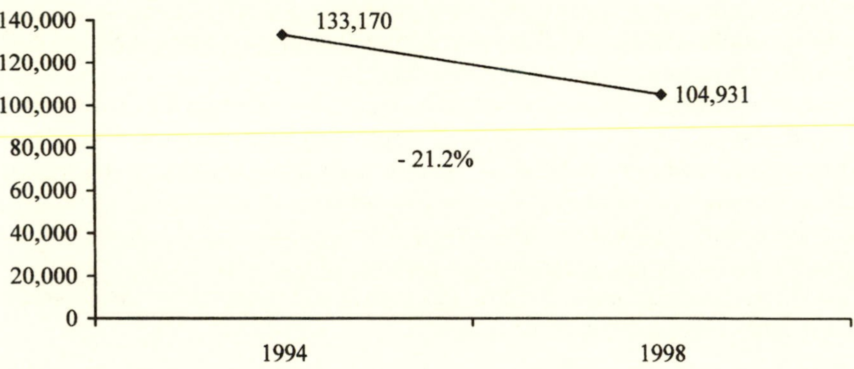

Source: Derived from U.S. Department of Justice, Federal Bureau of Investigation, *Crime in the United States: Uniform Crime Reports 1998* (Washington, D.C.: Government Printing Office, 1999), p. 216.

Similarly, for the five- and two-year trends—1994 to 1998 and 1997 to 1998, respectively—female arrests decreased at a lower rate than male arrests.[13] This might indicate that more females than males are continuing to leave home due to intolerable situations, such as sexual abuse, in spite of overall declines in teenage arrests for running away.

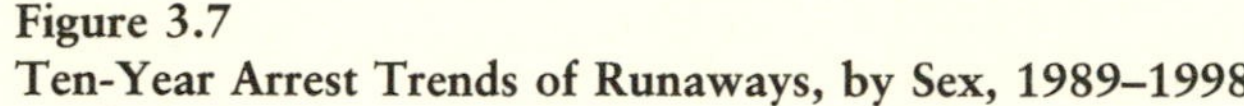

Figure 3.7
Ten-Year Arrest Trends of Runaways, by Sex, 1989–1998

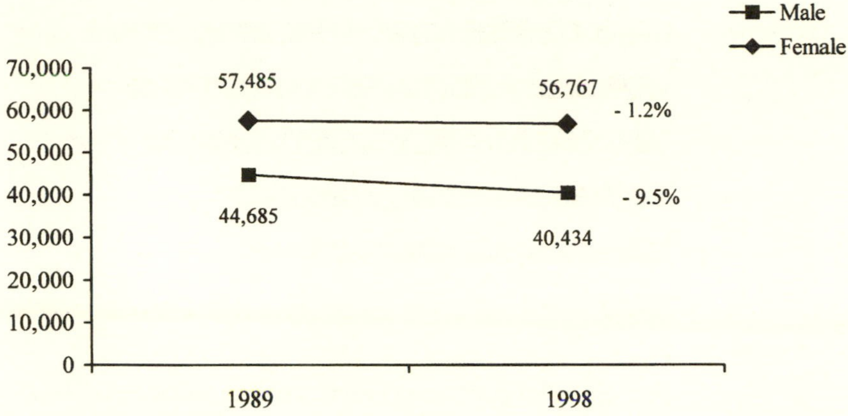

Source: Derived from U.S. Department of Justice, Federal Bureau of Investigation, *Crime in the United States: Uniform Crime Reports 1998* (Washington, D.C.: Government Printing Office, 1999), p. 215.

RUNAWAY-RELATED ARRESTS

Along with arrest statistics specifically on runaways, other official data reflects arrests of juveniles for offenses that are often associated with runaways and homeless youth such as drug abuse violations, prostitution, vandalism, and curfew and loitering law violations (see Figure 3.8). In 1998, persons under eighteen were arrested most often for runaway-related offenses. Over 146,000 persons under eighteen were arrested in the United States for drug abuse violations, more than 136,000 for curfew and loitering law violations, over 111,000 for liquor law violations, and more than 90,000 for vandalism. Though not all of these arrests were of runaway youth, studies show that there is a strong correlation between running away and certain offenses.[14] Other runaway-related offenses that juveniles are arrested for include drunkenness, disorderly conduct, and prostitution and commercialized vice. Prostitution-related offenses are most often associated with youth who run away and are without food, adequate clothing, shelter, or other basic needs. This correlation will be examined much more closely in Parts II and III. Overall, runaway-related arrests have been on the decline, similar to runaway arrests.[15]

RUNAWAYS AND POLICE CONTACT

A runaway's contact with the police occurs primarily through arrest, detention, and returning the runaway home or placing them in a juvenile

Figure 3.8
Arrests of Juveniles for Runaway-Related Offenses, 1998

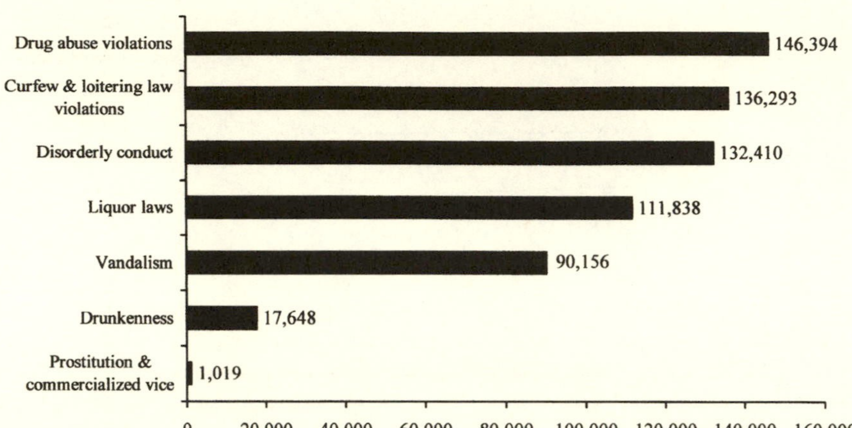

Source: Derived from U.S. Department of Justice, Federal Bureau of Investigation, *Crime in the United States: Uniform Crime Reports 1998* (Washington, D.C.: Government Printing Office, 1999), p. 220.

facility. The nature of this contact is based on a number of factors including reports of missing youth, the type of runaway episode, police department size, and varying laws with respect to dealing with runaway children.

Reports of Runaway Youth

Police investigations and arrests of children who run away from home often depend on reports of missing runaways by parents or caretakers. According to the National Incidence Studies, an estimated 40 percent of police involvement in runaway cases results from reports of runaway children by parents or guardians.[16] Law enforcement agencies investigate runaway cases far more often than family abductions, another form of missing children. In a study of police file reports of children who are missing from home, the ratio of runaway cases to family abductions was 55 to 1.[17] Because many runaways are, in fact, throwaways, these children are usually not reported as missing. Consequently, these runaways are unknown to police and are more likely to be arrested for prostitution, drug violations, or other offenses than running away.[18]

Police Response to Runaway Cases

The police response to reports of runaway children is based on a number of factors, including parental concern, information provided on the runaway, other police investigations, policies in the police department, subjectivity, and risk assessment. In many cases, police may view a runaway case as less of a police matter and more of a social work investigation. Hence, unless the runaway episode is perceived as being an immediate crisis, it may be given lower priority by some law enforcement agencies than parents would prefer. The larger the police department, the more likely it will have policies and procedures for dealing more effectively with investigating runaway cases. In most police agencies, reports of missing children who are very young or feared victims of kidnapping or foul play are given high priority.

Studies show that most reports of runaway children can be officially made without waiting periods. A mail survey of police departments found that only 2 percent of large police agencies had waiting periods before reports of running away could be considered official.[19] In more than three out of four reported runaway cases, an officer is sent to a suspected runaway's house to take a report.[20] Police response from that point on tends to vary from department to department. The following findings have emerged on police procedures in responding to cases of runaways:

- Sixty-three to 75 percent of police seek a photograph of the runaway, names of friends, and other information.
- Twenty percent of runaway cases result in an APB (All Points Bulletin).
- Ten percent of the initial police response results in additional officers being brought in on the investigation.
- Fifty-eight percent of the time police provide parents with a case number.
- In about 75 percent of the runaway cases, police make at least one other contact with the parent or caretaker following the initial report.
- Family characteristics such as race, ethnicity, sex, and income have little impact on police handling of runaway cases.[21]

Police and Homeless Youth

Police contact with homeless children is fairly limited, on the whole, given the scope of street kids and lack of police resources for investigating their circumstances. Generally, law enforcement agencies favor referral of runaway and throwaway youth to social service agencies more equipped to deal with them, including foster homes and group homes for abandoned or throwaway children. Only two in ten police departments report having written policies for handling homeless youth cases.[22]

Police are most likely to make contact with unreported homeless youth when on patrol, if they are a victim or offender of a criminal offense, or when the youth is in need of medical care.[23] Complications arise for many police departments in knowing what to do with runaways once in their custody. Almost two-thirds of police departments surveyed reported several obstacles to either returning runaways home or placing them in protective care facilities:

- A runaway's individual characteristics including age, mobility, and independence.
- Running away is considered a status offense rather than a criminal one.
- Throwaway children's parents or guardians are often uncooperative.
- Lack of shelters.
- Returning a runaway to an abusive home.
- The runaway's participation in criminal offenses.[24]

Police Custody and Runaway Laws

Police arrest and detainment of runaways is subject to various laws across the country, hampering the effectiveness of dealing with runaway cases. There are statistics that prohibit police taking suspected runaways into custody.[25] In most states, runaway children can only be detained for a limited amount of time. This usually ranges from three to twelve hours for in-state custody of runaways and up to seventy-two hours for out of state runaways.[26]

Around 40 percent of police departments report that the inability to hold runaways is a significant factor in the successful, or lack of, disposition of the cases.[27] This is especially true for repeat runaways and those from other jurisdictions where proper identification or return of the runaway might not be possible in the time permitted. The majority of law enforcement agencies favor being selective in holding runaway children, if they were legally permitted to, due to lack of police staff and adequate resources.[28] (See Chapter 15 for more on laws and runaways.)

SUMMARY

More than 165,000 juveniles are arrested as runaways annually. These include children who have been thrown out of the household by parents or guardians. Many runaways are arrested and charged with criminal offenses such as drug offenses and prostitution. Characteristically, most runaway youth tend to be female, white, older teens, and running from homes in cities and suburbs. Arrest trends indicate that fewer juveniles are being arrested for running away and related offenses than in past years.

The police count strongly on parental reports of runaway children to become involved in runaway cases. Around 40 percent of police runaway investigations result from reports of missing youth. Most law enforcement agencies do not have waiting periods for officially reporting runaways. However, investigations can vary from agency to agency. Runaway cases involving younger children are most likely to be given high priority and cases of repeat runaway offenders are less likely to be aggressively investigated. Inconsistent laws and lack of parental cooperation can make it difficult for the police to locate and/or detain runaway, throwaway, and homeless youth.

NOTES

1. U.S. Department of Justice, Federal Bureau of Investigation, *Crime in the United States: Uniform Crime Reports 1999* (Washington, D.C.: Government Printing Office, 1999).
2. Ibid., p. 210.
3. Ibid., p. 213.
4. Ibid., p. 227.
5. Ibid.
6. A. McCormack, M. D. Janus, and A. W. Burgess, "Runaway Youths and Sexual Victimization: Gender Differences in an Adolescent Runaway Population," *Child Abuse and Neglect* 10 (1986): 387–95.
7. *Uniform Crime Reports*, p. 226.
8. Vincent Schiraldi and Jason Zeidenberg, *Runaway Juvenile Crime? The Context of Juvenile Crime Arrests* (Washington, D.C.: Justice Policy Institute, 1998), p. 1.
9. *Uniform Crime Reports*, pp. 237, 247, 255, 265.
10. Ibid., pp. 235, 244, 253, 262.
11. Lindsay Crawford, "Troubled Teens Take to the Streets: Rebellious Youths with Nowhere to Turn Run Away from Their Problems and Their Homes," *Silver Chips Online* (April 13, 2000), p. 18.
12. Ibid.
13. *Uniform Crime Reports*, pp. 217, 219.
14. See, for example, R. Barri Flowers, *Drugs, Alcohol and Criminality in American Society* (Jefferson, N.C.: McFarland, 1999), p. 152.
15. *Uniform Crime Reports*, pp. 215, 217, 219.
16. U.S. Department of Justice, Office of Juvenile Justice and Delinquency Prevention, *Missing, Abducted, Runaway, and Thrownaway Children in America, First Report: Numbers and Characteristics, National Incidence Studies* (Washington, D.C.: Government Printing Office, 1990), p. 116.
17. U.S. Department of Justice, Office of Juvenile Justice and Delinquency Prevention, *Law Enforcement Policies and Practices Regarding Missing and Homeless*

Youth: Research Summary (Washington, D.C.: Government Printing Office, 1993), p. 5.

18. Flowers, *Drugs, Alcohol and Criminality in American Society*, p. 152; R. Barri Flowers, *The Prostitution of Women and Girls* (Jefferson, N.C.: McFarland, 1998), p. 75–77.

19. *Law Enforcement Polices and Practices*, p. 9.

20. Ibid.

21. Ibid., pp. 8–10.

22. Ibid., p. 11.

23. Ibid., p. 12.

24. Ibid.

25. Ibid.

26. Ibid., p. 14.

27. Ibid.

28. Ibid., p. 17.

Chapter 4

Why Teens Run Away from Home

Running away from home is a major step for even the most streetwise youth. Few runaways leave the comfort and familiarity of home without some compelling reasons. These are often related to domestic violence, sexual or physical abuse, drug problems, and other family dysfunction. Many children leave home due to school problems or other personal issues. Others are forced onto the streets by parents or caretakers who are unable or unwilling to handle the child's troubles or because of other family issues. Some children run away from juvenile institutions after having already had a history of running away from home. What these children all have in common is an overlapping set of factors that precipitates running away and leaving the secure environment of a household or institutional setting.

WHAT MAKES TEENAGERS RUN AWAY?

Runaway teens leave home for a number of reasons related to feeling uncomfortable, violated, threatened, unwanted, or rebellious. Researchers have found that running away can often be attributed to one or more of the following reasons:

- Poor home environment.
- Broken home (absence of at least one parent).
- Family crises.
- School problems.
- Mental illness.

- Emotional problems.
- Substance abuse.
- Sex (promiscuity, pregnancy, married).
- Boredom.
- Peer pressure.
- Lures (such as by someone on the Internet).[1]

In many instances, the runaway child has multiple reasons that result in the decision to leave home. These factors are often long-term, unresolved issues that reach a point of no return, either by the runaway or by the caretaker, resulting in the child being thrown away.[2]

Family dysfunction, parental neglect, family drug use, and implications of sexual activity by the runaway are seen as strong indicators of running away by youth. In a recent study of runaway children, the following disturbing characteristics emerged:

- Sixty percent of runaways had parents who abused alcohol and/or drugs.
- Seventy percent of the runaways used drugs prior to leaving home.
- One in four were born to mothers younger than seventeen years of age.
- Half of the runaways experienced physical or sexual abuse at home.
- One in four female runaways had been raped.
- Thirty-six percent had been pregnant at least once.
- Only 23 percent of female runaways used birth control.
- Half the male runaways under the age of fourteen were sexually active.
- Eighty percent of runaways had serious behavioral or emotional problems.
- Only 13 percent of the runaways were considered functionally literate.
- Only one-third ever sought help from a runaway shelter.[3]

According to experts, though many teens and preteens run away to escape an abusive, unhealthy environment, leaving home is largely a reflection of adolescent rebelliousness. Notes a child therapist: "Many runaways who feel that their family lives are too chaotic decide that they just have to live alone. They are rebellious and simply don't want to comply with the rules."[4]

DOMESTIC VIOLENCE

Domestic violence plays a significant role in teenagers running away from home. Defined as "a pattern of assaultive and coercive behaviors, including physical, sexual, and psychological attacks, as well as economic coercion, that adults or adolescents use against their intimate partners."[5] Domestic violence is a major problem in this country. The American Medical Association estimated that 4 million spouses are battered each year in the United States.[6] Similarly, a national health survey reported that 3.9 women—or 7 percent of all American women, married or living with someone—are beaten annually.[7] Murray Straus estimated that 65 percent of all married couples were participants in abusive behavior as victims or offenders, with 25 percent considered serious.[8] A woman is battered by her spouse every nine seconds in this country.[9]

The effect on children witnessing this domestic violence (who are often victims as well) can be devastating, leading many to flee the brutality and tension it produces within the entire household. The following tale of a runaway teen illustrates the tragedy of domestic violence:

> Meet Julie. Julie's 14. She ran away from home when she was 12. She saw her dad beat and almost kill her mother, and two more wives after that. Dad's working on wife number four. Julie's tried to warn her, but to no avail. She's seen the women in her father's life thrown down stairs, punched, choked. Good old dad also molested Julie. So much for a chance at life . . . [10]

SEXUAL AND PHYSICAL ABUSE

The relationship between child sexual and/or physical abuse and running away has been well documented. According to the National Network of Runaway and Youth Services, 70 percent of runaways in shelters had been sexually molested or abused at home.[11] Another study found that at least 90 percent of runaways were victims of severe child abuse.[12] Ann Hayman, the creator of the Mary Magdalene Project in Los Angeles, noted that runaway girls were typically subjected to "lots of incest, lots of alcoholism, lots of physical assault, lots of sexual battery."[13] Two-thirds of the runaway prostitutes Mimi Silbert studied were victims of child abuse and incest.[14]

The sexual abuse and battering experienced by young runaways can also be perpetrated by boyfriends and others they are not intimately involved with. Studies show that one in three females will be beaten by a boyfriend prior to reaching the age of eighteen.[15] In a survey of 500 female adolescents, virtually every one reported being the victim of dating violence.[16] Similarly, many runaways have experienced sexual assaults from intimates or acquaintances. It is estimated that half of all rape victims are teenagers, with the majority perpetrated by romantic partners or others known to the victim.[17]

The specter of maltreatment experienced by many teen runaways at the hands of parents or intimate partners can be seen in the following account of a runaway teenager:

> Debbie's 16. She ran away when she found out she was pregnant. Her baby weighed just over three-and-a-half pounds when she was born. Her father beat her; the father of the baby girl punched her while she was pregnant. Debbie slept on the street. A street too hard and too cold for anyone, much less a young woman about to give birth.[18]

SCHOOL PROBLEMS

Teenagers with school-related problems are at a higher risk to run away from home than teens who are well adjusted in school. Studies show that 13 percent of high school students have ever run away, while another 20 percent have thought about running away from home.[19] At risk youths for running away include those who have poor grades in school, school expulsions, social isolation from peers, and/or disciplinary problems in school or the home.[20] Many such teens tend to drop out of school and out of their families—taking to the streets and into a life of prostitution and other deviant behavior.

POVERTY

The rate of runaways from low income families is high. Approximately 40 percent of runaway homeless and street kids come from families on public assistance or living in public housing.[21] This is nearly twice the percentage of juveniles living in poverty in the general population.[22] Around 70 percent of the runaways in Louise Homer's study were from families on welfare.[23] Other studies have found a disproportionate number of runaway children from middle- and working-class backgrounds.[24]

MENTAL ILLNESS

A high percentage of runaways leave home with a number of mental disorders, including depression and schizophrenia. In a study of youth shelter runaways, Carol Canton and David Shaffer characterized 41 percent of the runaways as depressed and antisocial, 30 percent as depressed, and 18 percent as antisocial.[25] In comparing runaways and non-runaways, another study found that 85 percent of the runaways suffered from clinical depression while 21 percent had serious mental health problems.[26] The runaways were four times more likely to have emotional problems as the non-runaways. According to a Family and Youth Services Bureau (FYSB) study of homeless and shelter runaways, 71 percent of the homeless youth and 58 percent of the shelter runaways had spent time in an institution setting such as a psychiatric or mental facility.[27]

SUICIDE

Many runaway youth have a history of suicide attempts as a factor in leaving home. In one study, 50 percent of runaways had attempted or seriously considered committing suicide.[28] June Bucy noted the high rate of suicide among runaway girls.[29] The FYSB study found that 32 percent of runaways living on the streets and 26 percent of those in runaway shelters had ever attempted suicide.[30] Suicidal attempts were more likely among female and older teen runaways. Around 36 percent of shelter runaways attempting suicide were hospitalized following the most recent attempted suicide. The study further found that there was a higher proportion of runaway children who reported attempting suicide before leaving home than after leaving home.

SUBSTANCE ABUSE

Drug and alcohol abuse by runaways are seen as strongly related to runaway episodes. As many as seven in ten runaways abused drugs prior to leaving home.[31] Nearly half the runaway prostitutes were drinking alcohol before selling their bodies.[32] Many runaways had already developed a dependency for alcohol or drugs before taking to the streets.[33] In some instances, the substance abuse is a way to cope with problems while living at home, such as sexual abuse and family violence.[34] These youths, some already addicts or alcoholics, often "couch-hop from sofa to sofa and house to house. Some sleep in newspaper recycling bins or parking garages and ride the bus for hours when it's raining to stay dry."[35]

Drug use by family members is also linked to runaway children. The FYSB study concluded that familial substance abuse had an adverse affect on juvenile behavioral problems such as running away from home.[36] Approximately 45 percent of their homeless runaway sample and 31 percent of runaway shelter youth sample reported drug use by a family member in the month prior to the runaway leaving home. Around 24 percent of the street runaways reported it was the father using drugs, 33 percent the mother, and around 35 percent said it was their stepparents using drugs. For the shelter runaways, the percentages were approximately 19 percent of the fathers abusing drugs in the month before the youth left home, 18 percent of the mothers, and 27 percent of the stepparents. The study found a correlation between parental drug use and child drug use, as well as a relationship as a result to other destructive juvenile behavior such as suicide and delinquency.[37]

THROWAWAYS

Many runaway teens leave home not as a voluntary decision, but because parents or caretakers have forced them out of the house or abandoned them. Some studies have found that around half the children described as runaways are actually throwaways.[38] The FYSB found that overall more than half their sample group had either been driven out of the house or had parents who did not care that they were leaving.[39] Around 47 percent of the street runaways and shelter runaways reported being told to leave home by their parents, whereas around 41 percent of the runaways living on the streets and 35 percent in shelters reported parents who knew they were leaving home but did nothing to try and stop them. Throwaway kids are even more susceptible to familial conflicts and stresses than other runaway youth, and less likely to return home after leaving. (See also Chapter 2.) For many homeless teenagers, "on the street being physically or verbally abused, they become the throwaway group. Too invisible to even make the statistics."[40]

TEEN RUNAWAYS WHO ARE GAY

Gay runaway and throwaway teenagers have the same risk factors for leaving home as other runaway youth. But their sexual orientation issues pose additional precipitating causes for running away. According to Jenny Gable's essay on homeless gay youth, many " 'out of the closet' teens face angry homophobic parents who throw them out of the house when they are fourteen or fifteen. These youths . . . then end up in gay homeless shelters or counseling centers."[41]

However, a survey of 775 runaway teens in San Francisco, New York City, and Denver suggested that most youths leave home of their own accord, irrespective of sexual orientation or parental objection thereof.[42] Seventy-eight percent of the runaways indicated they left home on their own, while only 16 percent were thrown out. Nevertheless, the survey revealed that nearly six in ten teens ran away due to family conflicts and more than two in ten because of being abused or raped.

RUNAWAY ADVENTURERS

Not all runaway youth come from troubled, abusive families or are thrown away or abandoned. Some runaways actually leave home for life on the streets as part of a misguided sense of adventure and independence combined with teenage rebellion, precociousness, promiscuity, and a need for companionship. One expert on runaways noted: "The rule for runaway girls everywhere is often 'ball for bed'—meaning that implicit in an offer of lodging is the expectation of sexual intercourse."[43] A study of runaways found that their initial objectives were to "acquire a place to sleep and then look for adventure—get a crash pad and some kicks."[44] Some runaway adventurers experienced other problems at home, influencing the decision to run away.[45]

Many runaway adventurers seek the camaraderie, comfort, and acceptances that they lack at home. "The children who run look for companionship, friendship, and approval from those they meet. Many such youths are easy marks for gangs, drug pushers and pimps. Runaways often sell drugs or their bodies, and steal to support themselves."[46]

Some teenagers run away from home after having met someone on the Internet, often with promises of adventure, sex, and independence—lures too tempting to pass up for many caught between the boundaries of preadolescence and adulthood. The result is often anything but what was expected by the naïve and gullible runaway.

Few runaway kids, irrespective of the reason for leaving home, will find life elsewhere to be better. At the same time, for many runaways the life left behind was too difficult to return to. These youths face a tough road with few options for a satisfactory way around their dilemma.

SUMMARY

Teenagers usually run away from home because of an unstable family situation including domestic violence, child sexual or physical abuse, absence of one or both parents, impoverishment, and familial substance abuse. Some runaways leave because of school or personal problems, sexual identity issues, mental illness, peer pressure, or boredom. Many runaway youth are in reality thrown out of the home or otherwise abandoned by parents or guardians. Finally, there is a group of runaways who leave home for adventure, thrills, sexual experiences, or are lured by others through the Internet. Some of these children may also have underlying reasons for running away such as abuse or family violence. Whatever the reason a youth decides to or is forced to leave home, the result is often one of despair.

NOTES

1. R. Barri Flowers, *The Prostitution of Women and Girls* (Jefferson, N.C.: McFarland, 1998), p. 97; James A. Hildebrand, "Why Runaways Leave Home," *Police Science* 54 (1963): 211–16; C. J. English, "Leaving Home: A Typology of Runaways," *Society* 10 (1973): 22–24.

2. R. Barri Flowers, *The Victimization and Exploitation of Women and Chil-*

dren: A Study of Physical, Mental and Sexual Maltreatment in the United States (Jefferson, N.C.: McFarland, 1994), pp. 39–40.

3. Ibid., p. 44.

4. Lindsay Crawford, "Troubled Teens Take to the Streets: Rebellious Youths with Nowhere to Turn Run Away from Their Problems and Their Homes," *Silver Chips Online* (April 13, 2000), p. 2.

5. Quoted in R. Barri Flowers, *Domestic Crimes, Family Violence and Child Abuse: A Study of Contemporary American Society* (Jefferson, N.C.: McFarland, 2000), p. 16.

6. Ibid.

7. The Commonwealth Fund, "First Comprehensive National Health Survey of American Women Finds Them at Significant Risk," news release, New York, July 14, 1993.

8. Cited in Flowers, *The Victimization and Exploitation of Women and Children*, p. 30.

9. Flowers, *Domestic Crimes, Family Violence and Child Abuse*, p. 15.

10. Ray Johnson, "Dealing with Domestic Violence and Teen-age Runaways," *San Diego Union-Tribune* (October 22, 1997), p. B5.

11. Cited in Patricia Hersch, "Coming of Age on City Streets," *Psychology Today* (July 20, 1986): 31.

12. Stephanie Arbarbanel, "Women Who Make a Difference," *Family Circle* 107 (January 11, 1994), p. 11.

13. Quoted in ibid.

14. Mimi Silbert, "Delancey Street Study: Prostitution and Sexual Assault," summary of results, Delancey Street Foundation, San Francisco, 1982, p. 3.

15. S. Kuehl, "Legal Remedies for Teen Dating Violence," in Barbara Levy, ed., *Dating Violence: Young Women in Danger* (Seattle: Seal Press, 1998), p. 73.

16. Cited in Flowers, *Domestic Crimes, Family Violence and Child Abuse*, p. 88.

17. Ibid.

18. Johnson, "Dealing with Domestic Violence and Teen-age Runaways," p. B5.

19. Cited in Crawford, "Troubled Teens Take to the Streets," p. 1.

20. U.S. Department of Justice, Office of Juvenile Justice and Delinquency Prevention, *Prostitution of Children and Child-Sex Tourism: An Analysis of Domestic and International Responses* (Alexandria, Va.: National Center for Missing & Exploited Children, 1999), p. 3.

21. U.S. Department of Health and Human Services, Family Youth and Services Bureau, *Youth with Runaway, Throwaway, and Homeless Experiences: Prevalence, Drug Use, and Other At-Risk Behaviors* (Silver Springs, Md.: National Clearinghouse on Families & Youth, October 1995), p. 5.

22. Ibid.

23. Louise Homer, "Criminality-Based Resource for Runaway Girls," *Social Casework* 10 (1973): 474.

24. See, for example, Hildebrand, "Why Runaways Leave Home," pp. 211–16; Robert Shellow, "Suburban Runaways of the 1960s," *Monographs of the Society for Research in Child Development* 32 (1967): 17.

25. Cited in Hersch, "Coming of Age on City Streets," pp. 31–32.

26. Ibid., p. 32.

27. *Youth with Runaway, Throwaway, and Homeless Experiences*, p. 5.

28. Cited in Hersch, "Coming of Age on City Streets," pp. 31–32.

29. Cited in Dotson Rader, "I Want to Die So I Won't Hurt No More," *Parade Magazine* (August 18, 1985): 4.

30. *Youth with Runaway, Throwaway, and Homeless Experiences*, p. 5.

31. Flowers, *The Victimization and Exploitation of Women and Children*, p. 44.

32. Joan J. Johnson, *Teen Prostitution* (Danbury, Conn.: Franklin Watts, 1992), p. 97.

33. Flowers, *The Prostitution of Women and Girls*, pp. 93–97.

34. Judianne Densen-Gerber and S. F. Hutchinson, "Medical-Legal and Societal Problems Involving Children-Child Prostitution, Child Pornography and Drug-Related Abuse: Recommended Legislation," in Selwyn M. Smith, ed., *The Maltreatment of Children* (Baltimore: University Park Press, 1978), p. 322.

35. Martha Modeen, "Four Years after the Becca Bill Became Law, There Are Troubling Questions about How Well It Is Working," *HeraldNet* (June 27, 1999): 1.

36. *Youth with Runaway, Throwaway, and Homeless Experiences*, pp. 4–5.

37. Ibid.

38. Ibid., p. 2.

39. Ibid., p. 5.

40. Johnson, "Dealing with Domestic Violence and Teen-age Runaways," p. B5.

41. Frank York and Robert H. Knight, "Reality Check on Homeless Gay Teens," *Family Policy*, http://www.frc.org/fampol/fp98fcv.htm, 1998; Jenny Gable, "Problems Faced by Homosexual Youth," http://www.lmsa.edu/jgable/lbg/paper.html, 1995.

42. Cited in York and Knight, "Reality Check on Homeless Gay Teens."

43. Flowers, *The Prostitution of Women and Girls*, p. 97.

44. Ibid.

45. R. Barri Flowers, *Children and Criminality: The Child as Victim and Perpetrator* (Westport, Conn.: Greenwood Press, 1986), p. 133.

46. Robin Lloyd, *For Money or Love: Boy Prostitution in America* (New York: Ballantine, 1976), p. 58.

Chapter 5

The Perils for the Teenage Runaway

When teens run away or are forced to leave home, what awaits them is often just as bad, if not worse, than what they ran from. They usually find themselves quickly unable to meet basic needs such as food and shelter. In order to meet these needs, many runaways will be forced into selling their bodies, selling drugs, or other delinquent behavior. In the process of becoming child prostitutes and delinquents, runaways will encounter perils at almost every turn that will further rob them of their childhood and, in some cases, their life. These include AIDS, sexually transmitted diseases, pregnancy, sexual assault, theft, and other forms of victimization. An analysis of the victimization characteristics of runaway episodes found the following:

- Runaways twelve years of age and under were more likely to be sexually exploited than runaways age thirteen to seventeen.
- Preteen runaways were more likely to experience physical violence than runaways thirteen to fourteen years old.
- White runaways were more likely to be victims of violence away from home than black runaways.
- Runaways without a secure place to stay were more likely to be sexually exploited than runaways who stayed with friends or other family members.
- Runaways traveling between ten and fifty miles from home were more likely to be victims of violence than runaways going less than ten miles from home.

- Youth who ran away from home six or more times were more likely to be sexually exploited or victims of theft than those who ran away less than six times.[1]

Few, if any, runaways can be prepared for the consequences of being in an unsafe and dangerous environment outside the home.

RUNAWAYS' BASIC NEEDS

Runaway teens run not only from home but also from the basic necessities a stable home environment provides, such as food, clothing, shelter, and guidance. Within hours after leaving home, most runaways who take to the streets (as opposed to those who stay with a friend or relative) encounter problems in meeting their basic needs. According to a Family and Youth Services Bureau (FYSB) study, two-thirds of street runaways and one-third of those in runaway shelters reported difficulties in meeting the basic needs of food, clothing, shelter, and medical attention.[2] The study noted that a high percentage of runaway youth lacked other necessities when they were living at home such as family stability, support, and encouragement, or were otherwise victimized by child sexual abuse, child battering, mental abuse, or neglect.[3]

Unfortunately, this reality of conflicting vulnerabilities and crises for runaway children only further compounds the situation when out in the world on their own. "Once on the street, young people lack support and guidance in dealing with the negative feelings resulting from their family experiences and in obtaining and retaining a job. With no source of income, many cannot obtain basic necessities like food, clothing, and shelter."[4] This often vicious cycle forces runaways to do whatever they have to or are capable of to survive. With little in the way of marketable skills or talents, the majority must rely on their bodies to get them through one night after the next. Sadly, this can only come at a price no runaway should have to pay.

RUNAWAYS AND TEEN PROSTITUTION

Each year anywhere from several hundred thousand to over a million teenage runaways become teen prostitutes in the United States.[5] In a fifty-state study of teenage prostitution, most of the prostitutes were found to be runaways with substance abuse problems.[6] Runaway prostitutes are most likely to be female; however, studies show that male runaways are well represented among teenage prostitutes.[7] (See also Chapter 12.)

In almost all cases, runaway teens are forced into selling sexual favors after living on the streets, in alleys, or on park benches.[8] Girl runaways' entry into the world of prostitution tends to be influenced as much by the actions of pimps and johns as a means to meet basic necessities. In a *Psy-*

chology Today article, "Coming of Age on City Streets," the author writes: "Runaway girls, scared and alone, are welcomed by pimps who watch for them as they arrive at bus and train stations. They offer them a roof over their heads, a 'caring adult,' clothes, makeup and promises of love and belonging."[9]

The majority of runaway prostitutes fled from abusive environments before becoming homeless. According to Anastasia Volkonsky, who runs an organization combating sexual exploitation, the typical runaway turned streetwalker "experienced a major trauma: incest, domestic violence, rape, or parental abandonment. At an age widely considered too young to handle activities such as voting, drinking alcohol, driving, or holding down a job, these children survive by selling their bodies to strangers. These formative years will leave them with deep scars—should they survive to adulthood."[10]

SEXUAL ACTIVITY AMONG RUNAWAYS

Adolescence often involves sexual activity even for non-runaways with no serious family issues. Before the age of twenty, seven in ten females and eight in ten males in the United States have had sexual relations.[11] For teens living away from home, the incidence of sexual activity is even higher. Along with prostitution, runaways often engage in sexual relations without pay as a natural part of increased independence, puberty, and sexual experimentation.

In a survey on sexual practices of runaways in New York, San Francisco, and Denver, it was found that the average age a runaway girl lost her virginity was under fourteen, and the average age a runaway boy was no longer a virgin was under thirteen.[12] Group sex was a common occurrence among teen runaways. One-third of the boy runaways and one-fourth of the girl runaways had participated in sexual activity that involved more than two individuals. Among gay runaways, the survey reported that nearly four in ten girls and almost one in four boys admitted to having homosexual oral sex. Prostitution-related sexual relations was also a reflection of street life for a high percentage of the runaways.

Many runaway teens were sexually active prior to leaving home. The results have led to unwanted pregnancies and other serious implications such as AIDS. A study of female runaways living in shelters and on the street found that half of the street runaways and two-fifths of the shelter runaways had ever been pregnant.[13] Around one in ten of the runaways on the street and in shelters was pregnant when the study was conducted. Less than one in four runaway girls used birth control.[14]

The relationship between runaways and pregnancy was further established when studying male runways. While 13 percent of male teens with runaway experience admitted getting a female pregnant, only 2 percent of the males who had never run away reported getting a female pregnant.[15]

Another study found that half the male runaways under the age of fourteen were sexually active, thereby increasing the likelihood of impregnating a girl and contracting a sexually transmitted disease.[16]

RUNAWAYS, AIDS, AND SEXUAL DISEASES

Perhaps the biggest threat the runaway faces on the streets is exposure to the deadly AIDS (Acquired Immune Deficiency Syndrome) virus. The high risk lifestyle of the runaway prostitute makes them especially susceptible to contracting the disease. "They have sex with strangers. They use intravenous drugs or love somebody who does. The boys commit homosexual acts and the girls have lovers who earn a living that way."[17]

Some experts believe that runaways turned prostitutes will figure prominently in the next wave of the AIDS epidemic. Patricia Hersch wrote about the frightening relationship between runaway teens and AIDS:

> If geography is destiny, runaway and homeless kids gravitate to the very locations around the country where their risk is greatest. Not only are these kids at higher risk with every sexual contact . . . but they also have higher levels of sexually transmitted diseases. Often their immune systems are already compromised by repeated exposure to infections. . . . Sex more than anything puts runaway kids at risk for AIDS. . . . Their bodies usually become the currency of exchange. . . . There is . . . an epidemic of exposure, and many runaway kids, years hence, may pay horribly for the events of their troubled youth.[18]

It is estimated that as many as 200,000 runaways are at risk for contracting AIDS through prostitution and/or drug use in the United States each year.[19] Around 40 percent of homeless children may carry the AIDS virus, according to a medical worker at New York's largest runaway shelter, Covenant House.[20] Some experts believe the percentage may be even higher.[21] In a study of AIDS infection among runaways at Covenant House, 27 percent of the sample tested positive for HIV (Human Immunodeficiency Virus).[22] It was estimated that 15 percent of the 11,000 runaways passing through Covenant House each year would test HIV positive. However, for runaways engaged in frequent sexual activity, it was estimated that the rate of infection could surpass 50 percent.[23]

The regular sexual exploitation of runaway prostitutes by johns, pimps, and other sexual predators increases the likelihood of becoming infected with a sexually transmitted disease. Studies note a high rate of venereal diseases among runaways.[24] Many carry the diseases unknowingly and pass it to their customers or contract different strains from johns. Other runaways selling sexual favors "know they're flirting with disease. There's an epidemic of old venereal infections, crabs and chlamydia, secondary syphilis and super-gonorrhea, resistant to penicillin."[25]

RUNAWAYS AND SUBSTANCE ABUSE

Most runaway teens use alcohol and/or drugs while away from home. Some were drug or alcohol users before becoming runaways, while many others are introduced to these substances in the course of life and survival on the streets. About seven in ten runaways are substance abusers.[26] Similarly, seven in ten girl streetwalkers consume alcohol, while as many as one in two teen prostitutes is a regular drug user.[27] Many runaways turned prostitutes use mood altering drugs such as heroin and cocaine.[28] Runaways are introduced to drugs by pimps, customers, and other runaways, often becoming addicts before reaching adulthood.[29] The relationship between runaway use of drugs (especially IV drugs) and alcohol and having sex with many partners is seen by experts as being a "vicious" and often deadly combination in contracting AIDS and other diseases.[30]

A typical example of the runaway's road to prostitution and drug addiction can be seen in the following researcher's account of one runaway prostitute:

> At 9, Diane ran away from home. . . . By age 12, she was smoking pot. . . . By 16, she was a hooker and a junkie, sleeping under benches on the streets. . . . Everything had become incidental to the drugs—sex, friendships, plans, promises, security. . . . The first thing on her mind when she woke up was how long she would have to work for her first fix. On cocaine, she could turn tricks for 12- or 14-hour days, the most intense part of the high lasting 15 or 20 seconds.[31]

Few runaways ever seek or receive treatment for substance abuse problems. A survey of runaway substance abusers on the street and in shelters found that only 24 percent of the street runaways and 18 percent of the shelter runaways had ever received treatment for drug or alcohol abuse.[32] The survey further found that runaway substance abusers from families not on public assistance were more likely to receive treatment than those whose families were on public assistance.

RUNAWAYS AND VICTIMIZATION

Runaway children are frequently victimized through sexual exploitation, sexual assault, robberies, and other physical assaults. Sometimes even death occurs as a direct result of being placed in a dangerous, unstable environment. The runaway on the street is at once exposed to dangerous customers, drug addicts, violent or mentally ill homeless people, gang members, unpredictable elements and situations—all of which increases the risk of victimization.[33] The rate of suicidal tendencies among runaway teens is high.[34] There is a direct correlation between the experience of running away and teenage suicide.[35]

Many runaways who are infected with HIV or sexually transmitted diseases or are experiencing other medical problems do not receive proper medical attention, if any. This exacerbates an already perilous situation for runaways in not only surviving the mean streets but putting their health at risk. Because runaways are often caught between worlds, their physical well-being is endangered by the very nature of the life they are forced to live.

Studies show a strong association between runaways who abuse drugs or alcohol and victimization.[36] According to one expert: "Young people on the street are easily taken advantage of by adults. Their substance abuse makes them even more vulnerable or may be the result of having been victimized."[37] Runaway teens are also at high risk for assaultive crimes and robbery. In the FYSB study, one-third of homeless runaways and one-sixth of those staying in shelters reported being victims of assaults, robberies, or both.[38]

RUNAWAYS, DELINQUENCY, AND CRIMINALITY

Children who run away from home are not only at risk for victimization but may victimize others. The correlation between runaways and delinquent or criminal acts has been well established.[39] Most runaways must sell sexual favors to have money for basic necessities. Many turn to drug dealing to support drug habits or as an additional means to provide for food, clothing, and shelter.[40] Theft is a common practice among runaways. The FYSB reported that around four-fifths of their sample of street runaways and two-thirds of the shelter runaways had committed or attempted a theft.[41]

Runaways are also prone to committing violent crimes while on the streets. Researchers have found that there is a direct correlation between runaway violence, violence victimization as runaways, and violence experienced by the runaway prior to leaving home.[42] Around two-thirds of the homeless runaways and half of those in shelters surveyed by the FYSB reported carrying a weapon.[43] Approximately one in four street runaways and one in ten shelter runaways had committed an act of violence using a weapon.

SUMMARY

The runaway faces some serious challenges away from home. Lacking the basic necessities of food, clothing, shelter, and guidance, most who must live on the street turn to prostitution to survive. Others become more sexually promiscuous once on their own. Many become drug or alcohol abusers. This tripartite relationship exposes runaway youth to the AIDS virus, sexually transmitted diseases, pregnancy, and other health issues. Runaways are also at high risk to be sexually or physically assaulted, robbed, exposed to violence, suicidal, and without proper medical care. Substance abuse by runaways is significantly related to victimization.

Runaway children are commonly involved in delinquency or criminal acts as a regular part of street life. This includes theft, violence, and drug dealing. The serious implications of leaving or being thrown out of the home can readily be seen in the convergence of runaway victimization and deviance as a consequence.

NOTES

1. U.S. Department of Justice, Office of Juvenile Justice and Delinquency Prevention, *Law Enforcement Policies and Practices Regarding Missing Children and Homeless Youth: Research Summary* (Washington, D.C.: Government Printing Office, 1993), p. 14.
2. U.S. Department of Health and Human Services, Family and Youth Services Bureau, *Youth with Runaway, Throwaway, and Homeless Experiences: Prevalence, Drug Use, and Other At-Risk Behaviors* (Silver Springs, Md.: National Clearinghouse on Families & Youth, October 1995), p. 5.
3. Ibid.; R. Barri Flowers, *The Victimization and Exploitation of Women and Children: A Study of Physical, Mental and Sexual Maltreatment in the United States* (Jefferson, N.C.: McFarland, 1994), pp. 38–45.
4. Quoted in *Youth with Runaway, Throwaway, and Homeless Experiences*, pp. 5–6.
5. R. Barri Flowers, *The Prostitution of Women and Girls* (Jefferson, N.C.: McFarland, 1998), pp. 71, 89.
6. Sam Meddis, "Teen Prostitution Rising, Study Says," *USA Today* (April 23, 1984), p. 3A. See also R. Barri Flowers, *Sex Crimes, Predators, Perpetrators, Prostitutes, and Victims: An Examination of Sexual Criminality and Victimization* (Springfield, Ill.: Charles C. Thomas, 2000).
7. Flowers, *The Prostitution of Women and Girls*, pp. 71, 134–37; Flowers, *Sex Crimes, Predators, Perpetrators, Prostitutes, and Victims*; Robin Lloyd, *For Money or Love: Boy Prostitution in America* (New York: Ballantine, 1976).
8. Flowers, *The Victimization and Exploitation of Women and Children*, pp. 43, 82–85.
9. Patricia Hersch, "Coming of Age on City Streets," *Psychology Today* (January 1988): 32.
10. Anastasia Volkonsky, "Legalizing the 'Profession' Would Sanction the Abuse," *Insight on the News* 11 (1995): 21.
11. R. Barri Flowers, *The Adolescent Criminal: An Examination of Today's Juvenile Offender* (Jefferson, N.C.: McFarland, 1990), pp. 52–53.
12. Cited in Frank York and Robert H. Knight, "Reality Check on Homeless Gay Teens," *Family Policy*, http://www.frc.org/fampol/fp98fcv.htm, 1998.

13. *Youth with Runaway, Throwaway, and Homeless Experiences*, p. 7.

14. Flowers, *The Victimization and Exploitation of Women and Children*, p. 44.

15. *Youth with Runaway, Throwaway, and Homeless Experiences*, p. 7.

16. Cited in John Zaccaro, Jr., "Children of the Night," *Woman's Day* (March 29, 1988): 138.

17. Ibid., p. 137.

18. Hersch, "Coming of Age on City Streets," p. 35.

19. Ibid., p. 34.

20. Cited in Zaccaro, "Children of the Night," p. 137.

21. Flowers, *The Victimization and Exploitation of Women and Children*, p. 45.

22. Hersch, "Coming of Age on City Streets," p. 37.

23. Ibid.

24. Flowers, *The Victimization and Exploitation of Women and Children*, p. 43.

25. Zaccaro, "Children of the Night," p. 137.

26. Flowers, *The Prostitution of Women and Girls*, p. 93.

27. Ibid., pp. 84–85; D. Kelly Weisberg, *Children of the Night: A Study of Adolescent Prostitution* (Lexington, Mass.: Lexington Books, 1985), pp. 117–19.

28. Flowers, *The Adolescent Criminal*, pp. 59–60.

29. Flowers, *The Prostitution of Women and Girls*, pp. 84–85, 102–3, 130–31.

30. Ibid., pp. 30–36; Martin A. Plant, "Sex Work, Alcohol, Drugs, and AIDS," in Martin A. Plant, ed., *AIDS, Drugs, and Prostitution* (London: Routledge, 1990), pp. 1–17.

31. Myrna Kostash, "Surviving the Streets," *Chatelaine* 67 (October 1994): 103–4.

32. *Youth with Runaway, Throwaway, and Homeless Experiences*, p. 7.

33. Ibid., p. 6; Flowers, *The Victimization and Exploitation of Women and Children*, pp. 43–45.

34. Hersch, "Coming of Age on City Streets," pp. 31–32; Flowers, *The Prostitution of Women and Girls*, p. 87.

35. Flowers, *The Prostitution of Women and Girls*, pp. 93, 97–98.

36. Ibid., pp. 84–85.

37. Quoted in *Youth with Runaway, Throwaway, and Homeless Experiences*, p. 6.

38. Ibid.

39. Flowers, *The Adolescent Criminal*, pp. 51–52.

40. R. Barri Flowers, *Drugs, Alcohol and Criminality in American Society* (Jefferson, N.C.: McFarland, 1999), pp. 99–111.

41. *Youth with Runaway, Throwaway, and Homeless Experiences*, p. 6.

42. Ibid.; R. Barri Flowers, *Children and Criminality: The Child as Victim and Perpetrator* (Westport, Conn.: Greenwood Press, 1986), pp. 101–2.

43. *Youth with Runaway, Throwaway, and Homeless Experiences*, p. 6.

Chapter 6

Theoretical Approaches to Running Away and Teenage Prostitution

The question of why children run away from home and become engaged in a prostitution lifestyle has been explored through theoretical perspectives. Biologically, psychologically, and sociologically based theories have been applied to juvenile and young adult deviance and its causation. Some early theories such as those belonging to the biological positivistic school of thought have basically been rejected. Theories with social, cultural, or learning concepts are given more credibility in addressing teenage antisocial behavior. Most modern criminologists and theoreticians view such aberrations as multicausal, and approach it as such in attempting to explain.

The same is true in addressing prostitution in a theoretical framework. Many of the explanations for prostitution have moved away from biological premises to theories that tend to incorporate sociological, psychological, and economic points of view.

In spite of the acceptance of a number of current theories on juvenile delinquency and teen prostitution as sound by many professionals and experts in delinquent behavior, most such theories have shortcomings that cannot be dismissed when applying such causes to policy and practice.

DELINQUENCY THEORIES AND THE RUNAWAY

Theories on delinquency tend to focus primarily on inherited and learned antisocial behavior and the biological or sociological variables that contribute to this causation. Theoretical applications in juvenile deviance most relevant to the runaway juvenile offender include those that are biologically based, personality disorder theories, social control theories, and cultural transmission theories.

Biologically Based Theories

Biological theoretical perspectives on delinquency posit that it is primarily the result of biological influences. The biological positivistic school of thought originated with the work of Italian criminologist Cesare Lombroso. In his 1876 book, *L'Uomo Delinquente*, Lombroso advanced that delinquents were, in fact, products of atavism, or biological throwbacks to earlier genetic forms.[1] Influenced by Charles Darwin's theory of evolution, Lombroso believed that criminals could be differentiated from noncriminals by certain physical stigmata.[2]

Other early biological theorists continued to relate juvenile delinquency to biology and genetics. In the 1939 book, *Crime and the Man*, Ernest Hooton theorized that criminals could be distinguished by body types and, as such, were physically and mentally inferior to law-abiding citizens.[3] In the 1940s, William Sheldon sought to systematically relate body types (mesomorphics, in particular) to juvenile delinquency, contending that there were specific somatotype and personality differences between delinquents and non-delinquents.[4] Similarly, Sheldon Glueck and Eleanor Glueck followed up on Sheldon's principles in concluding that mesomorphs were disproportionately represented among institutionalized delinquents.[5]

Most early theories of juvenile antisocial behavior have since been discredited due to their unscientific basis, lack of control groups in the general population, and findings that failed to account for multiple causal factors in delinquency formation.

Modern biological positivism has been more promising in explaining juvenile deviance from the norm. Studies of twins have been undertaken to determine the relationship between genetics and delinquency. Concordance refers genetically to "the degree in which twins or related subject pairings both show a specific condition or behavior."[6] In his review of twin studies, Hans Eysench posited that the consistent disparity in concordance between identical and fraternal twins made heredity to be "beyond any doubt . . . an extremely important part in the genesis of criminal behavior."[7] However, some researchers have disputed this contention. For example, a study by Odd Dalgaard and Einar Kringlen found no significant differences in concordance rates between identical and fraternal twins.[8]

Adoption studies have also focused on a biological approach to delinquent behavior. One of the most comprehensive studies of adoptees was undertaken by Sarnoff Mednick, W. F. Gabrielli, and Bernard Hutchings. In comparing the conviction records of 14,427 adoptees to the conviction records of their biological and adoptive parents, it was concluded that the transmission of deviant tendencies through genetics increased the probability of children becoming involved in delinquent or criminal behavior.[9] In another study of adoptees, Hutchings and Mednick concluded there was a strong relationship between the criminality of male adoptees and that of their biological fathers.[10] However, the researchers noted the importance of environment in juvenile delinquency, finding that when biological and adoptive parents had criminal records, the chances of an adoptee becoming antisocial was that much greater.

Current biological research into delinquent and criminal behavior has been done in the behavior sciences, including such areas as biochemistry, endocrinology, immunology, and psychophysiology.[11] Though some results have proven to be interesting in relating biological variables to the understanding of juvenile deviance and other antisocial human behavior, the findings are still too new or inconclusive to properly evaluate.

Personality Disorder Theories

Personality disorder theories on delinquency tend to examine personality flaws and emotional problems in explaining juvenile antisocial or aberrant behavior. Some early theorists ascribed delinquency to emotional impairment or disturbances. In the 1930s, Cyril Burt found that 85 percent of the delinquents in his sample were emotionally impaired.[12] Similarly, in William Healy and Augusta Bronner's comparison of delinquent and nondelinquent siblings, the researchers posited that over 90 percent of the delinquents were unhappy, discontented, or "extremely emotionally disturbed because of emotion-provoking situations or experiences," compared to 13 percent of the control group.[13] Critics have largely rejected emotional variables as causal in delinquency, per se, pointing towards methodology weaknesses and subjectiveness in defining emotional problems.[14]

In the 1950s, an *Interpersonal Maturity Levels* (I-Levels) *System theory* was developed in explaining juvenile delinquency. According to the theory, there are seven stages of interpersonal maturity necessary for becoming socialized. I-Levels theorists postulated that delinquents were generally at lower levels of maturity than nondelinquents.[15] The I-Levels proposition has been criticized for its premise that adolescent offenders are less mature than nondelinquent adolescents and because of its lack of validity through "comprehensive comparative examinations of the maturity levels of nondelinquents."[16] Further, I-Levels research fails to account for the high incidence of self-reported delinquency among those who otherwise would not be labeled as delinquents.

Psychopathic personality theories have been used by some researchers in modern psychology to explain juvenile deviant behavior. William McCord and Joan McCord advanced that the origins of the psychopathic personality lie in brain damage, physical trauma, and extreme childhood emotional deprivation.[17] In seeking to relate psychopathic personalities to delinquency and adult criminality, Lee Robins did a follow-up study of 524 patients at a child guidance clinic three decades after their treatment. More than 70 percent of the juveniles being treated at the clinic had been referred by the juvenile court for "antisocial behavior" such as running away, truancy, and theft.[18] The implication was that the clinic delinquents (22 percent were diagnosed as sociopaths) generally had psychologically troubled, antisocial lives as adolescents and adults. There has been little empirical evidence to support relating psychopathy to delinquent behavior. In Herbert Quay's in-depth study of personality patterns of delinquents, the proportion that could be defined as psychopaths was relatively small.[19]

Intelligence quotient (IQ) theories have been used by some recent theorists in examining delinquency. Most notable is Travis Hirschi and Michael Hindelang's review of IQ research which led the two to contend that there is a strong relationship between delinquency and IQ, independent of such other factors as race and social class.[20] They found that a low IQ can affect school performance, which in turn can lead to running away and other deviant behavior by juveniles. R. Loeber and T. Dishion reached a similar conclusion in their review of the literature.[21] Though IQ may be related to delinquency when combined with other elements such as peer pressure, most criminologists do not support this theory because of its cultural biases and methodological weakness.

Social Control Theories

Social control theories explain antisocial behavior by youth "in terms of inadequate external social control and internalized social values for some juveniles, which creates a freedom in which delinquency becomes possible."[22] Control theorists are not so much concerned with the motivations to deviate from the norm but rather "the social institutions that produce conditions favorable to either violating or refraining from breaking the law."[23]

Social bonding theory may be the most influential social control theory. According to Hirschi in his book, *Causes of Delinquency*, the social bond that ties juveniles to the social order consists of four components: (1) *attachment* (to family and friends), (2) *commitment* (the devotion to social conformity), (3) *involvement* (in legitimate activities), and (4) *belief* (feelings regarding conformity).[24] The less one believes he or she should conform to social convention, the more likely the individual would be to become a nonconformist or law violator. Hirschi held that delinquent youth are without the intimate attachments, goals, and moral standards that connect most people to societal norms and values, hence allowing them to commit antisocial acts such as running away or prostitution.

Social bonding theory has been criticized for its reliance on attachment as a primary component to preventing delinquency, as many troubled youths' main attachments may be other delinquents. Another argument is that the theory is inadequate in explaining the variance in the frequency of delinquent acts. In spite of these weaknesses, many support social bonding theory in its basic tenets in addressing delinquency.

Containment theory is another social control theory that was advanced by Walter Reckless.[25] It contends that juveniles are restrained from committing antisocial acts by a combination of *inner containment* (a positive self-concept, self-components, well-developed superego, a high tolerance level, and positive goal orientation) and *outer containment* (positive social ties, strong parent supervision, and institutional support of the juvenile's positive self-concept). According to Reckless, these containments act as buffers against forces that encourage or influence antisocial behavior such as a delinquent subculture, temptations, and environment. Though both "inner and outer containment components were the most effective counter-delinquency measure, strong inner containment could compensate for defective or weak outer containment and vice versa."[26] Reckless's theory has been criticized mainly for its methodological shortcomings and questions concerning the validity of his self-concept measures.

Overall, social control theories appear to be successful in explaining certain dimensions of delinquent behavior such as "how we can comprehend the episodic delinquency of most adolescents and why even the most delinquent youths engage in delinquency only under certain circumstances."[27] Empirical studies tend to support their basic premise. However, the theories fail to adequately explain the role of internalized values and norms, or sufficiently account for the social-structural causes of delinquency.

Cultural Transmission Theories

Cultural transmission theories view juvenile delinquency as learned behavior—or a reflection of the norms, values, beliefs, and behavioral characteristics learned from those the juvenile interacts with. Thus, cultural transmission theory proposes that delinquency is caused primarily by conforming to a set of behavioral norms of a subculture that goes against conventional norms and values as they relate to behavior and obeying the law. Delinquent norms are regarded as intergenerational in the socialization process and techniques of perpetrating delinquent acts.

The most prominent cultural transmission theory is *differential association theory*.[28] Developed by Edwin Sutherland and outlined in his 1939 text, *Principles in Criminology*, the theory advances that delinquency is a learned behavior and as such, "persons who are selectively or differentially exposed to delinquent associates are likely to acquire that trait as well. The primary mechanism by which this occurs is attitude transference, meaning that individuals acquire attitudes of 'definitions' consistent with delinquency from significant others."[29] Sutherland held that a juvenile "becomes delinquent because of an excess of definitions favorable to violation of law over definitions unfavorable to violation of law."[30] Differential association theory contends that delinquency is a social rather than antisocial pattern of behavior, and that the probability of a person engaging in juvenile delinquent acts such as teen prostitution correlates directly with the priority, frequency, duration, and intensity of contact with antisocial elements or, conversely, social elements.

While differential association theory has wide support among criminologists and delinquency experts in explaining juvenile violations of the law, it has been attacked for its lack of clarity in some of its terminology, inability to be validated empirically, and failure to explain the origins of learned delinquency and criminality.

Social learning theory sought to modify differential association theory in explaining deviant behavior.[31] Developed in the late 1960s by Robert Burgess and Ronald Akers, social learning theory—also known as *differential-reinforcement theory*—proposes that juveniles learn deviant behavior such as running away and prostitution through social interaction with those "who constitute their primary source of reinforcement."[32] These social reinforcements are seen for the most part as "symbolic and verbal rewards for supporting group norms and expectations."[33] Social learning theory posits that the lesser role of nonsocial reinforcement, relating mostly to physiological variables, may be relevant for certain offenses such as juvenile substance abuse. According to Akers and colleagues, social learning theory "as a general perspective in deviance is part of a larger move towards incorporation of modern behaviorism into sociological theory. As such it is a theoretical perspective which is compatible with the more specific forays into the explanation of deviant behavior."[34]

Critics of social learning theory have argued that nonsocial reinforcers are stronger than social reinforcers in explaining deviant behavior. There has also been debate as to whether the theory can be sufficiently tested.[35] However, the basic learning premise of social control theory has been supported empirically.[36]

Labeling theory is another important theoretical approach to delinquency, relevant in particular to the runaway deviant or status offender.[37] Unlike other cultural transmission theories that primarily concern themselves with the juvenile's response to or interaction with deviant behavioral norms, labeling theory focuses mostly on "the societal responses to such persons, their behavior, and the results of this response."[38] According to the labeling proposition, juvenile deviance such as running away and other status offenses "does not emerge directly from an initial act of deviance. It is the imposition of the deviant label by a social audience and the reaction of the individual to this labeling that results in a deviant career."[39] Referring to labelers as "moral entrepreneurs, Howard Becker described the process of labeling:

> Social groups create deviance by making rules whose infractions constitute deviance, and by applying those rules to particular people and labeling them as outsiders. From this point of view, deviance is not a quality of the act a person commits, but rather a consequence of the application by others of rules and sanctions to an "offender." The deviant is one to whom the label has successfully been applied; deviant behavior is behavior that people so label.[40]

Labeling theorists contend that most juveniles commit acts that would constitute processing through the juvenile court system and are therefore labeled delinquent or "forced to join a deviant group because of newly reduced legitimate opportunities and a now negative self-image."[41] However, the labeling of youths as delinquent "is differentially applied by those who control social power," including lawmakers and law enforcement.[42] Consequently, juveniles occupying the low end of the social and economic strata often have the least power to resist the stigmatization of labeling.

While labeling theory has support among many as a valid theory in explaining the process of creating delinquency and self-perception as a delinquent, critics point towards methodological shortcomings and an inability to determine the circumstances that are necessary in order for a person or act to be labeled deviant.[43]

A *deterrence theory* has also been applied to status offenders, such as runaways, in explaining deviant behavior or lack of. Deterrence theory assumes that a youth "will not participate in deviant behavior if previously experienced punishment or if perceptions regarding the risk of punishment for a particular act suggests that the risks involved outweigh the potential rewards of the act."[44] Unlike labeling theory that "would predict that children processed through the courts will be more recidivistic than those diverted from the courts, deterrence theory would predict the opposite."[45]

Criticism has been leveled against deterrence theory and recidivism among youthful offenders because of methodological and interpretative difficulties. However, some studies have supported the deterrence perspective. In J. McCord's follow up study on juveniles involved in the Cambridge-Somerville youth program, the researcher found that those who had received a fine for their first conviction had a lower chance of recidivism than those who were simply released with no official processing through the juvenile court.[46] Other criminologists have found that deterrence from deviant behavior may vary from youth to youth, depending on the experience of the juvenile in deviant behavior or the dynamics of the deviant subculture the person belongs to.[47] With respect to deterrence theory, Sharla Rausch observed: "If status offenders have relatively little experience with delinquency or with juvenile courts, regular court processing might serve to deter them from, rather than to label and commit them to, further delinquency."[48]

PROSTITUTION THEORIES

Most of the theoretical approaches to prostitution have focused on female or general prostitution in terms of psychological, sociological, and economic explanations. Teenage prostitution is generally regarded in theory as being causative by functions in society.

Psychological Theories

Early psychological theories on prostitution were based mainly on the psychoanalytic writings of Sigmund Freud.[49] He regarded prostitutes as biologically deficient and therefore unable to resolve the Oedipus conflict. Freud believed that prostitutes were morally inferior and less able to control their impulses than others. Many Freudian disciples perceived prostituted females as frigid with "immature psychosexual development and severely deficient abject relationships."[50] However, in case studies of "sex delinquents and prostitutes [there] failed to indicate any general state of abnormality."[51] In a study by Jennifer James, prostitutes tended to experience a higher rate of orgasms than females in the general population, contradicting the indication of frigidity among prostitution involved females.[52]

Modern psychology and psychiatry have long since dismissed Freudian theories on prostitution as biased, psychologically unsound, and lacking of necessary social and economical variables. Current psychological research on prostitutes has focused on such mental disorders as depression, schizophrenia, and suicidal tendencies.[53]

Sociological Theories

Early sociological theories on prostitution were also fraught with gender biases and methodology problems. Sociologist William Thomas attributed female prostitution to a need for excitement and response, postulating that prostitution was the "most likely avenue to satisfy those needs."[54] One critic attacked his propositions as "sexist in that females were identified as offenders through sexual behavior."[55] In the 1950 work, *The Criminality of Women*, Otto Pollak held that female crimes were typically sexually motivated and that female sex criminals such as prostitutes were more of a hidden nature and thus inadequately accounted for in the statistics.[56] In rejecting his arguments, a writer noted: "Pollak's theories on causation were heavily influenced by Freudian analysis [and] therefore are subject to the same criticism."[57]

Modern sociologically based theories have explained prostitution in relation to the family, social structure, sexual pathology, and morality. Kingsley Davis's functionalist theory of prostitution proposed "the function served by prostitution is the protection of the family unit, maintenance of the chastity and purity of the 'respectable' citizenry."[58] Charles Winick and Paul Kinsie advanced in *The Lively Commerce* that the social structure is threatened by prostitution because "people tend to equate sexual activity with stable relationships, typified by the family."[59] In a social pathology proposition, Edwin Lemert described prostitution as a "formal extension of more generalized sexual pathology in our culture, of which sexual promiscuity and thinly disguised commercial exploitation of sex in informal context plays a large and important part."[60]

According to cultural transmission theories, teenage prostitution is the result of a "weakening of family and neighborhood control and the persistence and transmission from person to person of traditional delinquent activities."[61] Some evidence exists to support the introduction of many runaways and street youth into prostitution through other prostituted teenagers or from learned behavior.[62] Other cultural transmission theorists blame juvenile prostitution on "urban anonymity and the weakening of traditional and moral values."[63] This view further contends that prostitution is not a reflection of ecological factors, but can be seen on all occupational and income levels. The fact that runaways and teen prostitutes cross the socioeconomic strata, as do those that they service, lends credence to this perspective.

Economic Theories

Economic theorists attribute prostitution to economic influences that cause individuals to enter and remain in the sex-for-sale industry. Winick and Kinsey postulated that one's decision to enter into prostitution is based primarily on few opportunities in the work force and the recognition of the income potential prostitution presents.[64] Lemert held that a female's inferior power in society, including less control over material gains, makes prostitution a viable choice to balance the gender differential.[65] According to James, there are five aspects of the social and economic structure that lead females into prostitution:

- No other occupations are available to unskilled or low skilled females that provide a comparable income to that of prostitution.
- Practically no other occupations for unskilled or low skilled females provide the independent and adventurous lifestyle of prostitution.
- The traditional role of the female is virtually synonymous with the culturally defined female sex role that focuses on appearance, service, and sexuality.

- The cultural significance of wealth and material items leads some females to desire what is normally unavailable due to their socioeconomic position in society.
- The discrepancy between accepted male and female sex roles creates the "Madonna-whore" view of female sexuality; as a result, females who are sexually active outside their normal sex role expectations such as in prostitution, are labeled as deviants and lose their social status.[66]

Research on male prostitutes has found that boy prostitution is also closely tied to economic necessity or financial opportunity, irrespective of traditional sex roles or expectations.[67]

In her study of teenage prostitution, Joan Johnson describes money as a symbol for love among prostituted youth.[68] Many teens become addicted to the money made from prostitution, some selling sexual favors while still living under their parents' roof. Johnson suggests that because most teenage prostitutes lack self-esteem, earning money through prostitution "makes them feel good about themselves," as they are amazed that "people will pay for their bodies."[69]

SUMMARY

Theories explaining runaway behavior and teenage prostitution can be found in the biologically, psychologically, and sociologically based schools of thought. While much of the biological positivistic propositions on juvenile deviance have been abandoned, more recent work in the behavioral sciences has proven more promising. Delinquency theories tend to deal primarily with genetically transmitted behavior and learned behavior. Such theoretical views as social bonding, differential association, labeling, and deterrence theories have widespread acceptance for their principles in establishing the causes of deviant behavior among juveniles. Most modern criminologists subscribe to multiple theories in examining juvenile offenders and patterns of antisocial behavior such as running away and prostitution.

The theoretical causes of prostitution are reflected mostly in gender-based sociological and economic theories. Current psychological perspectives relate prostituted individuals to such mental disorders as depression, schizophrenia, and suicidal tendencies. Sociological theories explain prostitution in causal terms related to the family, social structure, immorality, and sexual exploitation. Economic theorists blame prostitution on economic conditions, financial deprivation, the social structure, sex role stereotypes, and the substituting of money for love.

NOTES

1. See Cesare Lombroso, *Crime, Its Causes and Remedies* (Boston: Little, Brown, 1918); Cesare Lombroso and William Ferrero, *Criminal Man* (Montclair, N.J.: Patterson Smith, 1972).

2. Lombroso and Ferrero, *Criminal Man*; R. Barri Flowers, *The Adolescent Criminal: An Examination of Today's Juvenile Offender* (Jefferson, N.C.: McFarland, 1990), pp. 111–12.

3. Ernest A. Hooton, *Crime and the Man* (Cambridge, Mass.: Harvard University Press, 1939).

4. William H. Sheldon, *Varieties of Temperament* (New York: Harper & Row, 1956).

5. Flowers, *The Adolescent Criminal*, pp. 112–13.

7. Hans J. Eysench, *The Inequality of Man* (San Diego: Edits Publishers, 1973), p. 167.

8. Odd S. Dalgaard and Einar Kringlen, "A Norwegian Twin Study of Criminality," *British Journal of Criminology* 16 (1976): 213–33.

9. Sarnoff A. Mednick, W. F. Gabrielli, and Bernard Hutchings, "Genetic Influences in Criminal Convictions: Evidence from an Adoption Cohort," *Science* 234 (1984): 891–94.

10. Bernard Hutchings and Sarnoff A. Mednick, "Registered Criminality in the Adoptive and Biological Parents of Registered Male Criminal Adoptees," in R. R. Fiene, D. Rosenthal, and H. Brill, eds., *Genetic Research in Psychiatry* (Baltimore: Johns Hopkins University Press, 1975).

11. Flowers, *The Adolescent Criminal*, p. 117. See also Andrea Dorfman, "The Criminal Mind: Body Chemistry and Nutrition May Lie at the Roots of Crime," *Science Digest* 92 (1984): 44; Diana H. Fishbein, "Biological Perspectives in Criminology," in Dean G. Rojek and Gary F. Jensen, eds., *Exploring Delinquency: Causes and Control* (Los Angeles: Roxbury, 1996), pp. 102–8.

12. Cyril Burt, *The Young Delinquent* (London: University of London Press, 1938).

13. Flowers, *The Adolescent Criminal*, p. 119; William Healy and Augusta F. Bronner, *New Light on Delinquency and Its Treatment* (New Haven, Conn.: Yale University Press, 1936).

14. Flowers, *The Adolescent Criminal*, p. 119.

15. Clyde Sullivan, Marguerite Q. Grant, and J. Douglas Grant, "The Development of Interpersonal Maturity: Applications to Delinquency," *Psychiatry* 20 (1957): 373–85.

16. Flowers, *The Adolescent Criminal*, p. 120.

17. William McCord and Joan McCord, *The Psychopath* (Princeton, N.J.: Van Nostrand, 1964).

18. Lee W. Robins, *Deviant Children Grown Up* (Baltimore: Williams and Wilkins, 1966).

19. Herbert C. Quay, "Crime Causation: Psychological Theories," in S. H. Kadish, ed., *Encyclopedia of Crime and Justice*, Vol. 1 (New York: Free Press, 1983), p. 340; Herbert C. Quay, "Patterns of Delinquent Behavior," in Herbert C. Quay,

ed., *Handbook of Juvenile Delinquency* (New York: Wiley-Interscience, 1987), pp. 118–38.

20. Travis Hirschi and Michael J. Hindelang, "Intelligence and Delinquency: A Revisionist Review," *American Sociological Review* 42 (1977): 571–86.

21. R. Loeber and T. Dishion, "Early Predictors of Male Delinquency: A Review," *Psychological Bulletin* 94 (1983): 68–99.

22. Flowers, *The Adolescent Criminal*, p. 124.

23. Ibid.

24. Travis Hirschi, *Causes of Delinquency* (Berkeley: University of California Press, 1969).

25. Walter C. Reckless, *The Crime Problem*, 5th ed. (Santa Monica, Calif.: Goodyear, 1973); Walter C. Reckless, Simon Dinitz, and Ellen Murray, "Self-Concept as an Insulator against Delinquency," in James E. Teele, ed., *Juvenile Delinquency: A Reader* (Itasca, Ill.: Peacock, 1970).

26. Flowers, *The Adolescent Criminal*, p. 126.

27. Ibid., pp. 126–27.

28. Edwin H. Sutherland, *Principles of Criminology* (Philadelphia: Lippincott, 1939).

29. E. Mark Warr, "Age, Peers, and Delinquency," in Dean G. Rojek and Gary F. Jensen, eds., *Exploring Delinquency: Causes and Control* (Los Angeles: Roxbury, 1996), p. 129.

30. Edwin H. Sutherland, *Criminology*, 4th ed. (Philadelphia: Lippincott, 1947), p. 6.

31. Robert L. Burgess and Ronald L. Akers, "A Differential Association-Reinforcement Theory of Criminal Behavior," *Social Problems* 14 (1966): 128–47; Ronald L. Akers, *Deviant Behavior: A Social Learning Approach*, 3rd ed. (Belmont, Calif.: Wadsworth, 1985).

32. Flowers, *The Adolescent Criminal*, p. 131.

33. Ibid.

34. Ronald L. Akers, Marvin D. Krohn, Lonn Lanza-Kaduce, and Marcia Radosevich, "Social Learning and Deviant Behavior: A Specific Test of a General Theory," in Dean G. Rojek and Gary F. Jensen, eds., *Exploring Delinquency: Causes and Control* (Los Angeles: Roxbury, 1996), p. 120.

35. Flowers, *The Adolescent Criminal*, p. 131.

36. See, for example, Werner Honig, *Operant Behavior: Areas of Research and Application* (New York: Appleton-Century-Crofts, 1966); Barry McLaughlin, *Learning and Social Behavior* (New York: Free Press, 1971); Arthur Staats, *Social Behaviorism* (Homewood, Ill.: Dorsey Press, 1975).

37. Edwin Schur, *Labeling Deviant Behavior* (New York: Harper & Row, 1972); Travis Hirschi, "Labeling Theory and Juvenile Delinquency: An Assessment of the Evidence," in W. R. Gove, ed., *The Labeling of Deviance: Evaluating a Perspective* (New York: John Wiley, 1975), pp. 181–203.

38. Flowers, *The Adolescent Criminal*, p. 131.

39. Sharla Rausch, "Court Processing versus Diversion of Status Offenders: A Test of Deterrence and Labeling Theories," in Dean G. Rojek and Gary F. Jensen, eds., *Exploring Delinquency: Causes and Control* (Los Angeles: Roxbury, 1996), p. 288.

40. Howard Becker, *Outsiders, Studies in the Sociology of Deviance* (New York: Macmillan, 1964), p. 9.
41. Rausch, "Court Processing versus Diversion of Status Offenders," p. 288.
42. Flowers, *The Adolescent Criminal*, p. 131.
43. Ibid., p. 132.
44. Rausch, "Court Processing versus Diversion of Status Offenders," p. 289.
45. Ibid.
46. J. McCord, "Myths and Realities about Criminal Sanctions," paper presented at the American Society of Criminology Convention, San Francisco, November 1980, p. 11.
47. B. Thorsell and L. Klemke, "The Labeling Process: Reinforcement or Deterrent," *Law & Society Review* 6 (1972): 393–403; C. Tittle, "Deterrents or Labeling?" *Social Forces* 53, 3 (1975): 399–410.
48. Rausch, "Court Processing versus Diversion of Status Offenders," p. 289.
49. Sigmund Freud, *New Introductory Lectures in Psychoanalysis* (New York: W. W. Norton, 1933).
50. R. Barri Flowers, *Women and Criminality: The Woman as Victim, Offender, and Practitioner* (Westport, Conn.: Greenwood Press, 1987), p. 121.
51. Ibid.
52. Jennifer James, "Motivations for Entrance into Prostitution," in Laura Crites, ed., *The Female Offender* (Lexington, Mass.: Lexington Books, 1976), p. 190.
53. R. Barri Flowers, *The Prostitution of Women and Girls* (Jefferson, N.C.: McFarland, 1998), p. 24; R. Barri Flowers, *Children and Criminality: The Child as Victim and Perpetrator* (Westport, Conn.: Greenwood Press, 1986), pp. 81–83.
54. Joy Pollock, "Early Theories of Female Criminality," in Lee H. Bowker, ed., *Women, Crime, and the Criminal Justice System* (Lexington, Mass.: Lexington Books, 1978), p. 45; William I. Thomas, *Sex and Society: Studies in the Social Psychology of Sex* (Boston: Little, Brown, 1907); William I. Thomas, *The Unadjusted Girl: With Cases and Standpoint for Behavior Analysis* (New York: Harper & Row, 1923).
55. Pollock, "Early Theories of Female Criminality," p. 45.
56. Otto Pollak, *The Criminality of Women* (Philadelphia: University of Philadelphia Press, 1950).
57. Pollock, "Early Theories of Female Criminality," p. 50.
58. Flowers, *Women and Criminality*, p. 121; Kingsley Davis, "The Sociology of Prostitution," *American Sociological Review* 2 (1937): 744–55.
59. Charles Winick and Paul M. Kinsie, *The Lively Commerce: Prostitution in the United States* (Chicago: Quadrangle Books, 1971).
60. Edwin M. Lemert, *Social Pathology* (New York: McGraw-Hill, 1951), p. 237.
61. Robert E. Faris, *Social Disorganization* (New York: Ronald Press, 1955).
62. Flowers, *The Prostitution of Women and Girls*, p. 80; Joan J. Johnson, *Teen Prostitution* (Danbury, Conn.: Franklin Watts, 1992), p. 87.
63. Flowers, *Women and Criminality*, p. 122; James, "Motivations for Entrance into Prostitution," p. 186; Norman Jackson, Richard O'Toole, and Gilbert Geis, "The Self-Image of the Prostitute," in John H. Gagnon and William Simon, eds., *Sexual Deviance* (New York: Harper & Row, 1967), p. 46.
64. Winick and Kinsie, *The Lively Commerce*, p. 271.

65. Lemert, *Social Pathology.*

66. James, "Motivations for Entrance into Prostitution," p. 194.

67. Flowers, *The Prostitution of Women and Girls*, pp. 138–42; Robin Lloyd, *For Money or Love: Boy Prostitution in America* (New York: Ballantine, 1966).

68. Johnson, *Teen Prostitution*, pp. 102–3.

69. Ibid., p. 103.

Chapter 7

Policy, Practice, and Response to Runaway and Prostitution Involved Teens

The problem of runaway and prostituted teenagers and the implications of such have resulted in a number of policy initiatives and responses in addressing the issues. Strategies for preventing children from running away and focusing on their needs as prostitution involved youth have been implemented through legislation, juvenile and criminal justice system efforts, and improvement in social service and child welfare programs. Efforts have also been made to respond to at-risk teens' medical and mental health needs, as well as to increase outreach programs to reduce the potential for running away from home and turning to a prostituted lifestyle. In spite of such positive approaches to the plight of runaway and sexually exploited youth, most experts agree that more effort is needed from policymakers, social services, community organizations, and the family to keep teenagers in a safe environment and rescue those who have slipped through the cracks.

FEDERAL POLICY

Federal programs aimed at responding to youth at risk for running away and teenage prostitution and those responsible for child abuse and child sexual exploitation can be seen in a number of important pieces of legislation since the mid-1970s. These include the Child Abuse Prevention and Treatment Act, the Juvenile Justice and Delinquency Prevention Act, the Protection of Children Against Sexual Exploitation Act, the Runaway and Homeless Youth Act, the Missing Children Act, and the creation of the National Center for Missing and Exploited Children.

Child Abuse Prevention and Treatment Act

The Child Abuse Prevention and Treatment Act was enacted in 1974 and amended in 1978 in response to increasing public concern about the growing numbers of abused, neglected, and exploited children in the United States.[1] In addition to defining child abuse and neglect, the Act provided for several programs aimed at combating these problems and their implications, including

> (1) the establishment of a National Center on Child Abuse and Neglect, (2) increasing public awareness on child maltreatment, detection, and reporting, (3) assisting states and local communities in developing more effective mechanisms for delivery of services to families, (4) providing training and technical assistance to state and local communities in dealing with the problems of child abuse and neglect, and (5) supporting research into causal and preventative measure in child victimization.[2]

For states to qualify for federal funds, they were required to meet certain criteria such as a uniform comprehensive definition of child abuse and neglect, investigation of child abuse reports, confidentiality of records, and the appointment of guardians ad litem for minors involved in child abuse or neglect judicial proceedings.

National Center on Child Abuse and Neglect (NCCAN)

The National Center on Child Abuse and Neglect was established by P.L. 93–247 in 1974 and reauthorized in 1988 under the Child Abuse Prevention, Adoption, and Family Services Act of 1988.[3] As the federal agency responsible for matters involving child abuse and neglect, the NCCAN administers grants to states and territories, organizations nationwide, and local agencies for research, service programs, and assistance with the identification, treatment, and prevention of child maltreatment.

National Child Abuse and Neglect Data System (NCANDS)

The National Child Abuse and Neglect Data System was established by NCCAN in response to the legislation enacted in 1988.[4] As part of the Administration on Children, Youth and Families (ACYF), NCANDS collects, analyzes, and disseminates data on child maltreatment from child protective services agencies. Through this data collection, ACYF, "seeks to provide information to concerned citizens, communities, child welfare practitioners, administrators, researchers, and policymakers so that data are available to inform practice and policy."[5]

Juvenile Justice and Delinquency Prevention Act

The Juvenile Justice and Delinquency Prevention Act was enacted in 1974 and amended in 1980 and 1996.[6] It was created to identify dependent and neglected children and status offenders—such as runaways—in order to divert them from institutionalization facilities used to house juvenile delinquents and adult offenders. The Act required (1) a comprehensive assessment of the existing juvenile justice system's effectiveness, (2) the impetus for development and implementation of innovative alternatives in the prevention of delinquency and diversion of status offenders from the juvenile justice system to deal more effectively with juvenile offenders.

> For states to receive federal funds, the Act mandated that juveniles who are charged with or who have committed offenses that would not be criminal if committed by an adult or offenses which do not constitute violations of valid court orders, or alien juveniles in custody, or such nonoffenders as dependent or neglected children, shall not be placed in secure detention facilities or secure correctional facilities, but must be placed in shelter facilities.[7]

However, federal regulations "have interpreted the Act to permit accused status offenders and nonoffenders to be held in secure juvenile facilities for up to twenty-four hours following initial contact with the police or the court."[8]

A *sight and sound separation* provision of the Act required that "juveniles alleged to be or found to be delinquent and [status offenders and nonoffenders] shall not be detained or confined in any institution in which they have contact with adult persons incarcerated because they have been convicted of a crime or are awaiting trial on criminal charges."[9]

The 1980 amendment to the Act, referred to as the *jail and lockup removal* requirement, further sought to protect juveniles from harm by stating that they shall not "be detained or confined in any jail or lockup for adults."[10] As amended in 1996, the Act further specified that states "clarify the sight and sound separation requirement—in nonresidential areas brief, accidental contact is not a reportable violation."[11]

Runaway and Homeless Youth Act

The Runaway and Homeless Youth Act (RHYA) was enacted in 1978, and amended in 1980, in order to provide assistance to local organization for operating temporary shelters for runaways.[12] The Act further addresses the seriousness of the problem of runaways and the implications thereof, such as teenage prostitution, substance abuse, child abuse, and delinquency. Grants were made available for the establishment and maintenance of runaway shelters by states, localities, and nonprofit organizations. To qualify for federal funding for a runaway shelter, requirements include (1) an accessible location to runaways, (2) a maximum capacity of twenty children, (3) an adequate staff-juvenile ratio, (4) sufficient plans to contact parents or relatives of the runaways and providing for his or her safe return home, and (5) maintenance of adequate statistical record keeping profiling runaway youths and their parents.

The 1980 amendment to the Act included the following provisions:

- Recognition that many so-called "runaways" are actually "throwaways" and, as such, were thrown out of the home or abandoned by parents or caretakers.
- Clarification of the requirements that shelter services be provided to the families of runaway, throwaway, and homeless youth in addition to the teens themselves.
- The addition of program authorities for establishing model programs designed to assist habitual runaways.[13]

Protection of Children Against Sexual Exploitation Act

The Protection of Children Against Sexual Exploitation Act was enacted in 1978 following extensive hearings in both the House and Senate.[14] Its purpose was to close the gaps existing in current federal statutes aimed at protecting children from sexual misuse and commercial sexual exploitation such as teenage prostitution and child pornography. The Act sought to halt the production and dissemination of child pornography by prohibiting interstate transporting of persons under the age of eighteen for purposes of sexual exploitation. Further, the legislation extended the federal government's power to prosecute producers and distributors of child pornography.

In specific,

> the law provides punishment for persons who use, employ, or persuade minors (defined as any persons under 16) to become involved in the production of visual or print materials that depict sexually explicit conduct if the producers know or have reason to know that the materials will be transported in interstate or foreign commerce or mailed. Punishment is also specifically provided for parents, legal guardians, or other persons having custody or control of minors and who knowingly permit a minor to participate in the production of such material.[15]

The Act also provided for stiff monetary penalties against pornographers, pimps, and others who sexually exploit children. (See also Chapter 15.)

Missing Children Act

The Missing Children Act, enacted in 1982, was a further effort to address the problem of children missing as a result of parental abduction, running away, being thrown away, kidnapped, or other circumstances.[16] The Act allows parents, guardians, or next of kin of missing children confirmation of an entry into the FBI's National Crime Information Center. Many local law enforcement agencies now have access to the computer, which assists them in identifying and locating children who are missing, while enabling parents to have their missing children registered nationwide, increasing the chances of them being found and returned home. The Act allows for intervention by the FBI after proof that a missing child has been abducted.

National Center for Missing and Exploited Children

The establishment of a permanent National Center for Missing and Exploited Children was mandated by law in 1984 in response to the continued problem of runaway teens and other missing and exploited youth.[17] The Center's objective was to start a national effort to try and halt the epidemic of displaced and missing children and the sexual exploitation of many through prostitution, child pornography, and molestation. It was also intended to serve as a central contact point for parents of missing children or those who may think they have seen them, or know their whereabouts, or otherwise have relevant information. Other key features the Center provides are assistance and expertise in education, public awareness, legislation, advocacy, and improving the effectiveness of the criminal justice system.

CHILD PROTECTIVE SERVICES

Child Protective Services (CPS) is the agency primarily responsible for evaluation, intervention, and prevention of child abuse and neglect cases in all fifty states, with an emphasis on the needs and well-being of abused and neglected children.[18] Many of these children end up running away from abusive situations and into juvenile prostitution and other aberrant behavior. The CPS agency's role in identifying such abuse or neglect includes

> receiving reports alleging that a child or children have been maltreated, determining whether such reports should be investigated or not, conducting an investigation or an assessment to determine

> whether a child has been maltreated or is at risk of maltreatment, and deciding whether to take any further action on behalf of protecting the child.[19]

While CPS seeks to maintain the integrity of the family, if the agency concludes that a child's health and well-being are in jeopardy, through the juvenile or family court, such a child or children can be removed from the home and put in foster care. The ultimate reunification of abusive or neglectful families and ensuring a stable environment for the maltreated child sometimes requires criminal prosecution of an abuser (often involving sexual or extreme physical abuse) in order to "ensure that the abuser accepts and follows through with treatment and to ensure that a criminal act is appropriately deterred."[20]

Child abuse reporting laws mandating or requiring the reporting of suspected child maltreatment exist in every state.

LAW ENFORCEMENT STRATEGIES

Law enforcement agencies have responded to the challenges faced in dealing with runaways and prostituted youth through various multijurisdictional and multidisciplinary approaches. Such preventative and intervention efforts often include specialized task forces, strike forces, and professional networks aimed at combating the problem of teen runaways and their sexual exploitation.

Task forces consisting of local and federal law enforcement, prosecutors, and community organizations pool their resources, skills, and expertise in developing strategies and techniques for identifying runaways and teenage prostitutes, returning them to a safe environment, and identifying and apprehending pimps, johns, child molesters, pornographers, and others who exploit them. Successful task force models include the Southern California Regional Sexual Assault and Exploitation Felony Enforcement (SAFE) Team,[21] and the South Florida Law Enforcement Effort Against Child Harm (LEACH) Task Force.[22] In Minnesota, a similar model is being established. The Pimp/Juvenile Prostitution Task Force will be comprised of representatives from local police agencies, the FBI, the Bureau of Criminal Apprehension, County Prosecutors, and community groups. They will work together toward a common goal of prevention, apprehension, and prosecution.[23]

Strike force models of cooperation among multijurisdictional law enforcement teams work towards quickly identifying sexual exploiters of children and arresting them. Efforts are also made to assist and protect prostituted and runaway youth after testifying against pimps, johns, pornographers, and others who sexually exploit them. An example of a successful strike force operation is the Federal Child Exploitation Strike Force out of Chicago.[24]

Networking between professionals in various disciplines in combating child maltreatment and sexual exploitation is an effective multijurisdictional approach. The sharing of knowledge, expertise, and resources can be especially important in identifying runaways and juvenile prostitutes, removing them from harm's way, and going after those who exploited or abused them. Successful networking models can be seen in such law enforcement alliances as the Massachusetts Child Exploitation Network,[25] the Dallas Police Department's Child Exploitation Unit,[26] and the Runaway and Homeless Youth Network in Pittsburgh.[27]

Multidisciplinary approaches to assisting at-risk teens through intervention, investigation, specialized training, and mutual cooperation among participating agencies and professionals in law enforcement have been successful in combating teenage prostitution and responding to the needs of exploited runaway youth. One example of a successful multijurisdictional effort involving federal, state, and local law enforcement was the 1997 conference sponsored by the Office of Juvenile Justice and Delinquency Prevention, "Combating the Trafficking of Youth for Prostitution: Forming Partnerships for Prevention, Protection and Prosecution."[28]

OUTREACH PROGRAMS

In response to the crisis of runaway and prostitution involved teenagers, various outreach programs have been established aimed at prevention and support through education, counseling, intervention, hotlines, and mobilizing community support and resources in helping at-risk youth. In combination with multijurisdictional and multidisciplinary practices, these efforts can be effective in reducing the number of teens who run away or are thrown away and their engagement in a prostitution lifestyle as well as rescuing them from sexual exploitation and targeting their exploiters for prosecution. Successful outreach programs include community youth shelters such as Covenant House and Children of the Night and national and international efforts like the National Committee to Prevent Child Abuse, the National Clearinghouse on Child Abuse and Neglect, the National Fingerprint Center for Missing Children, and End Child Prostitution, Child Pornography and Trafficking of Children for Sexual Purposes (ECPAT).[29]

SUMMARY

To address the issues of runaway and prostitution involved youth, policymakers, law enforcement, and national and community organizations have devised strategies to combat the running away of teenagers who often feel they have no place to turn and their subsequent sexual exploitation at the hands of pimps, johns, pornography, and other exploiters. Federal legislation such as the Child Abuse Prevention and Treatment Act, the Runaway and Homeless Youth Act, and the Protection of Children against Sexual Exploitation Act has paved the way for greater protection of juveniles from child abuse and child sexual misuse and exploitation, while creating greater penalties for offenders.

Child protective services agencies exist in all fifty states for identifying, evaluating, and intervening in suspected child abuse and neglect cases. Law enforcement strategies in responding to runaway and prostituted teens include multijurisdictional and multidisciplinary approaches. Outreach efforts are also aimed at combating the sexual exploitation of runaways and homeless youth through prevention, education, counseling, intervention, and community support.

NOTES

1. P.L. No. 100–294.
2. 42 U.S.C. §5101–5106 (1974); as amended by the Child Abuse Prevention and Treatment and Adoption Reform Act of 1978, P.L. No. 95–266, 92 Stat. 205 (1978).
3. P.L. No. 100–294.
4. U.S. Department of Health and Human Services, *National Child Abuse and Neglect Data System: Working Paper 2—1991 Summary Data Component* (Washington, D.C.: National Center on Child Abuse and Neglect, 1993), pp. 1, 6.
5. U.S. Department of Health and Human Services, Administration on Children, Youth and Families, *Child Maltreatment 1997: Reports from the States to the National Child Abuse and Neglect Data System* (Washington, D.C.: Government Printing Office, 1999), p. ix.
6. P.L. No. 93–415 (1974).
7. Ibid.
8. U.S. Department of Justice, Office of Justice Programs, *Juvenile Offenders and Victims: 1999 National Report* (Washington, D.C.: Office of Juvenile Justice and Delinquency Prevention, 1999), p. 207.
9. P.L. No. 93–415.
10. Ibid. as amended in 1980.
11. *Juvenile Offenders and Victims*, p. 88.
12. U.S.C. §5701–5702 Supp. II (1978).
13. Ibid.
14. 18 U.S.C. §2251, 2253–2254 (1978).
15. Ibid.
16. 128 Cong. Rec. 8, 566 (1982).
17. R. Barri Flowers, *The Adolescent Criminal: An Examination of Today's Juvenile Offender* (Jefferson, N.C.: McFarland, 1990), p. 203.
18. R. Barri Flowers, *Domestic Crimes, Family Violence and Child Abuse: A Study of Contemporary American Society* (Jefferson, N.C.: McFarland, 2000), pp. 228–29.

19. *Child Maltreatment 1997*, p. xi.

20. U.S. Department of Justice, *Child Abuse and Neglect: A Shared Community Concern* (Washington, D.C.: National Center on Child Abuse and Neglect, 1992), p. 10.

21. U.S. Department of Justice, Office of Juvenile Justice and Delinquency Prevention, *Prostitution of Children and Child-Sex Tourism: An Analysis of Domestic and International Responses* (Washington, D.C.: National Center for Missing & Exploited Children, 1999), p. 26; Sexual Assault and Exploitation Felony Enforcement Team, Los Angeles, Calif.

22. Law Enforcement Effort Against Child Harm Task Force, South Florida, Fort Lauderdale, Fla.

23. Cited in Minnesota Attorney General's Office, *The Hofstede Committee Report: Juvenile Prostitution in Minnesota*, http://www.ag.state.mn.us/home/files/news/hofstede.htm, August 23, 2000, p. 3.

24. *Prostitution of Children and Child-Sex Tourism*, p. 27.

25. Ibid.

26. Ibid.

27. Ibid.

28. Ibid., p. 28.

29. Flowers, *Domestic Crimes, Family Violence and Child Abuse*, p. 229.

Part II

The Dynamics of Teenage Prostitution

Chapter 8

The Nature of Teenage Prostitution

Teenage prostitution has reached epidemic proportions in this country with millions of teens engaged in selling their bodies for drugs, food, shelter, or other needs. Many of these child prostitutes are runaways or thrown out of the house, sexually or physically abused, and at high risk for exposure to the AIDS virus and numerous other diseases and illnesses. Pimps play a major role in the prostitution of girls, while boy prostitutes tend to be free agents in selling sexual favors. All teen prostitutes are forced to adjust to the harsh realities of the streets, which in turn dictates their involvement and degree of participation in the sex trade industry. Juvenile prostitutes are more likely than adult prostitutes to come into contact with law enforcement, while more girls than boys tend to face involvement with the criminal justice system. Understanding the dynamics of teenage prostitution will allow us to better respond to the social, psychological, and medical needs of street kids and reduce the overall incidence of child prostitution.

DEFINING PROSTITUTION

What is prostitution? How does it differ from other sexual relations? What makes a teenager engaging in prostitution different by definition from adult prostitution? What about girl prostitution versus boy prostitution? How is prostitution defined in terms of white slavery? The dictionary defines the prostitute as "one who solicits and accepts payment for sex acts" or "to offer oneself (or another) for sexual hire."[1] Hence the term *prostitution* is typically defined as "sexual relations that include some form of monetary payment or barter and are characterized by promiscuity and/or emotional apathy."[2] Paul Goldstein defined prostitution as "nonmarital sexual service for material gain,"[3] while Richard Goodall's definition is the selling of sexual favors by one who "earns a living wholly or in part by the more or less indiscriminate, willing, and emotionally indifferent provision of sexual services of any description to another, against payment, usually in advance but not necessarily in cash."[4]

Prostitution differs from other consensual sexual relations in that it is based primarily on money or other payment exchanging hands between the parties involved for the sexual acts to occur. Legally and historically, prostitution has been defined as a gender-specific offense—or one in which the offender is female. One early definition of prostitution by the U.S. Supreme Court defined it as "women who for hire or without hire offer their bodies to indiscriminate intercourse with men."[5] Today prostitution is often defined in gender-neutral terms and includes sexual intercourse along with oral copulation, sodomy, sexual acts between persons of the same gender, and adult and child prostitution.

Defining Child Prostitution

Child prostitution is defined as the use of or involvement of minors, usually persons under the age of eighteen, in "sexual acts with adults or other minors where no force is present, including intercourse, oral sex, anal sex, and sadomasochistic activities where payment is involved."[6] This differs from other types of child sexual exploitation such as incest and statutory rape in that the sexual favors are sold, thereby making it prostitution. Payment for child prostitutes includes cash as well as drugs, clothing, shelter, jewelry, or other material items.

The vast majority of child prostitutes are in their teens. According to research, the average age in which a juvenile enters prostitution is fourteen,[7] while the median age of a teenage prostitute is 15.5 years old.[8]

Much of the data suggests that most teenage prostitutes are female,[9] though an increase in male teenage prostitution has been reported by service providers.[10] Some studies have found that as many as two in every three teen prostitutes are girls.[11]

Defining White Slavery

White slavery is another type of prostitution in which teenage prostitutes are often participants. In contrast to voluntary or consensual prostitution, white slave prostitutes are forced into performing prostitution services—usually by a pimp, pornographer, or slave trader. Introduced at the 1902 Paris conference, the term *white slavery* refers to the trafficking of persons, typically girls and women, for sexual exploitation against their will.[12] Many females are lured into white slavery, then abducted and forced to be prostitutes. Though white slavery occurs most often in Southeast Asia and Europe, it also exists in the United States—involving both American females and those smuggled in from abroad.[13] These prostitutes can operate in massage parlors, nightclubs, houses of prostitution, or on the streets.

THE INCIDENCE OF TEEN PROSTITUTION

How big is the problem of teenage prostitution in the United States? Most sources indicate that the teen sex trade is a multimillion dollar business in this country, with hundreds of thousands to millions of girls and boys active participants. A report by the U.S. Department of Health and Human Services estimated that there are 300,000 prostitutes age seventeen and under operating on the streets of America.[14] Many of these are preteens as young as five years of age.[15] Law enforcement authorities have conservatively put the number of juvenile prostitutes at between 100,000 and 300,000.[16] Some experts on child prostitution believe that as many as half a million children younger than sixteen are selling sexual favors,[17] with that number doubling or tripling, depending on the source, when sixteen- and seventeen-year-old prostitutes are included.[18]

There is evidence that juvenile prostitution is on the rise in many parts of the country. According to a recent national survey of child prostitution, it has increased in 37 percent of the cities.[19] The growth is seen mostly with prostitutes age thirteen to seventeen, though many street kids selling sex were found to be much younger. These prostitute teens ply their trade largely in central business districts, arcades, and bus and train stations. Many are runaways, throwaways, and alcohol or drug dependent. Some are literally forced into prostitution through pimps, white slavery, and child sex ring operators.

TYPES OF TEENAGE PROSTITUTES

Teens that enter into prostitution can be broken down into different types depending on the circumstances of their prostituting, the length of commitment, and their involvement in the sex trade industry. Researchers Harry Benjamin and R.E.L. Masters divided prostitutes into two general types: voluntary and compulsive. Voluntary prostitutes' entrance into the business is a rational and free choice. Compulsive prostitutes sell sexual favors under compulsion because of "psychoneurotic" needs or narcotics addiction.[20] According to Paul Goldstein, an occupational commitment in prostitution exists based on the frequency of one's commitment. There are three types of prostitute occupational commitments: (1) temporary, (2) occasional, and (3) continual.[21]

- *Temporary prostitute*—a discreet act of prostitution that lasts no more than six months in a specific occupational milieu.

- *Occasional prostitute*—two or more discreet acts of prostitution in a particular occupational milieu, each of which lasts no more than six months in duration.
- *Continual prostitute*—prostitution that lasts more than six months in a specific occupational milieu on a steady basis.

Homeless Prostitutes

The number of homeless teenage prostitutes is growing across the country. One in three street kids resort to "survival prostitution" to attain the basic needs in life of food and shelter.[22] Homeless prostitutes—often runaways, throwaways, and drug-addicted youth—have been described by an expert on prostitute types as "at the bottom of the heap."[23] Studies show that a high percentage of homeless girls, in particular, end up selling their bodies for money, drugs, or other necessities.[24] Most homeless prostitutes are at increased risk for exposure to violence, arrest, and HIV infection.[25]

Streetwalkers

Streetwalkers are seen as the lowest form of prostitution, occupied primarily by females. The majority of teenage prostitutes fall into this category, with an estimated one in five streetwalkers younger than twenty.[26] Most of these are adolescent prostitutes. Few streetwalkers ever climb out of their occupational milieu in prostitution. Many have pimps, battle drug addiction, and have run away from abusive homes.

Drug-Addicted Prostitutes

Many juvenile prostitutes enter the business in order to support alcohol or drug habits. Others acquire substance abuse problems after entry into prostitution. Most drug abusing prostitutes occupy the lower level of the prostitution hierarchy, but also exist within every type of prostitution. It is estimated that as many as three-quarters of teenage prostitutes are regular drug users,[27] while virtually all prostituted juveniles have used some form of alcohol or drugs.[28] Teen crack addicts desperate for a fix are particularly vulnerable for sexual exploitation by pimps, johns, and drug dealers.[29] The relationship between high-risk, illicit sexual relations and substance abuse multiplies the teenage prostitute's risks related to drug addiction, delinquency, victimization, and exposure to the AIDS virus.[30]

Indentured Sexual Slaves

Some teenage girls involved in the sex trade industry in the United States become indentured sex slaves who are forced to prostitute themselves in order to pay off debts—sometimes debt incurred by parents or a pimp—to smugglers who use fear, threats, and intimidation to control young prostitutes. Sexual slavery operations are sometimes controlled by organized crime or gangs. In Asian communities, for example, thousands of female teenagers are smuggled into the country every year, where gang rapes and narcotics addiction are used to force them into indentured servitude as prostitutes.[31] Some crack addicted homeless youth and teenage street prostitutes find temporary shelter in crack houses where they, in effect, become "little more than indentured servants, if not outright slaves," in trading sex for drugs and shelter.[32]

TEENAGE PROSTITUTION AND THE RUNAWAY

Most teenagers who sell sexual favors are runaways and, conversely, most teens that leave home for good end up on the streets and must often turn to prostitution to survive. One study found that two in three teenage prostitutes were runaways.[33] Other data indicates that an even higher percentage of runaway girls turn to prostitution.[34] According to an expert on child prostitution: "The children who run look for companionship, friendship, and approval from those they meet. Many such youths are easy marks for gangs, drug pushers, and pimps. Runaways often sell drugs or their bodies and steal to support themselves."[35]

It is estimated that more than a million teenagers run away or are throwaways from home each year.[36] According to the National Center for Missing and Exploited Children, up to 77 percent of prostitution involved teens reported running away from home on at least one occasion.[37] Around 30 percent of runaway prostitutes were street kids or living in shelters.[38] Those not living on the streets were found, more often than not, to be living with other juvenile prostitutes, pimps, drug pushers, or others who prostituted them in order to provide shelter or other basic necessities.[39]

The runaway teen turned prostitute often leaves home due to a troubled existence such as school problems, learning difficulties, fighting, social isolation, parental substance abuse, and related problems. Many have been victims or witnesses to physical and emotional abuse, neglect, or domestic violence.[40] Studies show that sexual abuse, in particular, is a significant predictor of adolescent girl prostitution.[41] The correlation between child sexual abuse, running away, and prostitution has been well documented.[42] Sexual abuse seems to "indirectly increase the chance of prostitution by increasing the risk of running away."[43] As noted in a U.S. Department of Justice analysis of child prostitution: "It is not so much that sexual abuse leads to prostitution as it is that running away leads to prostitution."[44]

Writer Dotson Rader aptly described this tripartite relationship and its implications in his study of runaway prostitutes:

> I went to Los Angeles and talked to runaways cruising Hollywood Boulevard and Santa Monica. I interviewed a girl who said she had fled Milwaukee when she was twelve because her father and uncle raped her. Now, at fourteen, she lived in an abandoned bathhouse on Venice Beach with several other kids and pushes drugs. She was four months pregnant and didn't know by whom.[45]

HEALTH IMPLICATIONS FOR THE TEEN PROSTITUTE

Teenage prostitution carries with it a number of medical and health related risks, including serious bodily harm, internal injuries, drug and alcohol abuse, sexually transmitted diseases (STDs), exposure to HIV and AIDS, eating and sleep disorders, pregnancy, suicide, and mental illness. Many of these are examined in greater detail in other chapters. The lifestyle of prostituted youth particularly compromises their ability to maintain adequate and balanced nutritional needs. The typical teenage prostitute tends to eat irregularly and food that is lacking in important nutrients, while abundant in carbohydrates, fats, and caffeine.[46] Food money is often spent on cigarettes, alcohol, and drugs at the expense of a proper diet, which can lead to eating and sleep disorders, weakness of the body's immune system, and various other health problems.

Teen prostitutes, not too surprisingly, have a high rate of STDs, including gonorrhea, herpes, syphilis, hepatitis B, and HIV/AIDS infection.[47] These are typically the result of the multiple sexual partners common in the sex trade industry, and often combined with other high risk behaviors such as substance abuse and intravenous drug use. According to researchers, nearly 84 percent of all homeless youth participate in one or more AIDS risk behaviors.[48] An expert on prostitution involved youth noted that between half and two-thirds of teenage prostitutes contract STDs during the course of selling sexual favors.[49] One in three such teens do not use any form of protection in possibly preventing such diseases from attacking their bodies.

The rate of pregnancy among girl prostitutes is high.[50] Half of all female teenage prostitutes have been pregnant at least once, while 20 percent have experienced two or more pregnancies.[51] Studies show that those who have their babies tend to neglect them and place them in an unsafe environment where medical, psychological, and financial resources are often inaccessible for mother and child.[52]

MENTAL HEALTH DISORDERS AND TEENAGE PROSTITUTION

Prostituted teenagers face a number of mental health related issues including depression, personality disorders, thought disorders, and risk of suicide. Research shows that teens involved in street prostitution are twice as likely as other homeless kids to have mental problems.[53] Dissociate behaviors are often used by teen prostitutes as a survival mechanism, to attract new clients, or avoid extensive criminal records.[54] Prostitution involved street youth are more likely than other teenagers to be clinically depressed and twice as likely to experience a serious mental health disorder.[55]

The risk of suicide is great among teenage prostitutes, many of whom come from abusive, violent, and dysfunctional homes or who have a history of attempted suicide. Nearly seven in ten girl prostitutes and almost four in ten boy prostitutes have tried to commit suicide due to deep depression and the unbearable realties of the business.[56] In a self-report survey of runaway shelter youth involved in prostitution, 71 percent of the teens reported suicide ideation, 33 percent had formed a fatal strategy, and 14 percent admitted to previously attempting suicide.[57]

SUMMARY

Teenage prostitution involves paid sexual relations by or with a person in their teens. Anywhere from hundreds of thousands to millions of teenagers are active participants in prostitution in this country. More girls than boys enter the sex-for-sale business. Most prostituted youth are homeless, abused, runaways, or throwaways that sell sex on the streets for survival, drugs, or other needs. Some juvenile prostitutes are lured into sexual slavery by organized criminals, gangs, pimps, or drug dealers.

Many face a number of medical and health hazards in the business. These include serious physical injuries, eating deficiencies and disorders, alcohol and drug addiction, sexually transmitted diseases, and pregnancy. Teen prostitutes are also at high risk for mental disorders such as depression, personality disorders, dissociate behaviors, and attempted suicide.

NOTES

1. *American Heritage Dictionary*, 3rd ed. (New York: Dell, 1994), p. 664.

2. R. Barri Flowers, *The Prostitution of Women and Girls* (Jefferson, N.C.: McFarland, 1998), p. 6.

3. Paul J. Goldstein, *Prostitution and Drugs* (Lexington, Mass.: Lexington Books, 1979), p. 33.

4. Richard Goodall, *The Comfort of Sin: Prostitutes and Prostitution in the 1990s* (Kent, England: Renaissance Books, 1995), p. 1.

5. *U.S. v. Bitty*, 208 U.S. 393, 401 (1908); Charles Rosenbleet and Barbara J. Pariente, "The Prostitution of the Criminal Law," *American Criminal Law Review* 11 (1973): 373.

6. R. Barri Flowers, *The Victimization and Exploitation of Women and Children: A Study of Physical, Mental, and Sexual Maltreatment in the United States* (Jefferson, N.C.: McFarland, 1994), p. 82.

7. Mimi H. Silbert and Ayala M. Pines, "Occupational Hazards of Street Prostitutes," *Criminal Justice and Behavior* 8 (1981): 397.

8. U.S. Department of Justice, Office of Juvenile Justice and Delinquency Prevention, *Prostitution of Children and Child-Sex Tourism: An Analysis of Domestic and International Responses* (Alexandria, Va.: National Center for Missing & Exploited Children, 1999), p. 2.

9. Ibid.; Flowers, *The Prostitution of Women and Girls*, p. 71.

10. *Prostitution of Children and Child-Sex Tourism*, p. 2; R. Barri Flowers, *The Adolescent Criminal: An Examination of Today's Juvenile Offender* (Jefferson, N.C.: McFarland, 1990), pp. 60–62.

11. Flowers, *The Adolescent Criminal*, p. 55.

12. Joan J. Johnson, *Teen Prostitution* (Danbury, Conn.: Franklin Watts, 1992), p. 35.

13. Margot Hornblower, "The Skin Trade," *Time* 141 (June 21, 1993): 47; Susan Moran, "New World Havens of Oldest Profession," *Insight on the News* 9 (1993): 15.

14. Cited in Carol Smolenski, "Sex Tourism and the Sexual Exploitation of Children," *Christian Century* 112 (1995): 1079.

15. Flowers, *The Prostitution of Women and Girls*, p. 81.

16. Michael Satchel, "Kids for Sale: A Shocking Report on Child Prostitution across America," *Parade Magazine* (July 20, 1986): 4.

17. Flowers, *The Prostitution of Women and Girls*, p. 71.

18. Flowers, *The Adolescent Criminal*, pp. 54–55.

19. R. Barri Flowers, *Female Crime, Criminals and Cellmates: An Exploration of Female Criminality and Delinquency* (Jefferson, N.C.: McFarland, 1995), p. 149.

20. Harry Benjamin and R.E.L. Masters, *Prostitution and Morality* (New York: Julian Press, 1964).

21. Goldstein, *Prostitution and Drugs*, p. 34.

22. *Prostitution of Children and Child-Sex Tourism*, p. 2.

23. Flowers, *The Prostitution of Women and Girls*, p. 20.

24. *Prostitution of Children and Child-Sex Tourism*, pp. 2–8.

25. Flowers, *Female Crime, Criminals and Cellmates*, pp. 113–14.

26. Adrian W. LeBlanc, "I'm a Shadow," *Seventeen* 52 (March 1993): 216.

27. D. Kelly Weisberg, *Children of the Night: A Study of Adolescent Prostitution* (Lexington, Mass.: Lexington Books, 1985), pp. 117–19.

28. Gary L. Yates et al., "A Risk Profile Comparison of Homeless Youth Involved in Prostitution and Homeless Youth Not Involved," *Adolescent Health* 12 (1991): 547.

29. Evelina Giobbe, "An Analysis of Individual, Institutional and Cultural Pimping," *Michigan Journal of Gender and Law* 1 (1983): 43–44; "Crack: A Cheap and Deadly Cocaine Is a Spreading Menace," *Time* 127 (June 2, 1986): 18.

30. *Prostitution of Children and Child-Sex Tourism*, p. 9; Flowers, *The Prostitution of Women and Girls*, pp. 19–20.

31. Moran, "New World Havens of Oldest Profession," p. 14; Flowers, *The Prostitution of Women and Girls*, p. 19.

32. Giobbe, "An Analysis of Individual, Institutional and Cultural Pimping," p. 43.

33. Cited in Anastasia Volkonsky, "Legalizing the 'Profession' Would Sanction the Abuse," *Insight on the News* 11 (1995): 21.
34. Flowers, *Female Crime, Criminals and Cellmates*, pp. 141–56.
35. Robin Lloyd, *For Money or Love: Boy Prostitution in America* (New York: Ballantine, 1976), p. 58.
36. Flowers, *The Victimization and Exploitation of Women and Children*, p. 36.
37. Magnus J. Seng, "Child Sexual Abuse and Adolescent Prostitution: A Comparative Analysis," *Adolescence* 24 (1989): 671.
38. *Prostitution of Children and Child-Sex Tourism*, p. 3.
39. Yates et al., "A Risk Profile Comparison of Homeless Youth Involved in Prostitution."
40. Mimi H. Silbert and Ayala M. Pines, "Entrance into Prostitution," *Youth and Society* 13 (1982): 479–80.
41. Cathy S. Widom and Joseph B. Kuhns, "Childhood Victimization and Subsequent Risk for Promiscuity, Prostitution and Teenage Pregnancy: A Prospective Study," *American Journal of Public Health* 86 (1996): 1607–10.
42. Ibid.; Flowers, *The Victimization and Exploitation of Women and Children*, pp. 83–85.
43. *Prostitution of Children and Child-Sex Tourism*, p. 3; Ronald Simons and Les B. Whitbeck, "Sexual Abuse as a Precursor to Prostitution and Victimization among Adolescent and Adult Homeless Women," *Journal of Family Issues* 12 (1991): 373–75.
44. Seng, "Child Sexual Abuse and Adolescent Prostitution," p. 673.
45. Dotson Rader, "I Want to Die So I Won't Hurt No More," *Parade Magazine* (August 18, 1985): 5–6.
46. *Prostitution of Children and Child-Sex Tourism*, p. 7.
47. Ibid., p. 8; Clare Tattersall, *Drugs, Runaways, and Teen Prostitution* (New York: Rosen, 1999), pp. 28–30.
48. Cited in *Prostitution of Children and Child-Sex Tourism*, p. 8.
49. Tattersall, *Drugs, Runaways, and Teen Prostitution*, p. 28.
50. Yates et al., "A Risk Profile Comparison of Homeless Youth Involved in Prostitution," p. 548.
51. Tattersall, *Drugs, Runaways, and Teen Prostitution*, pp. 30–31.
52. Ibid.
53. *Prostitution of Children and Child-Sex Tourism*, p. 8.
54. Kathleen Barry, *The Prostitution of Sexuality* (New York: New York University Press, 1995), pp. 30–31; Evelina Giobbe, "Juvenile Prostitution: Profile of Recruitment," in Ann W. Burgess, ed., *Child Trauma I: Issues and Research* (New York: Garland, 1992), p. 127.
55. Yates et al., "A Risk Profile Comparison of Homeless Youth Involved in Prostitution," p. 547.
56. Tattersall, *Drugs, Runaways, and Teen Prostitution*, p. 31.
57. Debra Whitcomb, Edward De Vos, and Barbara E. Smith, *Program to Increase Understanding of Child Sexual Exploitation, Final Report* (Washington, D.C.: Education Development Center, Inc., and ABA Center on Children and the Law, 1998), p. 21.

Chapter 9

Teen Prostitutes, Arrest, and the Criminal Justice System

Every year in the United States thousands of teenagers are arrested and charged with prostitution. Many other prostitution involved youth are arrested for related offenses including runaways, drug violations, liquor law violations, larceny-theft, and curfew and loitering law violations. Girls are more likely than boys to be arrested for prostitution, as are older teens over younger ones. The arrest of teens for prostitution-related activities and police contact can vary depending on the police department and other factors. Police discretion often plays a big role in juvenile arrests for prostitution as does the individual policies, procedures, and practices of a local police department. Most experts recognize that only a fraction of teenagers engaged in prostitution are reflected in arrest figures and other involvement with the criminal justice system. Efforts have been made recently to crack down more on pimps, purveyors, and customers of teenage prostitutes. However, the relationship between underage prostitutes and police contact continues to be the most significant where it concerns teenage prostitution and the criminal and juvenile justice systems.

ARRESTS OF TEENAGE PROSTITUTES

Teens involved in prostitution not only face the hazards of street life and sexual exploitation, but also risk being arrested by the police as sex offenders and institutionalized. According to the *Uniform Crime Reports*, there were 3,869 arrests of persons under the age of twenty for prostitution and commercialized vice in the United States in 1998.[1] Many prostitution involved youth are arrested multiple times, while others manage to avoid

Table 9.1
Ten-Year Arrest Trends for Prostitution Involved Teenagers, 1989–1998

Total Arrests			Arrests of Persons Under 18 Years of Age		
1989	**1998**	**Percent Change**	**1989**	**1998**	**Percent Change**
65,072	63,098	–3.0%	996	935	–6.1%

Source: Derived from U.S. Department of Justice, Federal Bureau of Investigation, *Crime in the United States: Uniform Crime Reports 1998* (Washington, D.C.: Government Printing Office, 1999), p. 214.

arrest.[2] Other prostituted teens are arrested and charged with violent, drug, or property crimes.[3]

Recent findings suggest that overall prostitution arrests are on the decline, as are arrests for running away, which often leads to juvenile prostitution.[4] However, while estimates of teen prostitutes and runaway youth run as high as a million or more street kids who are forced into selling sex, arrest data per se does not accurately reflect the incidence, prevalence, and dynamics of teenage prostitution in America.[5] In one such example in San Diego, a nineteen-year-old female prostitute and "boss hooker" for a violent pimp was recently arrested and charged with pandering, assault, and other prostitution-related offenses. In spite of the fact that she had a "horrific history of child abuse"—including being sexually molested at age six, abandoned, and turned out by her pimp—a judge sentenced her to five years in prison.[6] Many young prostitute arrestees go from victim to convicted offender, only to repeat the process over and over.

Arrest Trends For Teen Prostitutes

Fewer teenagers are being arrested for prostitution, according to official long-term trends arrest data (see Table 9.1). From 1989 to 1998, arrests of persons under the age of eighteen for prostitution and commercialized vice dropped 6.1 percent. This decrease was more than twice the 3 percent overall decline in prostitution arrests during the ten year period. However, when breaking down arrests by sex, while arrests of females under eighteen dropped 21.2 percent and overall decreased 13.3 percent, male arrests rose for the period. Between 1989 and 1998, arrests of males under eighteen for prostitution and commercialized vice rose 17.1 percent and 16 percent for all males.[7]

Five-year arrest trends for persons under eighteen years of age show an increase for prostitution arrests for boys and girls (see Table 9.2). From

Table 9.2
Five-Year Arrest Trends for Prostitution Involved Teenagers, by Sex, 1994–1998

	Total			Under 18		
	1994	1998	Percent Change	1994	1998	Percent Change
Males	22,229	25,613	+14.9%	360	402	+11.7%
Females	35,882	35,155	–2.0%	378	467	+23.5%

Source: Derived from U.S. Department of Justice, Federal Bureau of Investigation, *Crime in the United States: Uniform Crime Reports 1998* (Washington, D.C.: Government Printing Office, 1999), p. 217.

1994 to 1998, arrests of males under eighteen for prostitution and commercialized vice increased 11.7 percent and rose 14.9 percent for all males. The increase was even greater for females under eighteen, rising 23.5 percent over the span, while overall female arrests decreased by 2 percent.

The rise in short-term arrest trends for prostitution involved teens may reflect a more concerted effort by law enforcement agencies nationwide in cracking down not only on teenage prostitutes but pimping and customers of prostitutes.[8] Further, arrest statistics must be kept in a proper context in examining the scope of teen sex workers, for it is almost "entirely dependent on the enforcement decisions and reporting of individual police departments. Each police department differs in its approach towards juvenile prostitution."[9]

Sex and Teenage Prostitute Arrestees

Teenage girls tend to be arrested more often for prostitution than teenage boys (see Figure 9.1). In 1998, there were 2,372 females under the age of twenty arrested for prostitution and commercialized vice, compared to 1,497 males under the age of twenty arrested. Sixty-one percent of teenagers arrested for prostitution charges were female, compared to 39 percent male. However, for teenagers younger than eighteen, arrests for boys and girls are similar. There were 513 arrests of females under the age of eighteen, compared to 506 arrests of males under eighteen in 1998.

These numbers suggest that juvenile prostitutes are more likely to be viewed in gender-neutral terms by law enforcement in arrest making decisions as opposed to older teens. More arrests of teenage girls may also reflect greater visibility of streetwalkers than prostituted young males, as well as the perception of the young female sex worker as a victim in greater need of intervention. Some examples making headlines of sexually exploited girls in prostitution give evidence of this concern:

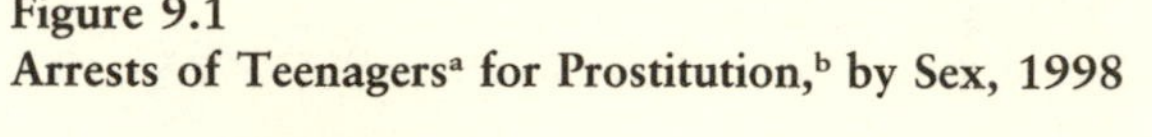

Figure 9.1
Arrests of Teenagers[a] for Prostitution,[b] by Sex, 1998

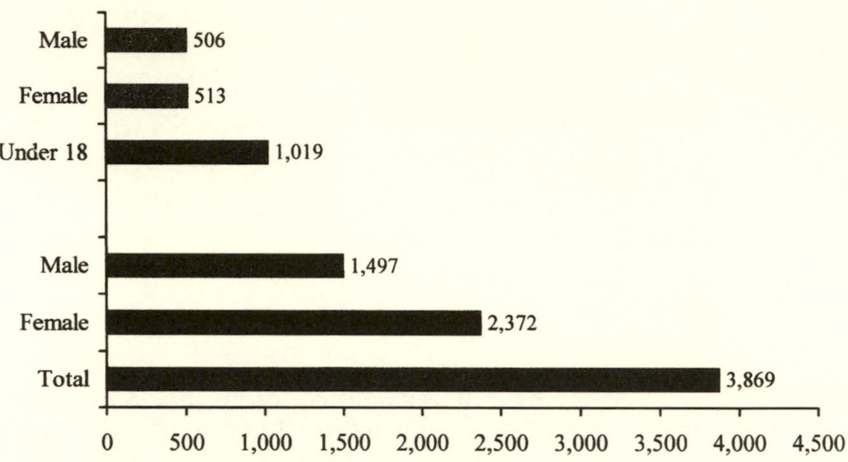

[a]Includes total arrests of persons under the age of twenty.
[b]Includes arrests for commercialized vice.
Source: Derived from U.S. Department of Justice, Federal Bureau of Investigation, *Crime in the United States: Uniform Crime Reports 1998* (Washington, D.C.: Government Printing Office, 1999), pp. 222, 224.

- A fourteen-year-old runaway girl turned prostitute was found shot to death in a San Diego hotel room. The suspect in the murder was her pimp whom she was attempting to leave.[10]
- In St. Paul, members of the King Mafia Crips gang were charged with forcing fourteen and fifteen-year-old girls into prostituting themselves with men in motels and hotels throughout the area.[11]
- A husband and wife received five years in prison for turning out their fourteen-year-old daughter as a streetwalker.[12]
- A prostitution ring in San Diego involving fourteen- to sixteen-year-old girls was broken up by authorities after going on for two years. The five people arrested were charged with pandering, pimping, and child abduction.[13]
- A sex slave ring in Fresno involving Southeast Asian girls age thirteen to sixteen who were being raped and sold into prostitution, resulted in raids in three states and charges against eighteen gang members.[14]

Age and Teenage Prostitute Arrestees

Teenagers arrested for prostitution are primarily older teens or non-juveniles. In 1998, 74.3 percent of all teenage prostitute arrestees were age

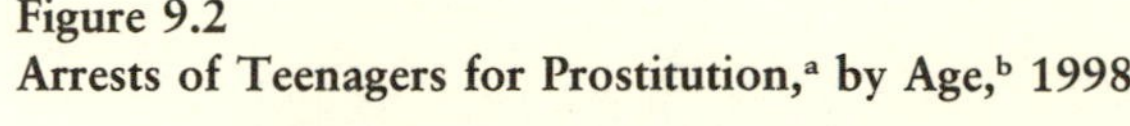

Figure 9.2
Arrests of Teenagers for Prostitution,[a] by Age,[b] 1998

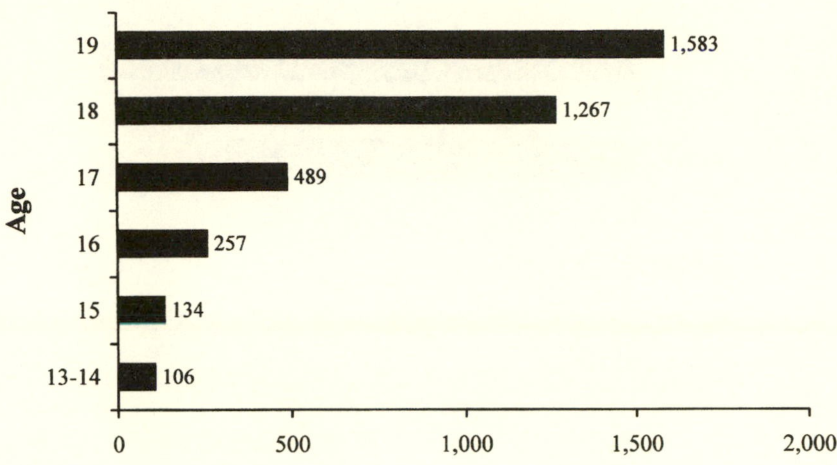

[a]Includes arrests for commercialized vice.
[b]Figures include thirty-three arrests of persons age twelve and under.
Source: Adapted from U.S. Department of Justice, Federal Bureau of Investigation, *Crime in the United States: Uniform Crime Reports 1998* (Washington, D.C.: Government Printing Office, 1999), p. 220.

eighteen and nineteen (see Figure 9.2). Among teens under eighteen, those seventeen and sixteen, respectively, had the highest incidence of arrests. Seventeen-year-old teens were more than three times as likely to be arrested for prostitution and commercialized vice as fifteen-year-olds. However, many young teenage runaways, throwaways, and street kids are also selling "survival sex" and subject to arrest and confinement, as illustrated by the following story of a teen prostitute:

> My parents kicked me out when I was 15. . . . One night a pimp approached me at a strip club and offered me $300 more to have sex with a trick in a van. . . . I needed the money, so I agreed to do it.[15]

Older teenage girls are far more likely than older teenage boys to be arrested for prostitution. There were nearly twice as many females age eighteen and nineteen arrested for prostitution and commercialized vice as males eighteen and nineteen in 1998.[16] The numbers leveled off for sixteen- and seventeen-year-olds, while more fifteen-year-old girls were arrested for prostitution than boys. However, more boys age thirteen to fourteen were arrested for prostitution than girls in that age category. The inconsistencies in the low teen ages for arrests may be due to a greater likelihood of young

Figure 9.3
Arrests of Teenagers[a] for Prostitution, by Race,[b] 1998

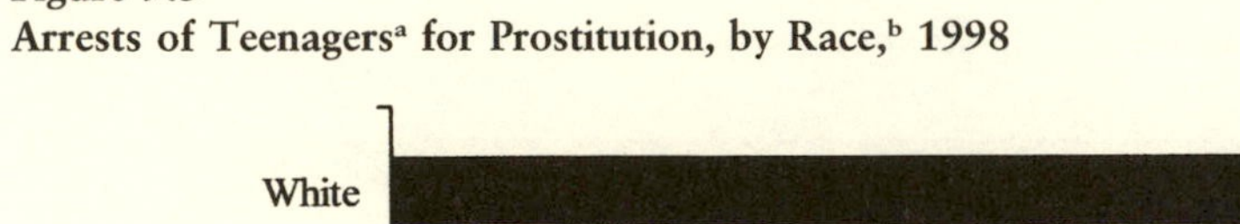

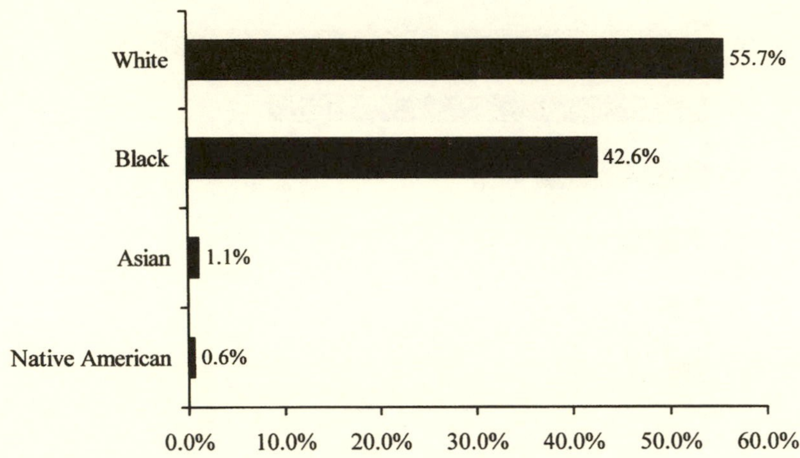

[a]Includes arrests for commercialized vice of persons under the age of eighteen.
[b]Native American includes American Indians and Alaskan Natives. Asian includes Asian or Pacific Islander.
Source: Adapted from U.S. Department of Justice, Federal Bureau of Investigation, *Crime in the United States: Uniform Crime Reports 1998* (Washington, D.C.: Government Printing Office, 1999), p. 229.

teenage girls being arrested as runaways and young teenage boys as juvenile delinquents.

Race and Teenage Prostitute Arrestees

Most teenagers arrested for prostitution are white or black. As shown in Figure 9.3, more than 55 percent of all persons under the age of eighteen arrested for prostitution and commercialized vice in 1998 were white. Almost 43 percent were black, with Asian youths accounting for around 1 percent and Native American teens less than a percent of the teen prostitution arrests. Blacks are disproportionately arrested for prostitution relative to their numbers in the population.

Black female teenage streetwalkers are the most susceptible juvenile prostitute subgroup to be arrested, as they tend to more often be "forced onto the streets and into blatant solicitation where the risk of arrest is highest."[17] studies reveal that black females are seven times more likely to be arrested for prostitution or commercialized vice as females of other races, with the greatest proportion of arrests taking place in inner cities where "living standards are low, the level of desperation high, and police prejudice endemic."[18] In a recent study of young prostituted women in New York City, half the streetwalkers were black, with 25 percent Hispanic, and 25 percent white.[19]

The sad realities of the cycle of prostitution, arrest, and the implications of the sexual exploitation of a back teenage prostitute were reported in a recent *San Diego Union-Tribune* newspaper article:

> The toll on young egos and bodies is tremendous. Children on the street survive by adopting brusque veneers that peel off slowly, if at all. San Diego police vice detectives . . . have been chipping away at the shell enveloping Peaches, a tall teenager whose exotic profile is reminiscent of an ebony Egyptian sculpture plucked from an ancient tomb.
>
> The detectives say Peaches is strong. But they know the toughness that helps girls like her survive on the street plays poorly in interviews. . . . "They all come across as very negative," [says a detective]. Peaches was a 16-year-old high school dropout living . . . with a girlfriend when a pimp named Dominique wheeled his flashy Cadillac El Dorado into her life.
>
> "He was the first man who was nice to me," she said. He bought her a leather coat and her first real pair of Levi's. In return, she sold her body. How many times? "I don't know," she shrugs. "Too many to count."[20]

Peaches was eventually able to get out of the business, but not before she was impregnated by her pimp-lover.

Community Size and Arrests of Teenage Prostitutes

Not too surprisingly, teenagers are arrested for prostitution-related activities predominantly in cities, where the sex-for-sale industry is most centered. FBI figures indicate that in 1998 there were 3,646 city arrests of persons under the age of twenty for prostitution and commercialized vice.[21] By comparison, in suburban areas, police arrested 460 persons younger than twenty, and in rural counties there were only 28 arrests of individuals age nineteen and under for prostitution in 1998.[22] There were nearly eight times as many teens arrested in cities for prostitution offenses as the suburbs, and 130 times as many as in rural areas.

However, arrests for teenage prostitution are rising at a much greater rate in the suburbs and rural America than in cities. As shown in Table 9.3, between 1997 and 1998, arrests of persons under eighteen for prostitution and commercialized vice rose 61 percent in suburban counties and 75 percent in rural counties, compared to just over 1 percent in cities. In suburban areas, which include suburban cities and counties, teenage arrests increased 19.6 percent. The rise in arrests of prostituted youth in suburbia

Table 9.3
Arrest Trends for Teen Prostitutes,[a] by Community Size, 1997–1998

	1997	1998	Percent Change
Cities	903	913	+1.1%
Suburban Counties	41	66	+61.0%
Rural Counties	8	14	+75.0%
Suburban Areas[b]	107	128	+19.6%

[a]Includes arrests for commercialized vice for persons under the age of eighteen.
[b]Includes suburban city and county law enforcement agencies inside of metropolitan areas.
Source: Derived from U.S. Department of Justice, Federal Bureau of Investigation, *Crime in the United States: Uniform Crime Reports 1998* (Washington, D.C.: Government Printing Office, 1999), pp. 231, 240, 249, 258.

reflects the expansion of the problem of teen prostitution beyond the city limits. According to a report on teenage prostitution in Minnesota:

> Juvenile prostitution can happen to virtually anyone's child. This is illustrated by the growing number of suburban teenage girls involved in prostitution. While living with parents in what appears to be stable families, these teens are recruited into prostitution by pimps who find them in such places as the Mall of America and the Minnesota City Center. Often parents fail to notice the subtle signs—the girls wear pagers, cell phones, have older boyfriends. . . .
>
> A young girl from Eden Prairie, living with her parents and going to high school . . . met a boy a few years older who introduced her to drugs. In order to pay for the drugs her "boyfriend" provided her, she was prostituted to men throughout the Minneapolis and St. Paul metropolitan area. . . . The number of suburban teen prostitutes, like this girl, is difficult to determine. These kids often do not appear to be in immediate need of help.[23]

TEENAGE PROSTITUTES AND THE CRIMINAL JUSTICE SYSTEM

Teenage girl prostitutes are much more likely than teenage boy prostitutes to come into contact with the police or other parts of the criminal justice system. Some studies have reported that 75 percent of all teenage girls involved in prostitution have had some contact with police officers, courts, or corrections.[24] Comparatively, it has been estimated that as many as 70 percent of teenage male prostitutes never come into contact with the criminal justice system.[25] However, according to juvenile prostitution researcher D. Kelly Weisberg, prostitution involved boys have a high rate of contact with the criminal and juvenile justice systems. She reported that approximately two-thirds of the teenage male prostitutes in her sample had been arrested on at least one occasion, with prostitution-related crimes comprising of one-third of the arrests.[26]

The majority of teenagers arrested for prostitution actually spend little time in detention, according to Lois Lee, who runs Children of the Night, a shelter for teen prostitutes in Van Nuys, California. She points out that "juvenile authorities turn these kids back onto the streets almost as fast as they are brought in," while explaining that "social service agencies want little to do with street prostitutes."[27] Hence, many such prostituted youth end up back on the streets selling sexual favors until they are arrested again.

Teen prostitutes tend to face arrest much more often than the men who solicit them for sex. Researchers have found that only two male johns are arrested for every eight prostitutes arrested.[28] In Portland, Oregon, for example, there were 402 arrests of persons charged with prostitution and commercialized vice in 1995. By comparison, only eighteen arrests were made for pimping, and ten for solicitation of a prostitute.[29] This disparity can be seen across the country.

However, for most teenagers involved in prostitution, contact with the criminal and juvenile justice systems results from other acts of delinquency or criminal behavior. Young prostitutes often engage in petty theft, drug abuse and dealing, robbery, and assaultive crimes as part of the prostitution subculture and survival mentality on the streets.[30] Sometimes they act on their own or under the influence of drugs or alcohol, other times in pairs or groups, or under the command of pimps or johns. Unfortunately for many teen prostitutes, this can result in arrest, conviction, and incarceration. The abused child turned runaway and prostitute can often end up as a convicted felon sent to an adult prison.

SUMMARY

Thousands of teenagers are arrested for prostitution and commercialized vice in the United Sates each year. Many are arrested multiple times, only to return to selling their bodies for food, shelter, drugs, or money. Girls and older teens are arrested and charged with prostitution more often than boys and younger teens. More than half the youth arrested for prostitution are white, with blacks constituting over 40 percent of the arrestees.

Prostituted teens are far more likely to be arrested in cities than suburban or rural areas. However, short-term trends show a much greater increase in suburban and rural arrests for teenage prostitution than in cities. Overall, ten-year arrest trends indicate a decline in prostitution arrests. Five-year arrest trends suggest an increase in arrests of persons under eighteen for prostitution and commercialized vice.

Girls tend to come into contact with the criminal justice system more often than boys. However, teenage prostitutes are far more likely to be arrested than their customers or pimps. For most prostitution involved teens, other delinquent or criminal acts—such as theft, drug violations, and crimes of violence—are responsible for their contact with the police, courts, or corrections.

NOTES

1. U.S. Department of Justice, Federal Bureau of Investigation, *Crime in the United States: Uniform Crime Reports 1998* (Washington, D.C.: Government Printing Office, 1999), p. 220.

2. R. Barri Flowers, *The Prostitution of Women and Girls* (Jefferson, N.C.: McFarland, 1998), pp. 72–78; D. Kelly Weisberg, *Children of the Night: A Study of Adolescent Prostitution* (Lexington, Mass.: Lexington Books, 1985), p. 75.

3. Flowers, *The Prostitution of Women and Girls*, pp. 75–76; R. Barri Flowers, *The Adolescent Criminal: An Examination of Today's Juvenile Offender* (Jefferson, N.C.: McFarland, 1990), pp. 62–63.

4. *Uniform Crime Reports*, pp. 214, 216, 218; Flowers, *The Prostitution of Women and Girls*, pp. 76–78, 90.

5. Flowers, *The Prostitution of Women and Girls*, pp. 79–99. See also Robin Lloyd, *For Money or Love; Boy Prostitution in America* (New York: Ballantine, 1976); Clare Tattersall, *Drugs, Runaways, and Teen Prostitution* (New York: Rosen, 1999).

6. Bill Callahan, "Pimp's 'Boss Hooker' Gets Five Years in Prison," *San Diego Union-Tribune* (July 30, 1998), p. B2.

7. *Uniform Crime Reports*, p. 215.

8. Flowers, *The Prostitution of Women and Girls*, pp. 127–28, 146.

9. Minnesota Attorney General's Office, *The Hofstede Committee Report: Juvenile Prostitution in Minnesota*, http://www.ag.state.mn.us/home/files/news/hofstede.htm, August 23, 2000, p. 6.

10. Kelly Thornton, "Girl, 14, Finds Her Life on the Streets Has an Abrupt, Deadly Ending," *San Diego Union-Tribune* (February 5, 1994), p. B2.

11. *The Hofstede Committee Report*, p. 6.

12. "Daughter Forced into Prostitution," *Associated Press* (December 5, 1993).

13. Joe Hughes, "Five Arrested in Teen Prostitution Case," *San Diego Union-Tribune* (November 28, 1996), p. B3.

14. Matthew Yi, "Police Say Sex-Slave Ring Is Broken Up," *Associated Press* (November 14, 1998).

15. *The Hofstede Committee Report*, p. 6.

16. *Uniform Crime Reports*, pp. 222, 224.

17. Marilyn G. Haft, "Hustling for Rights," in Laura Crites, ed., *The Female Offender* (Lexington, Mass.: Lexington Books, 1976), p. 212.

18. Ibid.

19. Cited in Barbara Goldsmith, "Women on the Edge: A Reporter at Large," *New Yorker* 69 (April 26, 1993): 65–66.

20. Bill Callahan, "Prisoners without Chains: For Teen-agers like Peaches, Coming Back Is an Uphill Battle," *San Diego Union-Tribune* (June 21, 1998), p. A19.

21. *Uniform Crime Reports*, p. 233.

22. Ibid., pp. 251, 260.

23. *The Hofstede Committee Report*, p. 5.

24. Weisberg, *Children of the Night*, pp. 124–28.

25. Cited in Tamara Stieber, "The Boys Who Sell Sex to Men in San Francisco," *Sacramento Bee* (March 4, 1984), p. A22.

26. Weisberg, *Children of the Night*, p. 75.

27. Callahan, "Prisoners without Chains."

28. Flowers, *The Prostitution of Women and Girls*, p. 127.

29. Laura Trujillo, "Escort Services Thriving Industry in Portland Area," *Oregonian* (June 7, 1996), p. B1.

30. Flowers, *The Prostitution of Women and Girls*, pp. 85–86; Ronald Simons and Les B. Whitbeck, "Sexual Abuse as a Precursor to Prostitution and Victimization among Adolescent and Adult Homeless Women," *Journal of Family Issues* 12 (1991): 370; Les B. Whitbeck and Ronald L. Simons, "Life on the Streets: The Victimization of Runaway and Homeless Adolescents," *Youth and Society* 22 (1990): 113; A. Brannigan and Erin Gibbs Van Brunschott, "Youthful Prostitution and Child Sexual Trauma," *International Journal of Law and Psychiatry* 20 (1997): 344.

Chapter 10

Girl Prostitution

Every year anywhere from tens to hundreds of thousands of teenage girls enter the sex-for-sale business in the United States. Many of these are runaways from sexually, physically, or mentally abusive homes. Over a million children run away or are thrown away annually. Ninety percent of these, by some estimates, will turn to prostitution as a means to survive.[1] Girls are especially vulnerable to being turned out by pimps or sexually exploited by operators in the sex trade industry. Most young female prostitutes will abuse alcohol and drugs, be abused by pimps and customers, and face a high risk for AIDS infection and other hazards of the profession. Few will emerge without serious emotional and physical scars.

THE EXTENT OF GIRL PROSTITUTION

There is much debate among experts on just how many girl prostitutes are active as sex workers at any given time in the United States. It is generally believed that there are at least 1 million teenage prostitutes plying their trade annually.[2] Some estimate that twice as many children are engaged in prostitution nationally.[3] Studies suggest that up to two-thirds of underage prostitutes are female.[4] The vast majority of prostitution involved girls are runaways. More than two-thirds of all runaway girls will end up as prostitutes.[5] Both runaway and prostituted girls are more likely than their male counterparts to be arrested and otherwise involved in the criminal and juvenile justice systems (see Chapter 9).

Most girl prostitutes ply their trade as streetwalkers. However, teenage girls can also be found selling sex as call girls through escort services, massage parlors, brothels, hotels, and nightclubs.[6] They provide a range of services including sexual intercourse, "oral sex, anal sex, homosexual activities, multiple partner sex, sadomasochistic activities, urination or defecation, and obscenity related sexual performances."[7] The degradation and sexual exploitation of the girl prostitute in the sex trade can be seen in the following depiction of a fourteen-year-old pimp-controlled runaway prostitute and cocaine user named Marlena:

> "I had been sleeping on a park bench for three nights. . . . The fourth night . . . I met a man named Troy, who was really good to me at first. . . . Little did I know that my problems were about to begin."
>
> . . . Troy sometimes filmed Marlena when she was with customers. He also asked her to perform sexual acts with other boys and girls for the camera.
>
> . . . "I had sex with a lot [of] men," says Marlena, "and it was easier and easier each time. I felt numb and empty. I earned just two dollars for each man."[8]

A GIRL'S ENTRANCE INTO PROSTITUTION

Prostituted girls can be as young as five or six. However, according to Jennifer James, the median age of a girl prostitute is 16.9 years.[9] Most girls are in fact younger when entering prostitution. In their study of teenage prostitution, Mimi Silbert and Ayala Pines found the average age of a girl's first prostitute experience to be fourteen.[10] Other researchers have supported this conclusion.[11]

Although a small percentage of girl prostitutes enter the business as independent operators, the vast majority are brought into the child sex trade by pimps, pornographers, johns, family members, and even other young prostitutes. Studies indicate that pimps are primarily responsible for turning girls out. As many as 90 percent of teenage female prostitutes were coerced or charmed into selling sexual favors by a pimp.[12] One self-report study found that virtually every girl prostitute surveyed was associated with a pimp, directly or indirectly.[13] (See Chapter 11.)

Girls are also drawn into prostitution by family members or acquaintances. In four out of every ten cases of girls becoming prostitutes, the person most responsible for that entry was a relative such as her father, mother, or a sister.[14] Notes one researcher on child sexual exploitation: "Pimps lurk in cars in the shadows, calculating the night's take. But not all pimps are gangsters. Often it is the father who sits in the backup car or mother who negotiates the deal for her daughter."[15] In some instances, the family member responsible for bringing a girl into prostitution may also be a prostitute.

Ten percent of girl prostitutes are believed to have entered the business after being propositioned by a john.[16] Another 20 percent of girl runaways become prostitutes through their association with other street kids and teenage prostitutes.[17] Oftentimes these girls are actually recruiting prostitutes for pimps. In some cases, they are merely offering the struggling runaway or street youth an alternative to selling drugs, stealing, or starving.

Most girl prostitutes enter the profession as part-time prostitutes, usually as a quick means to earn money for food, cigarettes, alcohol, drugs, or shelter. For many teens, this turns into a full-time occupation. Researchers have found that the typical girl prostitute will be turning tricks as a full-time way of life within eight months to a year after her initial experience as a prostitute.[18]

The conditions in which a girl becomes a full-time prostitute were described in *The Prostitution of Women and Girls*:

> Girl prostitutes undergo a change in self-image. . . . Adapting to the reality of being prostitutes, along with the negative self-image this brings, adolescent females become, in effect, what they are labeled by society: sluts, whores, or hookers. The more they become a part of the prostitution subculture . . . the more they come to regard themselves as prostitutes and the more committed they become to working the streets, selling their bodies full-time.[19]

THE GIRL STREETWALKER

It is estimated that at least one-fifth of all streetwalker prostitutes are teenage girls.[20] By some estimates, streetwalkers represent up to three-quarters of all sex workers.[21] Streetwalkers occupy the lowest rung of the prostitution hierarchy. Typically they ply their trade on busy, neon lit street corners in red light districts of inner cities, wearing "ankle-length coyote and raccoon coats over Victoria's Secret-type chemises of shimmering satin, black stockings, and five-inch red heels or boots" or "G-strings with sparkling pasties on their nipples or in lace panties and bras."[22] One article mentioned streetwalking prostitutes' "strolls" or "tracks" on the streets in seeking to attract johns.[23] The teenage streetwalker's sexual services range from fellatio to masturbating to intercourse. One study found that 75 percent of streetwalkers' sexual contacts involve fellatio, or oral copulation only.[24] According to an expert on teenage prostitution, the girl sex worker's primary service is oral sex because "it is what her customers want and the most practical for working in cars. It's also quick, which is a concern, because street prostitution is illegal, and when the cops show up, it is sometimes necessary to run."[25]

James divides streetwalkers into to two classes: (1) true prostitutes and (2) part-timers.[26] True prostitutes include outlaws, rip-off artists, hypes, ladies, old-timers, and thoroughbreds:

- *Outlaws*—prostitutes who operate independent of pimps.
- *Rip-off artists*—thieves disguised as prostitutes; prostitution is not their primary source of income.
- *Hypes*—prostitutes who are in the business to support drug habits.
- *Ladies*—prostitutes identified as such by their class, carriage, finesse, and professional way in which they conduct themselves.
- *Old-timers*—seasoned prostitutes who lack the class of ladies.
- *Thoroughbreds*—young and professional prostitutes.

Part-timers include girl prostitutes who have no style and amateurs or "hos." True prostitutes and part-time prostitutes are not mutually exclusive. Rather, they reflect different behavioral dimensions of the streetwalker prostitution subculture, "as opposed to complete behavioral types, each having elements from all streetwalker modes of behavior."[27]

Young female streetwalkers are especially susceptible to the persuasive charms and dominance of a pimp. They are also more likely than other types of prostitutes to experience violence, drug addiction, and other hazards as part of the job.[28]

GIRL PROSTITUTES, RACE, ETHNICITY, AND NATIONALITY

Girl prostitutes in the United States come in every racial and ethnic persuasion, as well as nationality. Some female teen sex workers migrated or were forced to come here from Europe, Asia, South America, and elsewhere. Studies indicate that the vast majority of prostitution involved girls are white. In studies done in Minneapolis[29] and San Francisco,[30] 80 percent of the prostitutes were white. Sixty-two percent of James's sample of girl prostitutes were white.[31]

Black girls make up the second largest racial group of female teenage prostitutes, with estimates of between 10 and 50 percent of those sampled.[32] The larger the prostitute sample, the lower the percentage of black girl sex workers tended to be.

The number of other minority girl prostitutes is low by comparison. Various studies have shown the representation of Hispanic and Native American girl prostitutes to be anywhere from 2 to 11 percent of female juvenile prostitutes.[33]

Although Asian girl prostitution is believed to be relatively small in this country (as opposed to in Asia), there has been an increase in prostituted Asian girls in recent years. Many have been lured into the United States by Asian gangs from the Philippines, Vietnam, and other parts of Asia, often to work as indentured sex slaves.[34]

GIRL PROSTITUTION AND CLASS

Common wisdom is that girl prostitutes are more likely to come from lower-class environments. However, research has shown mixed results with respect to the relationship between girl prostitution and class. A number of studies with small samples have indicated a higher incidence of girl prostitutes from working- or lower-class backgrounds.[35] Studies involving larger sample groups have found that most adolescent female prostitutes come from middle- and upper-middle class families.[36] In a study of girl prostitutes in Minnesota, almost one in four had parents with some college education.[37] Seventy percent of Silbert's sample of teen prostitutes were from families with average or above average income levels.[38] James made a similar finding, reporting a "phenomenal" rise in the number of "affluent and overindulged" girl prostitutes.[39]

GIRL PROSTITUTES AND FAMILY DYSFUNCTION

Most girl prostitutes come from families characterized by divorce, separation, discord, and other dysfunction. Eighty-five percent of the girl prostitutes in Maura Crowley's study reported that at least one parent was absent during their upbringing.[40] The Huckleberry House Project reported that 70 percent of its sample had come from broken homes.[41] A similar finding was reached by James.[42] A number of other researchers have also related the absence of one or both parents as a factor in juvenile prostitution.[43]

Other studies have focused on the relationship between teenage prostitution and a parental relationship beset by conflict and stress. The Huckleberry House researchers found that most girl prostitutes did not have a positive, caring relationship with their parents.[44] In a study of teenage prostitution, Diana Gray found that 75 percent of girl sex workers described the relationship with their parents as "poor" or "very bad."[45] Crowley reported that mothers were nearly twice as likely as fathers to be responsible for the child-parent dysfunction.[46] Forty-two percent of mothers, compared to 25 percent of fathers, were considered by the girl prostitute as the blame for the poor parental relationship.

GIRL PROSTITUTION AND CHILD ABUSE

There is a strong correlation between girls entering prostitution and various forms of child abuse—including sexual, physical, and emotional.[47] A high percentage of girl prostitutes have been victims of incest, rape, beatings, neglect, and other domestic violence and related problems. The Huckleberry House Project reported that 90 percent of the girl prostitutes had been sexually molested.[48] Two-thirds of the sample in Silbert's study were incest and child abuse victims.[49] Sexual abuse has been found to be a strong predictor of prostitution involvement for girls,[50] increasing the chance of running away and right into the commercial sex trade industry.[51]

Child physical abuse is also likely to be a contributory factor in the prostitution of girls. One study found that at least 90 percent of girl runaways turned prostitutes were victims of "severe" child abuse.[52] Two in every three adolescent female prostitutes in the Crowley[53] and Huckleberry House[54] studies disclosed being physically assaulted at home.

SUBSTANCE ABUSE AMONG GIRL PROSTITUTES

Drug and alcohol use and misuse are common among prostitution involved girls. Studies show that virtually all teen prostitutes in the sex-for-sale industry have at some time used alcohol or drugs.[55] It is estimated that between one-fifth and one-half of all juvenile prostitutes are regular drug users.[56] As many as 70 percent of girl prostitutes drink alcohol.[57]

Marijuana is the most popular drug among teenage prostitutes.[58] However, many prostituted youth use other mood-altering drugs such as cocaine, heroin, and LSD (lysergic acid diethylamide).[59] Girl prostitutes are often introduced to drugs by pimps, johns, and other prostitutes, sometimes leading to addiction. Some female teen prostitutes report using alcohol in order to "deaden memories" associated with childhood sexual or physical abuse; whereas others turn to drugs in order to "desensitize present experiences."[60]

Researchers have discovered that girl prostitutes' dependency on drugs varies according to the drug, described as follows:

> Heroin use may help a prostitute adjust to a life she resents; increase her ability to withstand emotional and physical stress; help her relax. . . . Heroin seems to relax the anal sphincter muscles. Prostitutes who are heroin addicts are likely to have minimal problems in engaging in anal intercourse. . . . Cocaine and other stimulants have been reported to increase the confidence of streetwalkers to solicit strangers on the street and . . . enable massage parlor prostitutes to maintain their energy level. . . . Valium aided some call girls in "getting through the day." . . . New York [prostitutes] got "protection from insults to their bodies and minds" by drinking steadily.[61]

GIRL PROSTITUTION AND SEXUAL ADVENTURE

Although the evidence is overwhelming that the vast majority of prostituted girls enter the profession as runaways or substance abusers in need of money to pay for food, shelter, or addiction, not all girl prostitutes are in such dire straits. Indeed, one study found that only 5 percent of girl sex workers were forced into prostitution, per se, by violent pimps or customers, or circumstances that made this a necessary choice.[62] Some evidence suggests that a growing number of teenage girls are sexual adventurers, engaging in prostitution not as the result of child abuse, dissatisfaction, domestic violence, mental illness, or related factors, but rather for the sexual excitement it brings. Dorothy Bracey found that many young females become prostitutes because they have friends who are prostitutes.[63] A self-report survey of youth engaging in prostitution activities actually found that more than half the respondents were living with parents or families during the most recent plying of their trade.[64]

For many prostitution involved girls, the combination of money and sexual enjoyment seem to go hand in hand in motivating them to sell their bodies. As one article put it, "a lot of kids take to prostitution as an 'on and off job'—when you need a few bucks."[65] According to a social worker who counsels girl prostitutes: "Sex is no longer for love and procreation, but solely for enjoyment. But this leads to fleeting sexual contacts, which turn out to be meaningless. What gives them meaning is the profit."[66]

Teenage girls out for sexual adventure and income can also be seen in the following observation by an expert on teen prostitution:

> There are more younger hookers, thirteen and fourteen year olds. They just don't care. It's a way they can have all the clothes they want, all the blue jeans and shoes they want. . . . Girls sell their bodies to get money. It if was legal and had a tax on it, they would find something else.[67]

The rise in prostitution among affluent girls was noted by James: "It is basically entertaining to dress up with your friends and go down on the street and con, cajole, and be the aggressor. The extravagant sensations from the illegality, projected immorality, and danger of prostitution is a relief from the neutrality of suburbia."[68]

Sexual addiction and the temptations of the sex industry itself are seen by some as powerful lures for many adolescent girls to become involved in prostitution. Learning about "sex, sexual acts, the male and female bodies, and the pleasures of orgasm—and getting paid for it—can make leaving the business much harder than entering it."[69]

GIRL PROSTITUTION AND HIV INFECTION

Girl prostitutes are at risk for a variety of sexually or intravenous drug transmitted diseases. The most deadly of these is exposure to the HIV virus, which can lead to full blown AIDS. One study found that nearly 84 percent of street kids are involved in at least one high risk behavior for AIDS infection such as prostitution, multiple sexual partners, multiple drug use, and intravenous drug use.[70]

Girl sex workers are especially vulnerable to contracting HIV and other infectious diseases because of their youth, immaturity, and inability to resist customers who engage in unsafe, high risk, sexual practices. Studies show that HIV is often passed "through unprotected, vaginal and anal intercourse and through the sharing of 'works' with infected substance abusers."[71] The risk of HIV infection is high even among girl prostitutes whose sexual contacts are limited to oral sex, "an activity that clearly puts [them] more at risk than a man: common sense tells us that the AIDS virus gains easy entry through mouth lacerations from crack smoking."[72]

The strong correlation between streetwalkers and HIV has been well documented. In a University of Miami study of infected prostitutes, 41 percent of the streetwalkers tested HIV positive.[73] In a study of streetwalkers and female intravenous drug users, 46 percent tested positive for HIV.[74] According to Covenant House, the largest runaway shelter in New York City, girls who engage in prostitution every night may have a rate of HIV infection that exceeds 50 percent.[75]

In *Teen Prostitution*, Joan Johnson describes the horrific process of becoming infected with HIV and AIDS.

> The virus multiplies and spreads . . . can attach itself to the body's vital T-cells and at the same time evade the body's defensive army of antibodies. . . . Colds become pneumonia. Tumors grow and multiply. Stomach aches become stomach ulcers. Yeast infections flourish unabated in the mouth or vagina. . . . Eventually, sick all the time, unable to eat or hold down food, in constant pain, and totally debilitated, the AIDS victim dies.[76]

GIRL PROSTITUTES AND OTHER VICTIMIZATION

The risk of victimization among prostitution involved girls is high. Runaway girls turned into street prostitutes face constant peril including rape and other sexual assaults, physical attacks, robberies, and even murder. Studies show that girl streetwalkers are far more likely to experience sexual violence than boy streetwalkers.[77] Perpetrators of victimized girls include pimps, clients, drug addicts, thieves, and other sex industry workers. Many sexual serial murderers target young runaways and streetwalkers as their prey.[78]

Prostituted girls experience a high rate of physical and mental problems such as pelvic inflammatory disease, pregnancy, eating and personality disorders, sleep deprivation, depression, and suicide.[79]

SUMMARY

Girl prostitutes may account for as much as two-thirds of the teenage prostitution subculture. Most girls who enter prostitution are runaways in their early teens. They often run away from abusive or dysfunctional homes and enter the profession as part-time prostitutes. As many as nine out of ten prostitution involved girls are recruited into the business by pimps. However, some girl prostitutes are turned out by relatives, acquaintances, or other prostitutes.

The majority of girls involved in prostitution are streetwalkers, and have been identified as *true prostitutes* and *part-timers*. Most prostituted girls are white, followed by black and Hispanic. Asian girl prostitutes are often brought into this country illegally to serve as sex slaves. Class does not appear to be a significant factor among prostitutes; however, family dysfunction has been shown to be an important contributory factor.

Most girl prostitutes abuse drugs and alcohol, while some are characterized as sexual adventurers, engaging in prostitution for enjoyment and money. All prostitution involved girls are at high risk for HIV infection, sexual assaults, abuse, and related physical and mental victimization.

NOTES

1. Clare Tattersall, *Drugs, Runaways, and Teen Prostitution* (New York: Rosen, 1999), p. 16.
2. R. Barri Flowers, *The Prostitution of Women and Girls* (Jefferson, N.C.: McFarland, 1998), p. 71.
3. Ibid.
4. R. Barri Flowers, *The Adolescent Criminal: An Examination of Today's Juvenile Offender* (Jefferson, N.C.: McFarland, 1990), p. 55.
5. Ibid., pp. 49–55; Tatersall, *Drugs, Runaways, and Teen Prostitution*, p. 8; Anastasia Volkonsky, "Legalizing the 'Profession' Would Sanction the Abuse," *Insight on the News* 11 (1995): 21.
6. Flowers, *The Prostitution of Women and Girls*, p. 79.
7. Flowers, *The Adolescent Criminal*, p. 58. See also D. Kelly Weisberg, *Children of the Night: A Study of Adolescent Prostitution* (Lexington, Mass.: Lexington Books, 1985), p. 107.
8. Tattersall, *Drugs, Runaways, and Teen Prostitution*, pp. 8, 13, 16, 37.
9. Jennifer James, *Entrance into Juvenile Prostitution* (Washington, D.C.: National Institute of Mental Health, 1980), p. 17.
10. Mimi H. Silbert and Ayala M. Pines, "Occupational Hazards of Street Prostitutes," *Criminal Justice and Behavior* 8 (1981): 397.
11. James, *Entrance into Juvenile Prostitution*, p. 29; Weisberg, *Children of the Night*, p. 94.
12. Joan J. Johnson, *Teen Prostitution* (Danbury, Conn.: Franklin Watts, 1992), p. 75.
13. Cited in ibid., p. 78.

14. Ibid., p. 87.
15. Margot Hornblower, "The Skin Trade," *Time* 141 (June 21, 1993): 44.
16. Flowers, *The Prostitution of Women and Girls*, p. 80.
17. Ibid.
18. Johnson, *Teen Prostitution*, p. 108.
19. Flowers, *The Prostitution of Women and Girls*, p. 80.
20. Ibid., p. 79.
21. Adrian N. LeBlanc, "I'm a Shadow," *Seventeen* 52 (March 1993): 216.
22. Barbara Goldsmith, "Women on the Edge: A Reporter at Large," *New Yorker* 69 (April 26, 1993), p. 66.
23. Ibid.
24. Cited in ibid., p. 65.
25. LeBlanc, "I'm a Shadow," p. 216.
26. Jennifer James, "Two Domains of Streetwalker Argot," *Anthropological Linguistics* 14 (1972): 174–75.
27. Flowers, *The Prostitution of Women and Girls*, p. 50.
28. Ibid., pp. 51–53, 84, 102–4, 130.
29. "The Enablers," *Juvenile Prostitution in Minnesota: The Report of a Research Project* (St. Paul: The Enablers, 1978), p. 18.
30. Sparky Harlan, Luanne L. Rodgers, and Brian Slattery, *Male and Female Adolescent Prostitution: Huckleberry House Sexual Minority Youth Services Project* (Washington, D.C.: U.S. Department of Health and Human Services, 1981), p. 7.
31. James, *Entrance into Juvenile Prostitution*, p. 19.
32. Ibid.; Flowers, *The Adolescent Criminal*, p. 56; "The Enablers," *Juvenile Prostitution in Minnesota*, p. 18.
33. James, *Entrance into Juvenile Prostitution*, p. 10; Mimi H. Silbert, *Sexual Assault of Prostitutes: Phase One* (Washington, D.C.: National Institute of Mental Health, 1980), p. 10.
34. Susan Moran, "New World Havens of Oldest Profession," *Insight on the News* 9 (1993): 12–16.
35. Flowers, *The Adolescent Criminal*, p. 56; Dorothy H. Bracey, *"Baby-Pros": Preliminary Profiles of Juvenile Prostitutes* (New York: John Jay Press, 1979), p. 19.
36. Flowers, *The Prostitution of Women and Girls*, p. 82.
37. Ellen Hale, "Center Studies Causes of Juvenile Prostitution," *Gannet News Service* (May 21, 1981).
38. Silbert, *Sexual Assault of Prostitutes*, p. 15.
39. James, *Entrance into Juvenile Prostitution*, p. 18; Jennifer James, *Entrance into Juvenile Prostitution: Progress Report, June 1978* (Washington, D.C.: National Institute of Mental Health, 1978), p. 53.
40. Maura G. Crowley, "Female Runaway Behavior and Its Relationship to Prostitution," Master's thesis, Sam Houston State University, Institute of Contemporary Corrections and Behavioral Sciences, 1977.
41. Harlan, Rodgers, and Slattery, *Male and Female Adolescent Prostitution*, p. 14.
42. James, *Entrance into Juvenile Prostitution*, p. 88.
43. See, for example, C. S. Widom and M. A. Ames, "Criminal Consequences of Childhood Sexual Victimization," *Child Abuse & Neglect* 18, 4 (1994): 303–18; David Finkelhor, *Sexually Victimized Children* (New York: Free Press, 1979);

I. Gibsonainyette, D. I. Templer, R. Brown, and L. Veaco, "Adolescent Female Prostitutes," *Archives of Sexual Behavior* 17, 5 (1988): 431–38.

44. Harlan, Rodgers, and Slattery, *Male and Female Adolescent Prostitution*, p. 15.

45. Diana Gray, "Turning Out: A Study of Teenage Prostitution," Master's thesis, University of Washington, 1971, p. 25.

46. Crowley, "Female Runaway Behavior," pp. 74–77.

47. Flowers, *The Prostitution of Women and Girls*, p. 83; R. Barri Flowers, *The Victimization and Exploitation of Women and Children: A Study of Physical, Mental, and Sexual Maltreatment in the United States* (Jefferson, N.C.: McFarland, 1994), pp. 83–85.

48. Harlan, Rodgers, and Slattery, *Male and Female Adolescent Prostitution*, p. 21.

49. Mimi H. Silbert, "Delancey Street Study: Prostitution and Sexual Assault," summary of results, Delancey Street Foundation, San Francisco, 1982, p. 3.

50. Cathy S. Widom and Joseph B. Kuhns, "Childhood Victimization and Subsequent Risk for Promiscuity, Prostitution and Teenage Pregnancy," *American Journal of Public Health* 86 (1996): 1607–10.

51. Ronald Simons and Les B. Whitbeck, "Sexual Abuse as a Precursor to Prostitution and Victimization among Adolescent and Adult Homeless Women," *Journal of Family Issues* 12 (1991): 375; Magnus J. Seng, "Child Sexual Abuse and Adolescent Prostitution: A Comparative Analysis," *Adolescence* 24 (1989): 673.

52. Stephanie Abarbanel, "Women Who Make a Difference," *Family Circle* 107 (January 11, 1994): 11.

53. Crowley, "Female Runaway Behavior," p. 63.

54. Harlan, Rodgers, and Slattery, *Male and Female Adolescent Prostitution*, p. 15.

55. Flowers, *The Prostitution of Women and Girls*, p. 84; R. Barri Flowers, *Drugs, Alcohol and Criminality in American Society* (Jefferson, N.C.: McFarland, 1999), p. 150.

56. Weisberg, *Children of the Night*, pp. 117–19; Flowers, *The Adolescent Criminal*, pp. 59–60.

57. Paul W. Haberman and Michael M. Baden, *Alcohol, Other Drugs, and Violent Death* (New York: Oxford University Press, 1978), pp. 18–19.

58. Crowley, "Female Runaway Behavior," p. 80; R. Barri Flowers, *Female Crime, Criminals and Cellmates: An Exploration of Female Criminality and Delinquency* (Jefferson, N.C.: McFarland, 1995), p. 153.

59. Flowers, *The Adolescent Criminal*, p. 59; U.S. Department of Justice, *Prostitution of Children and Child-Sex Tourism: An Analysis of Domestic and International Responses* (Alexandria, Va.: National Center for Missing & Exploited Children, 1999), p. 9.

60. Flowers, *Female Crime, Criminals and Cellmates*, p. 153; Flowers, *The Prostitution of Women and Girls*, p. 85; Judianne Densen-Gerber and S. F. Hutchinson, "Medical-Legal and Societal Problems Involving Children-Child Prostitution, Child Pornography, and Drug-Related Abuse: Recommended Legislation," in Selwyn M. Smith, ed., *The Maltreatment of Children* (Baltimore: University Park Press, 1978), p. 322.

61. Paul J. Goldstein, *Prostitution and Drugs* (Lexington, Mass.: Lexington Books, 1979), pp. 117–18.

62. "The Enablers," *Juvenile Prostitution in Minnesota*, p. 57.

63. Bracey, *"Baby-Pros,"* p. 23.

64. *Prostitution of Children and Child-Sex Tourism*, p. 3.

65. Quoted in Hale, "Center Studies Causes of Juvenile Prostitution."

66. Quoted in Flowers, *The Adolescent Criminal*, p. 59.

67. Quoted in Clemens Bartollas, *Juvenile Delinquency* (New York: John Wiley & Sons, 1985), p. 342.

68. James, *Entrance into Juvenile Prostitution: Progress Report.*

69. Flowers, *The Prostitution of Women and Girls*, p. 87.

70. *Prostitution of Children and Child-Sex Tourism*, p. 8.

71. Goldsmith, "Women on the Edge," p. 65.

72. Ibid.

73. Cited in Flowers, *The Adolescent Criminal*, p. 63.

74. Cited in Goldsmith, "Women on the Edge," p. 74.

75. Patricia Hersch, "Coming of Age on City Streets," *Psychology Today* (January 1988): 37.

76. Johnson, *Teen Prostitution*, pp. 124–25.

77. Les B. Whitbeck and Ronald L. Simons, "Life on the Streets: The Victimization of Runaway and Homeless Adolescents," *Youth and Society* 22 (1990): 119.

78. See, for example, Brian Lane and Wilfred Gregg, *The Encyclopedia of Serial Killers* (New York: Berkley, 1995).

79. Flowers, *The Prostitution of Women and Girls*, p. 87; *Prostitution of Children and Child-Sex Tourism*, pp. 4–8; Tattersall, *Drugs, Runaways, and Teen Prostitution*, pp. 28–32.

Chapter 11

The Pimp's Role in Teenage Prostitution

The pimp plays a crucial role in the dynamics of teenage prostitution. Although virtually nonexistent in the adolescent male prostitution subculture, pimps are intricately involved in the lives of most prostituted girls. This relationship usually begins upon entry into prostitution and continues throughout the life of a girl prostitute. Most have run away from sexually abusive or otherwise dysfunctional homes straight into the arms of the manipulative and cunning pimp who seizes the opportunity for sexually exploiting vulnerable, needy girls. A combination of psychological and physical tactics are used by a pimp to keep a girl in his stable, combined with drugs, seduction, and the harsh realities of the streets. Few girl prostitutes emerge from the pimp controlled commercial sex trade without serious bodily and emotional scars.

THE PIMP AND THE GIRL'S ENTRANCE INTO PROSTITUTION

Unlike boy prostitution and adult female prostitution where the role of the pimp is more limited, if a factor at all, pimps are an important part of the life of prostitution involved girls. Pimps are thought to command anywhere from 80 to 95 percent of teenage female prostitution.[1] Most girls come into the business as a direct result of the persuasive or coercive powers of a pimp. Studies show that as many as 90 percent of all girl prostitutes either began selling sexual favors under the direction of a pimp, or become involved with one over the course of prostituting themselves.[2] One self-report survey found that virtually every teenage streetwalker respondent had some ties with a pimp.[3] Runaways and homeless youth are disproportionately targeted by pimps because of being "naïve and easy to control."[4] Others at risk include girls who have a low self-esteem, are depressed, lonely, rebellious, or substance abusers.

Pimps do not always go directly after vulnerable girls. Many entice girls into the business through procurers who are often other runaways or prostitutes. One out of five teenage girls enter prostitution through their association with other prostitution engaged teenagers.[5] In some instances, the pimp or procurer is a member of the prostituted girl's own family, including parents and siblings.[6]

Pimps and their recruiters or "runners" often scour bus and train stations, shopping malls, coffee shops, arcades, street corners, and anywhere that runaway, wayward, and lost kids hang out or end up. Prospects for sex workers are relatively easy to spot as they often look hungry, disheveled, confused, distant, disoriented, scared, and in need of a friend. Most have been abused, witnessed family violence, tossed out of the house, or run away from a destructive environment. Pimps have no trouble using this to their advantage in playing the supportive, caring adult willing to be everything the girl never had at home—quickly winning her confidence, love, and loyalty. An expert on pimps and prostitution described the typical pattern of seduction:

> It often starts out with romance. Seduced at malls and in schoolyards, courted with restaurant meals and expensive gifts, the girls eventually find themselves cut off from their families and being asked to "return a favor." They are all, after all, very young. But the pimps also choose their targets well—girls from broken homes, girls living on the streets, girls who are just somehow troubled.[7]

Unlike the attractive, fit, sexy, smart images of runaways-turned-prostitutes often portrayed in Hollywood or fiction, in reality most pimps do not go after these types of girls who are likely to be more secure and confident in who they are. Instead, pimps seek out young females who are rather unattractive, insecure, and not particularly sexy. These girls are likely to be on the chubby side, asexual, limited in their social skills, and not very comfortable with males, especially boys their own age.

A police detective working vice put into perspective the reason why pimps are so successful in their recruitment of susceptible girls: "The kids that are stable and know what their lives are about will tell these guys to hit the road. But kids who are vulnerable and hungry take up their offers of food, clothing, and a relationship and once the girls are with them, they are the pimp's property."[8]

According to teen prostitution researcher Joan Johnson, the pimp relies on the two most powerful human emotions to manipulate targeted girls into prostituting themselves: love and fear.[9] If he is successful in tapping into these in taking advantage of the girl's weaknesses, she almost always will respond like the child she is and fall into the trap of believing the pimp truly has her best interests—love, support, and security—at heart.

Pimps often tighten their emotional grip on the girl being groomed for prostitution by initiating a sexual relationship and essentially taking control of every aspect of her life until she becomes physically, emotionally, and spiritually dependent upon him. The fact that so many prostitution involved girls have run away from abusive, violent, uncaring families makes it that much easier to succumb to the well-established techniques and charms of the pimp.

Having gained psychological control of his new recruit through kindness, sex, drugs, money, gifts, and even jealousy, the pimp then begins to insist that she have sex with others *for him* as proof of her love. This soon turns into sex for money, as the vulnerable prostituted victim will do virtually anything to win approval from her pimp-lover. He has then succeeded in turning her out and securing her loyalty and a ready source of income.

TYPES OF PIMPS

The dictionary defines the pimp as "one who procures customers for a prostitute." In fact, most pimps school prostitutes in the techniques to attract and obtain their own clients, usually as streetwalkers, while the pimps lurk in the shadows waiting to collect money from their stable of working girls. The vast majority of pimps are adult males. In spite of the stereotype image of the urban African American male pimp "wearing flashy clothes, hats, and jewelry and driving a Cadillac or other large status symbol car,"[10] pimps can be any racial or ethnic persuasion and can ply their trade in the suburbs or rural areas as well as the inner cities. Indeed, most of the businessman pimps operating escort services, massage parlors, and strip clubs across the nation are white males. Pimps can also be teenage males or women—sometimes working in cooperation with adult male pimps. Female pimps are, in many instances, former prostitutes who use their knowledge of the business to get young runaways and prostitutes to become part of their stable.

Pimps are often involved with other types of criminal activities such as drug use and dealing, robbery, assault, organized crime, criminal gangs, and murder. Most have criminal records or are otherwise recidivists. According to Johnson, there are three primary types of pimps: (1) the *popcorn pimp*, (2) the *player pimp*, and (3) the *Mack pimp*.[11] Popcorn pimps tend to be the least successful type of pimp. They work largely with teenage girls, have little money, and few roots. These pimps are often highly competitive with other popcorn pimps in recruiting girls who are primarily runaways. Popcorn pimps are more likely to be violent towards the girls in their stable and experience a higher turnover rate of prostitutes than their more successful counterparts.

The player pimp is, by and large, more stable and successful than the popcorn pimp, less violent, and more reliant on using psychological tactics to control his stable. Players tend to have a few prostitutes and one "special" girl that they live with. According to an expert on the pimp subculture, a successful player or "mid-range" pimp can earn in excess of $200,000 every year.[12]

Mack pimps are regarded as the elite class of pimps. The men who occupy this status generally have a much larger number of female prostitutes in their stable and have one as the pimp's "lady." The Mack pimp often combines street smarts with sharp business acumen—investing prostitution profits in legitimate investments. Most Mack pimps are able to live a comfortable suburban lifestyle while maintaining a low profile, making it more difficult for authorities to gather evidence, arrest them, and put them out of business.

Some criminal justice professionals contend that the business of pimping is often intergenerational.[13] Aside from being handed down the knowledge of pimping, pimps also learn the tricks of the commercial sex trade from other pimps, prostitutes, and customers. Among pimps at the lower level, a fraternity of sorts exists, encouraging sharing and cooperation between members.

PIMPS AND VIOLENCE AGAINST GIRL PROSTITUTES

Pimp violence against the girls in their stable is common, according to many experts and self-report surveys of prostitutes.[14] However, research indicates that most girls entering the prostitution business are not physically forced by pimps into prostituting themselves. According to Jennifer James's findings on a violence-coercive relationship between a pimp and girl entering prostitution: "It is not true that pimps force [them] to work against their will, seduce young girls, turn [them] into drug addicts for the purpose of control, give no sexual satisfaction . . . keep them from ever leaving their stable, and are never married to prostitutes who work for them."[15] Indeed, one study found that only 5 percent of all prostituted girls were actually forced into selling sexual favors due to a pimp's violence, threats, or intimidation.[16] Similar findings were reported in Dorothy Bracey's study of juvenile prostitutes.[17]

Most such girls are seen as entering prostitution less from violence by pimps than the severe isolation most runaways and street youth feel in their estrangement from family and lack of a sense of belonging.[18] However, once a girl does become a part of a pimp's stable of prostitutes, "she is generally subject to his rules, regulations, and manipulation which includes falling in love, working for him, believing him, giving him much of her earnings, and violence."[19]

Female teenage prostitutes frequently experience violence at the hands of their pimps who use verbal abuse, physical assaults, rape, and threats to keep the girls in their stable from being disrespectful, holding back on them, or leaving. Sometimes the violence is merely to reassert the pimp's authority and control, while reinforcing the prostitute's low self-esteem, psychological dependence, and loyalty. A study of young female prostitutes found them to be the victims of "extreme sexual, physical, and psychological abuse" from pimps and johns.[20] More than two-thirds of streetwalker prostitutes in a self-report survey said they were regularly assaulted by their pimps,[21] while in a study of prostitution, it was found that physical assaults occurred in more than half the associations between a prostitute and pimp.[22] The physical violence prostitutes endure from pimps includes being hit by fists, slapped, burned, and beaten with "coat hangers to lashings with a six-foot bull whip."[23] Some prostitutes have accused their pimps of "severe violence, torture and attempted murder."[24] The mortality rate for prostitution involved females is forty times the national average, as reported by the U.S. Department of Justice.[25]

Prostitutes are at greatest risk for pimp violence when threatening or attempting to leave his stable. One young streetwalker recalled what her pimp did when she tried to quit the business: "He told me to take my clothes off. I wouldn't so he punched me so hard he lifted me off the ground. . . . My skin split. Blood was spraying and it was like a horror movie."[26]

The relationship between a girl prostitute and her pimp has been compared to that between a battered woman and her spouse batterer.[27] Many young female sex workers undergo repeated assaults at the hands of their pimp—unable to break free because of emotional or financial dependence, declarations of love and sorrow, or other means the pimp uses to maintain complete dominance and control. This includes further abuse, threats, intimidation, sometimes even threatening bodily harm to the girl prostitute's family, and drug dependence. The gripping psychological hold and violence-coercive control a pimp often has over a prostituted girl can be seen in the following example:

> In New York City, a girl's pimp kept her on the street six nights a week. She hated being a prostitute, but the pimp was the only person who had shown her any kindness. When she could stand it no longer and told him she had to quit, he broke her jaw. At the hospital where her jaw was wired shut, she was given pain pills and told to rest. But her pimp put her on the street the next night.
>
> Later she tried to commit suicide using the pills, but she vomited, breaking the wires in her jaw. Her pimp would not allow her to return

to the hospital and sent her back on the street. . . . She turned herself in to the police.

When asked her age, she replied, "I'll be fifteen tomorrow."[28]

KEEPING THE PROSTITUTED GIRL TIED TO A PIMP

How do pimps maintain the loyalty of girls in their stable? Violence is the primary means for ensuring that a girl will not leave a pimp for either another pimp or home. This can include actual physical violence and the threat of such through verbal abuse and intimidation. However, most pimps will use violence mainly as a last resort to keep young prostitutes from fleeing. They are more likely to rely on psychological manipulation of the prostitute through charm, affection, gifts, promises, pretense of love, and even by getting the girl pregnant. The baby is used as a pawn by the pimp to bind the prostituted girl to him—threatening to never let her have the child or even doing bodily harm to the child should the girl ever leave.[29] Many pimps also turn the girls in their stable into drug addicts, thereby using their dependence to keep them in virtual sexual bondage.[30] Other means typically used by pimps to control prostitutes include:

- Getting prostituted girls to sell drugs or commit other crimes.
- Using child pornography to break the will of girl prostitutes, while normalizing the prostitution itself in "seasoning" the prostitute victim.
- Establishing an environment of complete emotional deprivation.
- Changing the identity of prostitution involved girls and cutting off all ties with family or friends.
- Humiliating and insulting them.
- Using jealousy to create possessiveness and obsessiveness in the love struck girl prostitute.
- Random violence to maintain authority and control.

Love is perhaps the single most effective tool a pimp will use to his advantage in keeping the girl prostitute under his control. Since most runaway and prostituted girls are already psychologically vulnerable to feeling love for someone that appears to really care for them, the pimp has little problem capturing the girl prostitute's heart and soul. If he can then "successfully convince her of *his love*, the pimp can convince her of almost anything—including that she should stay with him *and* that he needs other girls for sex, prostitution, and profit."[31]

In spite of this feeling of love for a pimp that rules many prostitution involved girls, studies reveal that it does not last forever. In one survey, only 4 percent of girl prostitutes said they were in love with their pimp.[32] For many girl sex workers, early love toward a pimp often turns into hatred and deep resentment.[33] This is not too surprising, considering the range of emotions the prostituted girl is put through over the typical course of a relationship with a pimp.

Most girl prostitutes do not stay very long with the pimp that turned them out, much less for their lifetime as a prostitute. Over two-thirds of girls engaged in prostitution switch from one pimp to another in a short period of time, usually within a few months.[34] Ninety percent will leave a pimp within a year.[35] Often when a girl switches pimps, her new pimp requires she pay a fee to guarantee her safety from her former pimp, who may acquire the services of a bounty hunter or "tracker" to retrieve his "property."[36] During their early years of prostitution, many girls may have up to four pimps before settling on one, working for themselves, or leaving the business altogether in a revolving cycle of prostitute and pimp interrelations.[37]

PIMPS, JOHNS, AND GIRL PROSTITUTION

Pimps are largely responsible for girl prostitutes' involvement with johns. Though most streetwalkers do much of the work in enticing potential customers and arranging for the sex-for-pay, pimps are often involved in the details of the prostitute-john relationship. This includes determining the location where the girls in their stable will ply their trade (usually on street corners or neighborhoods controlled by the pimp), how much they will charge the john, what earnings the prostituted girls get to keep, and even bailing them out of jail during frequent arrests for prostitution-related charges. Under orders from a pimp, some girl prostitutes will rob johns of money, drugs, or other possessions, giving it to the pimp.[38] Should the prostitute deviate from any of her pimp's directions (including being arrested), she is subject to being beaten, raped, losing what little money she earns, or other punishment.

Pimps often use pornographic performances by the prostitution involved girls they control to advertise them to clients, who then use the pornography for their own sexual satisfaction, in addition to the prostitution services provided by the pimp.[39]

The tripartite relationship between pimps, prostitutes, and johns often includes sexually transmitted diseases. Studies have found that prostituted girls typically have high risk unprotected sexual relations with pimps, who routinely have multiple partners and a high rate of intravenous drug use.[40] These same girls have been shown to commonly engage in sexual practices with multiple paid clients, often without safeguards against venereal infections and HIV.[41] When drug use, including intravenous, by many johns is factored in, prostitution involved girls' sexual contact with pimps and johns puts them at a particularly vulnerable crossroads for infection with one sexual disease or another.

SUMMARY

Girl prostitution is predominantly controlled by pimps. The vast majority of prostituted female teens enter the business through the charms, coercion, and manipulation of a pimp or someone who works for the pimp. While pimps are mostly males, women and teenage boys can also turn girls out. Pimps come in all races and occupy various levels of the socioeconomic strata. The primary types of pimps have been identified as popcorn pimps, player pimps, and Mack pimps. Pimping can be passed from generation to generation and tends to operate like a fraternity on the lower levels.

Prostituted girls are kept in a pimp's stable through violence, intimidation, drugs, use of pornography, pregnancy, fear, and love. Most girl prostitutes go through a number of pimps over the life of their prostitution. A tripartite relationship between pimps, prostitutes, and johns puts girl sex workers at high risk for sexually transmitted diseases and other health hazards.

NOTES

1. Kathleen Barry, *The Prostitution of Sexuality* (New York: New York University Press, 1995), p. 198.
2. R. Barri Flowers, *The Prostitution of Women and Girls* (Jefferson, N.C.: McFarland, 1998), p. 101.
3. Cited in Joan J. Johnson, *Teen Prostitution* (Danbury, Conn.: Franklin Watts, 1992), p. 78.
4. U.S. Department of Justice, Office of Juvenile Justice and Delinquency Prevention, *Prostitution of Children and Child-Sex Tourism: An Analysis of Domestic and International Responses* (Alexandria, Va.: National Center for Missing & Exploited Children, 1999), p. 4; Gregory A. Loken, "Child Prostitution," in U.S. Department of Justice, *Child Pornography and Prostitution: Background and Legal Analysis* (Alexandria, Va.: National Center for Missing & Exploited Children, 1987).
5. Johnson, *Teen Prostitution*, p. 87.
6. R. Barri Flowers, *Female Crime, Criminals and Cellmates: An Exploration of Female Criminality and Delinquency* (Jefferson, N.C.: McFarland, 1995), p. 152.
7. Deborah Jones, "Pimped," *Chatelaine* 67 (November 1994): 111.
8. Ibid.
9. Johnson, *Teen Prostitution*, p. 79.
10. Flowers, *The Prostitution of Women and Girls*, p. 100.
11. Johnson, *Teen Prostitution*, pp. 76–77.
12. Cited in ibid., p. 77.
13. Flowers, *The Prostitution of Women and Girls*, p. 102.
14. Ibid., pp. 103–4; *Prostitution of Children and Child-Sex Tourism*, pp. 4–5;

Barry, *The Prostitution of Sexuality*, p. 202; Minouche Kandel, "Whores in Court: Judicial Processing of Prostitutes in the Boston Municipal Court in 1990," *Yale Journal of Law & Feminism* 4 (1992): 329; Clare Tattersall, *Drugs, Runaways, and Teen Prostitution* (New York: Rosen, 1999), pp. 31–32.

15. Quoted in Lee H. Bowker, *Women, Crime, and the Criminal Justice System* (Lexington, Mass.: Lexington Books, 1978), p. 55. See also Jennifer James, "Prostitute-Pimp Relationships," *Medical Aspects of Human Sexuality* 7 (1973): 147–63.

16. "The Enablers," *Juvenile Prostitution in Minnesota: The Report of a Research Project* (St. Paul: The Enablers, 1978), p. 57.

17. Dorothy H. Bracey, *"Baby-Pros": Preliminary Profiles of Juvenile Prostitutes* (New York: John Jay Press, 1979), p. 23.

18. Flowers, *The Prostitution of Women and Girls*, pp. 100–101; *Prostitution of Children and Child-Sex Tourism*, pp. 4–5; Evelina Giobbe, "An Analysis of Individual, Institutional and Cultural Pimping," *Michigan Journal of Gender and Law* 1 (1993): 46–47.

19. R. Barri Flowers, *The Adolescent Criminal: An Examination of Today's Juvenile Offender* (Jefferson, N.C.: McFarland, 1990), p. 58.

20. Flowers, *The Prostitution of Women and Girls*, p. 103.

21. Anastasia Volkonsky, "Legalizing the 'Profession' Would Sanction the Abuse," *Insight on the News* 11 (1995): 20.

22. Kandel, "Whores in Court," p. 329.

23. Quoted in Flowers, *The Prostitution of Women and Girls*, p. 51.

24. Volkonsky, "Legalizing the 'Profession' Would Sanction the Abuse," p. 20.

25. Cited in ibid.

26. Quoted in Jones, "Pimped," p. 112.

27. Giobbe, "An Analysis of Individual, Institutional and Cultural Pimping," pp. 33, 46.

28. John G. Hubbell, "Child Prostitution: How It Can Be Stopped," *Reader's Digest* (June 1984): 202, 205.

29. Flowers, *The Prostitution of Women and Girls*, p. 102; Johnson, *Teen Prostitution*, p. 84.

30. Flowers, *The Adolescent Criminal*, pp. 57–60.

31. Flowers, *The Prostitution of Women and Girls*, p. 103.

32. Cited in Johnson, *Teen Prostitution*, p. 83.

33. Flowers, *The Prostitution of Women and Girls*, p. 103.

34. Ibid.

35. Ibid.

36. *Prostitution of Children and Child-Sex Tourism*, p. 5; Giobbe, "Analysis of Individual, Institutional and Cultural Pimping," p. 48.

37. Flowers, *The Prostitution of Women and Girls*, p. 103; Johnson, *Teen Prostitution*, pp. 83–84.

38. Flowers, *The Prostitution of Women and Girls*, pp. 85–86.

39. Ibid., p. 13; *Prostitution of Children and Child-Sex Tourism*, p. 6; Cathy S. Widom and Joseph B. Kuhns, "Childhood Victimization and Subsequent Risk for Promiscuity, Prostitution and Teenage Pregnancy: A Prospective Study," *American Journal of Public Health* 86 (1996): 1611.

40. Flowers, *The Prostitution of Women and Girls*, p. 104; Johnson, *Teen Prostitution*, p. 127.

41. Flowers, *The Prostitution of Women and Girls*, pp. 130–31; Barbara Goldsmith, "Women on the Edge: A Reporter at Large," *New Yorker* 69 (April 26, 1993): 65.

Chapter 12

Boy Prostitution

Male prostitution has generally received less attention in the literature than female prostitution. This is apparently a reflection of the common belief that females constitute the majority of people prostituting themselves, therefore justifying the greater attention. Girl prostitutes, in particular, have been thought to represent as many as two-thirds of all child prostitutes. However, some researchers now believe that there may be as many boys active in the sex trade industry as girls. Moreover, with the advent of AIDS, greater focus has been placed on male prostitution, its incidence, and impact on the spread of the deadly virus. Recent studies suggest that young male prostitutes are less likely to be involved with the criminal justice system than their female counterparts, and less likely to return home once leaving for life on the streets.

THE EXTENT OF BOY PROSTITUTION

How big is the problem of boy prostitution in the United States? Most studies have found that the vast majority of youth engaged in prostitution are female.[1] Experts are now beginning to question this assumption, finding that male teenage runaways-turned-street hustlers may account for an equal number of juvenile prostitutes as runaway girls selling their bodies.[2] The strong correlation between runaways and prostitution has been discussed in Chapters 4 and 8. An apropos example of self-reported prostitution by a boy throwaway can be seen in the following account as told by a reporter studying runaway children:

> I met Nicky at Miss Brown's, an all-night coffee shop on San Francisco's Polk Street. . . . His voice was somewhat high and unsteady.

> He was 16. He told me he was originally from Portland. . . . His parents were divorced, and his step-mother had thrown him out when he was 14.
>
> "I didn't know what to do," he said. "I was just a kid. Finally another kid told me about Camp—that's an area in Portland where all the boys and girls sell themselves. So I did, and I lived in a dirty hotel. Then I got beat up by pimps a couple of times, and I came here to San Francisco and got involved down here. I've been here a year or two, I guess."[3]

The most noted estimate on the extent of boy prostitution in this country came from Robin Lloyd in his groundbreaking book on male prostitution, *For Money or Love: Boy Prostitution in America*. He estimated that there were 300,000 boy prostitutes under the age of sixteen nationwide.[4] Researchers have reported that the number of prostitutes may double or even triple when including sixteen- and seventeen-year-olds.[5] The proportion of boy prostitutes appears to be higher in larger cities;[6] however, an increase in the prostitution of teenage males has also been reported in smaller cities.[7]

THE CHICKEN AND CHICKEN HAWK

Boy prostitutes are typically referred to on the streets as *chickens*, while homosexual men that solicit young male prostitutes are known as *chicken hawks* or *chicken queens*. In law enforcement and psychiatry, these men are seen as child molesters and pedophiles. Much of the teenage male prostitution occurs in large cities with a significant population of gay males.[8] Young prostituted boys can also be found practicing their trade in the ever growing suburbs and rural areas across America.[9] An example of a chicken–chicken hawk encounter can be seen in the following description by a police detective working in the sex offenses unit of his department:

> The boy will usually find a set of marble steps, sit, and observe passing cars. Eye contact is the key. The "chicken hawk" will stare at the boy he feels could be a "hustler." If a period of eye contact is made between both, the "chicken hawk" will still circle the block several times, making eye contact at each passing. Finally the "chicken hawk" will nod and, if the boy returns the nod, a deal is in the making. At times, the "chickens" would work as teams, usually two together. If the customer wanted two boys, he would use hand signals, indicating how many boys he wanted and how much he was paying.[10]

Although most chicken hawks prefer boy prostitutes, many will seek out male hustlers of any age. Some pedophiles prefer chickens that fall within a particular age range and "will not pick up any boys who might be older or younger than he desires."[11] A profile of the chicken hawk is shown as follows:

- He is often middle aged.
- Relates to children usually better than adults.
- He sees the chicken as the sexual aggressor.
- He is often single, but some are married.
- Is typically nonviolent.
- Usually associates with fellow child molesters and chicken hawks.
- He was often himself a victim of child molestation.
- He pretends to be the chicken's friend.
- Is usually a white-collar professional or worker.[12]

Gay customers of male prostitutes have typically been shown to be middle aged and physically unattractive. Most of these men tend to be interested in "bizarre and unusual sex acts which would not meet with acceptance in conventional gay society."[13] Authorities on male prostitution report that male prostitutes and the men who seek them out tend to have a "deep hatred" towards each other—both wrestling "with conflicting emotions during their time together, often creating fantasies that are acted out in the course of the sexual encounter."[14]

CHARACTERIZING THE BOY PROSTITUTE

Like girls in the sex trade industry, boy prostitutes come from every walk of life and background, including "delinquent school dropouts to well-educated, refined college students; they come from inner city projects and middle-class suburbs, from completely disintegrated families and from effective, loving families."[15] The first national study of adolescent male prostitution was undertaken by the Urban and Rural Systems Associates of San Francisco.[16] They reported the following characteristics of boy prostitutes:

- Boy prostitutes sell sexual favors primarily for financial reasons, to explore their sexuality, and/or make contact with homosexual men.
- Money is the most important motivating factor for teenage males to become and remain prostitutes.
- The average age of a boy prostitute is sixteen.
- The majority of male juvenile prostitutes are runaways or were thrown out of the home.

- A high percentage of boy prostitutes come from broken homes or dysfunctional families.
- Most prostitution involved boys have been victimized by child sexual, physical, or mental abuse.
- Male teen prostitutes have a high rate of high school dropout or poor school performance.
- Delinquency and criminality are frequent patterns of behavior among boy prostitutes.
- Gay-identified prostituted male youth find the lifestyle to be initially exciting.
- Pimps are virtually nonexistent in the boy prostitution subculture.

Most boy prostitutes are preteen when they have their first paid sexual encounter. A study of male prostitution found the average age of a prostitute's first homosexual experience to be 9.6 years.[17] Three-fifths of the prostitutes reported receiving some type of payment for their services. On average, the male customer was at least five years older in a boy prostitute's first sexual engagement.[18] Official data show that most boys arrested for prostitution and commercialized vice are older teens.[19] (See also Chapter 9.)

The majority of boy prostitutes entered the sex-for-sale business as runaways. Two-thirds of full-time male prostitutes in one study had run away from home prior to prostituting themselves.[20] Of those whose first sexual experience was with a male, over half reported being seduced, while two-thirds were paid to engage in sexual relations.

It is estimated that as many as half of all boy prostitutes are "thrown out of their houses because of sexual identity issues."[21] One study reported that two-thirds of the male prostitutes considered themselves to be either homosexual or bisexual.[22] However, apparently most male prostitutes do not label themselves as homosexual but rather regard their sexual activities as done solely for the money or other payment, such as drugs.[23] In a study where nearly 75 percent of the males involved in prostitution were seen as homosexual, only 6 percent of the subjects identified themselves as gay.[24]

Most boys who sell sex are streetwalkers. In D. Kelly Weisberg's study of adolescent prostitution, 94 percent of her sample of boy prostitutes plied their trade on the streets.[25] However, boy brothels exist where young male prostitutes live and work. They are usually operated by owner-pimps or madams. According to Joan Johnson, boy brothel prostitutes are at the lowest level of the teenage male prostitute hierarchy.[26]

Researchers have found that most male prostitutes tend to be self-destructive, unstable, immature, irresponsible, and have high levels of psychopathology.[27] They have also been shown to have a high rate of drug addiction, sexually transmitted diseases, and suicide.[28]

TYPOLOGIES OF BOY PROSTITUTES

Researchers have identified a number of subgroups of boy prostitutes. According to S. Caukins and N. Coombs, there are four types of adolescent male prostitutes: (1) street hustlers, (2) bar hustlers, (3) call boys, and (4) kept boys.[29] These were defined in a psychosocial study as follows:

- *Street hustlers*—typically drifters who sometimes support a family through prostitution.
- *Bar hustlers*—often drifters who support a wife and/or children.
- *Call boys*—often operate as companions to upscale johns for social affairs such as dinner or a play.
- *Kept boys*—usually houseboys who also perform various nonsexual household chores.[30]

Caukins and Coombs found that a "gay sex market thrives in every big city . . . a profit oriented street corner college for the recruiting, training, and selling of boys and men to older, affluent homosexuals."[31]

In a study of male prostitutes and intravenous drug use, Dan Waldorf and Sheigla Murphy classified boy prostitutes into two general typologies: hustlers and call boys.[32] Hustlers found clients in places typically frequented by chickens and chicken hawks—arcades, gay bars, adult bookstores, and theaters. The researchers subdivided hustlers into three categories:

- *Trade hustlers*—often heterosexual or bisexual males who sell sex for money. Most do not acknowledge being gay or admit to enjoying sexual relations with their male customers.
- *Drag queen hustlers*—transvestites and transsexual prostitutes who specialize in oral sex. They are commonly active in known gay red-light areas.
- *Youth hustlers*—young, admitted homosexual males who seem to be naïve and innocent, but are often experienced in a number of paid sexual relationships.

Call boys are less a reflection of erotic styles as the way in which johns are located, as well as the kinds of sexual services offered them. Waldorf and Murphy subdivided call boys into four groups:

- *Call book boys*—typically identify themselves as homosexual or bisexual. They tend to find customers from a call book or have regular clients. Drag queen call girls are transvestite males working from a call book.

- *Models and escorts*—males who locate clients by advertising in general or special interest publications. They often develop a network of regular customers and may also have a call book.
- *Erotic masseurs*—males who find new clients through advertising even while having a regular clientele. Most are certified by licensed massage schools, combining massages with sexual services for fees that are typically lower than those charged by call males.
- *Porn industry stars*—these males represent the elite or highest paid of the male prostitute subculture, and include erotic dancers and porn starts. Johns are typically solicited at work and sexually serviced outside of work.[33]

Weisberg broke boy prostitutes into two distinct subcultures: peer-delinquent subculture and gay subculture:

> For youth in the first subculture, prostitution is an integral aspect of delinquent street life. These adolescents engage indiscriminately in prostitution, drug dealing, panhandling, and petty criminal activity. They sell their sexual favors habitually as a way of making money, viewing prostitution as just one aspect of "hustling"—as the term is used to mean procuring more than one gives.
>
> Youth in the gay subculture engage in prostitution for different reasons. Prostitution is one outlet for their sexuality. They find in the gay male subculture a means of identification, and prostitution satisfies their needs for social interaction with gay persons and for sexual partners. Simultaneously, it provides a way of making money, since the purchase and sale of sexual activity is a product of the sexual mores of that community.[34]

These subcultures are further subdivided into four categories of boy prostitutes: (1) situational, (2) habitual, (3) vocational, and (4) avocational prostitutes:

- *Situational prostitutes*—male teens who participate in prostitution only on certain occasions and who view prostitution as merely an occasional pastime.
- *Habitual prostitutes*—adolescent males who are active in inner city street life, including prostitution, drug dealing, robbery, and petty theft.
- *Vocational prostitutes*—male juveniles who view child prostitution as either a career or a means to advance to one and who regard themselves as professionals.

- *Avocational prostitutes*—vocational boy prostitutes who see selling sexual favors as strictly a part-time occupation.[35]

In Johnson's study of teenage prostitution, most boy prostitutes were identified as street hustlers, who were gay, bisexual, and heterosexual.[36] Many were further described as aggressive, drug addicted, and unattractive. Other prostitution involved male youth were categorized as transvestite boy prostitutes and upper-class adolescent male prostitutes.[37] The latter was seen as often better looking, better dressed, and more self-confident than street hustlers. Most upper-class boy prostitutes ply their trade through escort services or their own call boy service.

SUBSTANCE ABUSE AMONG BOY PROSTITUTES

The rate of substance abuse is high for both boy and girl prostitutes. More than three-quarters of teenage prostitutes abuse alcohol or drugs, while virtually all admit to drinking alcohol or taking drugs.[38] Alcohol and marijuana are the most commonly used substances by prostituted youth, though other drugs such as cocaine, heroin, amphetamines, and LSD are also frequently used.[39]

According to the Huckleberry House Youth Services Project, 83 percent of the boy prostitutes had tried marijuana and 77 percent were regular users.[40] Another study of young male prostitutes found that 42 percent could be classified as heavy drinkers or alcoholics, while 29 percent were regular users of hard drugs.[41]

The use of crack cocaine by teenage prostitutes and homeless kids can be especially harmful, addictive, and contribute to the spread of underage prostitution. Some crack houses double as "sex-for-drugs" centers. One study found that juvenile crack use in poor inner city neighborhoods has increased the incidence of teenage prostitution at the street level.[42]

BOY PROSTITUTION AND AIDS

Compared to female prostitution, relatively few studies have been done on the relationship between male prostitution and the AIDS virus. Existing data suggests that the rate of infection in male prostitutes is high.[43] AIDS and its precursor, HIV, are most commonly spread in two ways in the male prostitution subculture: (1) through the sharing of dirty needles and tainted blood between intravenous drug users and (2) the passing of AIDS infected bodily fluids, often through anal intercourse. Given the high rate of intravenous drug use and multiple partner homosexual or bisexual relations among male prostitutes, they may be at greater risk for becoming exposed to the AIDS virus than female prostitutes.[44]

Recent studies on the correlation between male prostitution and HIV infection give rise to the seriousness of the problem. A study of eighty-four prostituted males at a New York City venereal clinic revealed that 53 percent of those involved in homosexual prostitution tested HIV-seropositive, while 10 percent of the prostitutes whose clients were female tested positive.[45] In a study of male prostitutes and intravenous drug users in Italy, 11 percent of the prostitutes and 49 percent of the intravenous drug addicts tested positive for HIV.[46] In both studies, researchers found male prostitutes to be a high risk population for contracting and spreading HIV.

VIOLENCE AND BOY PROSTITUTION

Most prostituted youth are exposed to violence on a daily basis. This includes physical and sexual assaults and robberies from pimps, customers, drug addicts or dealers, muggers, and other prostitutes. Some teenage prostitutes are killed by their attackers—including sexual predators or sexual serial murderers who target young prostitutes.[47] Boy prostitutes are as "at risk" as girl prostitutes for being victimized in the course of plying their trade on the streets or even in work elsewhere, such as a boy brothel. Much of the violence experienced by teen prostitutes goes unreported due to fear of reprisal or of law enforcement authorities who may arrest them and/or return them to abusive homes.[48]

The violence prostitution involved youth are at risk for can be seen in the following example of a boy prostitute, as told to teenage prostitution researcher Clare Tattersall:

> Simon, a fifteen year old male prostitute from Texas, says, "I was repeatedly beaten up by johns. Twice I was taken to a field, raped at knifepoint, and kicked so badly that I couldn't work for days afterwards. I was often beaten up by johns who tried to get their money back after the act and I have been raped I don't know how many times."[49]

SUMMARY

Boy prostitution may be as prevalent as girl prostitution in this country. Every year tens of thousands of young males enter the sex trade, often as runaways or throwaways from homes that may be abusive or otherwise dysfunctional. Boy prostitutes are known in the male prostitution subculture as chickens and their customers as chicken hawks. The average age of a boy prostitute is sixteen, though many were much younger when they had their first prostitution experience. Types of boy prostitutes identified by experts include street hustlers, bar hustlers, call boys, and kept boys. Some are further seen as situational, habitual, vocational, or avocational prostitutes.

The vast majority of prostituted boys sell sexual favors on the street, though there are some boy brothels. Most prostitution involved young males abuse alcohol or drugs and are at high risk for exposure to the AIDS virus. There is also a high rate of sexual assaults, muggings, and other violence among boy prostitutes, sometimes perpetrated by other male prostitutes or sex workers.

NOTES

1. R. Barri Flowers, *The Prostitution of Women and Girls* (Jefferson, N.C.: McFarland, 1998), p. 71; Debra Whitcomb, Edward De Vos, and Barbara E. Smith, *Program to Increase Understanding of Child Sexual Exploitation, Final Report* (Washington, D.C.: Education Development Center, Inc., and ABA Center on Children and the Law, 1998), p. 65.
2. R. Barri Flowers, *The Victimization and Exploitation of Women and Children: A Study of Physical, Mental and Sexual Maltreatment in the United States* (Jefferson, N.C.: McFarland, 1994), p. 82.
3. Dotson Rader, "I Want to Die So I Won't Hurt No More," *Parade Magazine* (August 18, 1985): 5–6.
4. Robin Lloyd, *For Money or Love: Boy Prostitution in America* (New York: Ballantine, 1976), pp. 58–72.
5. Flowers, *The Victimization and Exploitation of Women and Children*, p. 82; Judianne Densen-Gerber and S. F. Hutchinson, "Medical-Legal and Societal Problems Involving Children, Child Prostitution, Child Pornography, and Drug-Related Abuse: Recommended Legislation," in Selwyn M. Smith, ed., *The Maltreatment of Children* (Baltimore: University Park Press, 1978), p. 318.
6. U.S. Department of Justice, Office of Juvenile Justice and Delinquency Prevention, *Prostitution of Children and Child-Sex Tourism* (Alexandria, Va.: National Center for Missing & Exploited Children, 1999), p. 2.
7. Ibid.
8. Flowers, *The Prostitution of Women and Girls*, p. 140.
9. Ibid.
10. Quoted in Alfred Danna, "Juvenile Male Prostitution: How Can We Reduce the Problem?" *USA Today* 113 (May 1988): 87.
11. Ibid., p. 88.
12. Flowers, *The Victimization and Exploitation of Women and Children*, p. 87.
13. S. Caukins and N. Coombs, "The Psychodynamics of Male Prostitution," *American Journal of Psychotherapy* 30 (1976): 446, 450; Richard Green, *Sexual Science and the Law* (Cambridge: Mass. Harvard University Press, 1992), p. 194.
14. Flowers, *The Prostitution of Women and Girls*, p. 138; Joan J. Johnson, *Teen Prostitution* (Danbury, Conn.: Franklin Watts, 1992), p. 11.
15. Donald M. Allen, "Young Male Prostitutes: A Psychosocial Study," *Archives of Sexual Behavior* 9 (1980): 418.
16. Cited in Hilary Abramson, "Sociologists Try to Reach Young Hustlers," *Sacramento Bee* (September 3, 1984), p. A8.
17. N. Coombs, "Male Prostitution: A Psychosocial View of Behavior," *American Journal of Orthopsychiatry* 44 (1974): 782–89.

18. C. Earls and H. David, "A Psychosocial Study of Male Prostitution," *Archives of Sexual Behavior* 18 (1989): 401–19.

19. U.S. Department of Justice, Federal Bureau of Investigation, *Crime in the United States: Uniform Crime Reports 1998* (Washington, D.C.: Government Printing Office, 1999), p. 222.

20. Allen, "Young Male Prostitutes," pp. 409–18.

21. Tamar Stieber, "The Boys Who Sell Sex to Men in San Francisco," *Sacramento Bee* (March 4, 1984), p. A22.

22. Earls and David, "A Psychosocial Study of Male Prostitution," pp. 401–19.

23. Caukins and Coombs, "The Psychodynamics of Male Prostitution," p. 446; Green, *Sexual Science and the Law*, p. 194.

24. Coombs, "Male Prostitution," pp. 782–89.

25. D. Kelly Weisberg, *Children of the Night: A Study of Adolescent Prostitution* (Lexington, Mass.: Lexington Books, 1985), p. 61.

26. Johnson, *Teen Prostitution*, p. 100.

27. See, for example, Flowers, *The Prostitution of Women and Girls*, p. 138; Caukins and Coombs, "The Psychodynamics of Male Prostitution," p. 450; D. MacNamara, "Male Prostitution in American Cities: A Socioeconomic or Pathological Phenomenon?" *American Journal of Orthopsychiatry* 35 (1965): 204.

28. Caukins and Coombs, "The Psychodynamics of Male Prostitution," p. 450; Clare Tattersall, *Drugs, Runaways, and Teen Prostitution* (New York: Rosen, 1999), p. 31.

29. Caukins and Coombs, "The Psychodynamics of Male Prostitution," pp. 441–51.

30. Allen, "Young Male Prostitutes," pp. 399–426.

31. Caukins and Coombs, "The Psychodynamics of Male Prostitution," p. 441.

32. Dan Waldorf and Sheigla Murphy, "Intravenous Drug Use and Syringe-Sharing Practices of Call Men and Hustlers," in Martin A. Plant, ed., *AIDS, Drugs, and Prostitution* (London: Routledge, 1990), pp. 109–31.

33. Ibid.

34. Weisberg, *Children of the Night*, p. 19.

35. Ibid., p. 40.

36. Johnson, *Teen Prostitution*, p. 110.

37. Ibid.; Flowers, *The Prostitution of Women and Girls*, p. 142.

38. Gary L. Yates et al., "A Risk Profile Comparison of Homeless Youth Involved in Prostitution and Homeless Youth Not Involved," *Journal of Adolescent Health* 12 (1991): 547.

39. *Prostitution of Children and Child-Sex Tourism*, p. 9.

40. Sparky Harlan, Luanne L. Rodgers, and Brian Slattery, *Male and Female Adolescent Prostitution: Huckleberry House Sexual Minority Youth Services Project* (Washington, D.C.: U.S. Department of Health and Human Services, 1981), p. 22.

41. Allen, "Young Male Prostitutes," pp. 399–426.

42. Kathleen Barry, *The Prostitution of Sexuality* (New York: New York University Press, 1995), p. 41.

43. Waldorf and Murphy, "Intravenous Drug Use and Syringe-Sharing Practices of Call Men and Hustlers," pp. 109–27.

44. Flowers, *The Prostitution of Women and Girls*, p. 143; *Prostitution of Children and Child-Sex Tourism*, p. 8.

45. M. A. Chiasson, A. R. Lifson, R. L. Stoneburner, W. Ewing, D. Hilderbrandt, and H. W. Jaffe, "HIV-1 Seroprevalence in Male and Female Prostitutes in New York City," Abstracts from the Sixth International Conference on AIDS, Stockholm, Sweden, June 1988.

46. U. Tirelli, D. Erranto, and D. Serraino, "HIV-1 Seroprevalence in Male Prostitutes in Northeastern Italy," *Journal of Acquired Immune Deficiency Syndrome* 1 (1988): 414–15.

47. See, for example, David Lester, *Serial Killers: The Insatiable Passion* (Philadelphia: The Charles Press, 1995).

48. *Prostitution of Children and Child-Sex Tourism*, pp. 6–7.

49. Tattersall, *Drugs, Runaways, and Teen Prostitution*, p. 23.

Part III

Correlates of Running Away and Teenage Prostitution

Chapter 13

Child Sexual Abuse

The sexual abuse of children by family, acquaintances, or stranger perpetrators has been shown in many studies to be directly related to teenage prostitution and other child sexploitation. Girls who have been sexually abused, in particular, are more likely to enter prostitution and other high risk sexual activities than sexually abused boys, or girls who have not been abused sexually. Child sexual abuse often leads to running away from home, which in turn increases the likelihood that the runaway will become involved in prostitution, pornography, and other survival sexual activities. The implications of sexual abuse on the prostituted child can be enormous, including drug addiction, dangerous sexual relations with multiple persons, sexual abuse perpetrated by strangers, HIV infection, depression, and attempted suicide.

DEFINING CHILD SEXUAL ABUSE

What is child sexual abuse? Who are child sexual abusers? Who are the likely victims? Child sexual abuse has been defined legally through the Child Abuse Prevention and Treatment Act as

> the employment, use, persuasion, inducement, enticement, or coercion of any child to engage in, or assist any other person to engage in, any sexually explicit conduct or simulation of such conduct for the purpose of producing any visual depiction of such conduct, or (b) the rape, molestation, prostitution, or other such form of sexual exploitation of children, or incest with children.[1]

In a report sponsored by the American Bar Association, the Legal Resource Center for Child Advocacy and Protection, the American Public Welfare Association, and the American Enterprise Institute, definitional guidelines for child sexual abuse and exploitation were suggested to child protective services agencies. Sexual abuse was defined as "vaginal, anal, or oral intercourse; vaginal or anal penetrations; or other forms of contact for sexual purposes."[2] The definition of sexual exploitation was the use of "a child in prostitution, pornography, or other sexually exploitative activities."[3]

Child sexual abuse can encompass a number of different forms of sexual victimization and exploitation. These include incestuous relations, child molestation, forcible and statutory rape, child prostitution, and child pornography. Children are sexually abused by parents, guardians, friends, caretakers, acquaintances, and complete strangers. Though most child sexual abusers are adult males, they can also be adult females and children. The following outlines the primary types of child sexual abuse and its perpetrators:

- *Familial Child Sexual Abuse*. Perpetrated by a nuclear family member such as a father/father substitute, mother/mother substitute, brother, or sister.
- *Extended Familial Child Sexual Abuse*. Perpetrated by a non-nuclear family member such as a grandparent, uncle, aunt, or cousin.
- *Caretaker Child Sexual Abuse*. Perpetrated by a child caretaker such as a babysitter, nanny, or day care worker.
- *Acquaintance Child Sexual Abuse*. Perpetrated by someone acquainted with the child such as an adult family friend, scout leader, neighbor, or postman.
- *Peer Child Sexual Abuse*. Perpetrated by another child, usually older, that is a non-family member.
- *Stranger Child Sexual Abuse*. Perpetrated by someone that is a stranger to the child victim.
- *Ritualistic Child Sexual Abuse*. Perpetrated by a person involved with the practice of ritualism or satanism.[4]

Child victims of sexual abuse can range from totally accidental victimization where there is "little victimogenesis to seductive sexual partner with extensive victimogenesis."[5] In many cases of child sexual abuse, the victimized child

> may consent to the sexual victimization unintentionally or unwittingly, or offer only passive resistance; in other cases of sex exploi-

tation, the victim and offender are in a symbiotic relationship or form a cooperative dyad. At its worst, the sexually abused child is completely powerless, vulnerable, and exploited by the powerful, nonvulnerable exploiter.[6]

THE EXTENT OF CHILD SEXUAL ABUSE

Many experts believe that millions of children are being affected by sexual abuse in the United States each year. However, uniform, accurate figures of its incidence are hard to come by, given differing measuring devices and the secrecy associated with child sexual abuse. In a recent fifty-state survey of child maltreatment by the National Committee for Prevention of Child Abuse, it was found that an estimated 17 percent of all cases of child abuse and neglect involved sexual abuse.[7] According to the National Child Abuse and Neglect Data System, there are around 130,000 reports of child sexual abuse substantiated each year.[8] In an examination of nineteen prevalence studies of child sexual abuse, the rate of victimization ranged from 6 to 62 percent for females and 3 to 31 percent for males.[9] In his study of child sexual abuse, David Finkelhor reported that as many as 52 percent of the adult females and 9 percent of the adult males sampled disclosed being victims of child sexual abuse.[10]

Estimates of incest alone in the United States range from tens of thousands to well over a million cases annually.[11] One study estimated that anywhere from 11 to 33 million people were involved in incestuous relations nationally.[12] As many as one in three people may be victims of incest before reaching the age of eighteen, according to researchers.[13] In a report released by the Family Violence Research Program at the University of New Hampshire, an estimate of between 5 and 15 percent of the female population under seventeen years of age were thought to be incest victims or sexually exploited through other means.[14]

Child molestation, or pedophilia, may be at least as prevalent as incestuous sexual abuse, if not more common. It is estimated that 2 million children are the sexual victims of pedophiles in the United States annually.[15] Hundreds of thousands of other children are at risk daily from sexual abuse by other sexual predators, pimps, pornographers, and sex offenders.[16]

Most experts on child sexual abuse agree that the vast majority of cases go unreported and, thus, are unknown to researchers, medical personnel, and the authorities.[17]

CHILDREN AT RISK FOR SEXUAL ABUSE

No child can feel totally safe from sexual abuse, given its range, nature, and potential abusers. However, researchers have found that some children are more at risk than others to be sexually abused. The following characteristics have been identified for children most vulnerable to child sexual abuse:

- Girls are at greater risk than boys.
- Preteens are more susceptible than teens.
- The absence of one or more parents/guardians.
- The existence of a family cycle of sexual or physical abuse.
- A victim of emotional abuse.
- Being a stepchild.
- Being the oldest child in the family.
- Alcohol or drug abuse in the family.
- In a dysfunctional, unstable family.
- Where there is a lack of family bonding.
- Not being in a loving, supportive family environment.[18]

The American Humane Association (AHA) reported the average age of a sexually abused child to be 9.3 years of age.[19] In nearly eight in ten cases of sexual abuse, the victim was female. The AHA found that the sexual abuse of girls appeared to increase relative to chronological age. According to the National Incidence Study, the rate of child sexual abuse is highest for girls age twelve to seventeen.[20] The Child Victimization Study found that child sexual abuse cases involved mostly male abusers and young female victims and were more likely to take place among middle class families than child physical abuse or neglect cases.[21]

Studies show that victims of intrafamilial child sexual abuse are at greater risk for subsequent sexual abuse than children sexually abused by someone outside the family.[22] Some research has shown that adult female incest victims often may unconsciously "seek abusive environments in which they are subsequently victimized (through rape or spousal [rape]) and are frequently unable to protect their own children from being abused."[23]

Learned behavior through transgenerational child sexual abuse is believed by some to place children at increased risk for both abuse and becoming sexual abusers from generation to generation, resulting in "an escalating geometric progression of abuse."[24]

CHILD SEXUAL ABUSE AND TEENAGE PROSTITUTION

The relationship between child sexual abuse and teenage prostitution has been well documented in the literature.[25] Children who are sexually abused are at increased risk to run away from home; in turn, most long-term runaways will become prostituted youth.[26] Girls who are sexually abused are more likely than boys to leave home as a direct consequence and engage in a prostitution lifestyle.[27] The National Network of Runaway and Youth Services estimated that seven in ten runaways in youth shelters have been sexually abused.[28] Ann Hayman of the Mary Magdalene Project in Los Angeles, posited that the vast majority of runaway girl prostitutes were sexually battered and incest victims.[29]

Studies have shown that virtually all prostitution involved girls experienced sexual molestation or other abuse prior to entering prostitution.[30] According to the Huckleberry House Project's study of adolescent prostitution, 90 percent of girl prostitutes were sexually abused.[31] Mimi Silbert found that two-thirds of the girl prostitutes in her sample were incest or child abuse victims.[32] This tragic correlation was noted by Ian Sparks, director of The Children's Society: "These children have been sexually abused and are acting out their pain and feelings of worthlessness. Their friends may be prostitutes and so they stand and watch. They get drawn in."[33]

Teenage boy prostitutes have also been the victims of frequent sexual abuse prior to leaving home. In a study of adolescent male prostitution, the Urban and Rural Systems Associates of San Francisco found a high rate of childhood sexual molestation and runaway behavior.[34] Other research has pointed to the dysfunctional family life of prostituted young males, including incestuous relations and drug abuse.[35] One study found that the average boy prostitute's first paid homosexual experience occurred when under ten years of age.[36] Another study found that the boy prostitute's initial sexual encounter was with a john who was at least five years older on average.[37]

Sexually abused young male runaways are often propositioned for sex by older chicken hawks on an exclusive basis. Notes one researcher: "If the boy is desperate enough, he'll take the customer up on his offer . . . [of] food and shelter. . . . Many young boys count themselves lucky to find a dutch uncle [or] sugar daddy."[38] However, most prostituted male youth leaving an abusive environment enter a life of street prostitution through the encouragement and participation of other boy prostitutes.[39]

INTRAFAMILIAL CHILD SEXUAL ABUSE

Teenage prostitution is most closely associated with intrafamilial child sexual abuse or incest, generally defined as "sexual intercourse between relatives within the prohibited degrees of relationship defined by the law."[40] These days child sexual abuse usually refers to any sexual acts, including fondling, oral sex, sodomy, and masturbation between a young minor and any nuclear family member, such as a father or stepfather, or a non-nuclear family member, such as an uncle or grandfather.

The typical active aggressor in an incestuous relationship is an older male, while the passive victim tends to be a young female. An estimated

90 to 97 percent of all incest cases involve a male perpetrator, while females constitute 85 percent of incest victims.[41] Approximately 78 percent of all reported incest today is that of father-daughter, 8 percent sibling-sibling, 1 percent mother-son, and the balance involving multiple incestuous family members.[42]

While natural fathers constitute the majority of offenders in intrafamilial father-daughter child sexual abuse, a high proportion of such cases involve stepfather-stepdaughter.[43] Many incestuous men also sexually molest other children aside from their own.[44] Incestuous males have been identified by researchers as *passive-dependent* and *aggressive-dominant*[45] and subcategorized as *sexually preoccupied, adolescent regressives, instrumental self-gratifiers, emotionally dependent*, and *angry retaliators.*[46]

The ratio of female to male victims of incest has been estimated to be ten to one.[47] Female incest victims are usually the oldest or only daughter, often entering adolescence, and ranging in age from five to sixteen years old, with a median age of 8.5.[48] The clear association between incest victimization, running away, and prostitution can be seen in the following tragic account of a female teenage prostitute with AIDS:

> A victim of childhood incest, Wendy ran away at age fifteen. Miami police have arrested her seventeen times for prostitution [and] now is a known AIDS carrier. . . . The authorities cannot hold her longer than the maximum amount of time for prostituting, so as soon as her time is up, Wendy once again returns to hustling. . . . Wendy averages five johns a day. "Ten," she says, "if things are hopping."[49]

EXTRAFAMILIAL CHILD SEXUAL ABUSE

Another prevalent type of child sexual abuse related to teenage prostitution is extrafamilial sexual abuse, or that which is perpetrated by someone outside the child's family. Generally known as child molestation or pedophilia, this usually refers to sexual desires and misconduct by an adult towards a child. Child molestation typically consists of "nonviolent sexual contact with a child including genital viewing or fondling, orogenital contact, penetration, and any other immoral or indecent behavior involving sexual activity between an adult and child."[50] In an eighteen-month investigation of child molestation cases, it was revealed that:

- Child molestation is more prevalent than other types of child abuse.
- Female victims outnumber male victims by ten to one.
- A sexual molestation victim's median age is eleven.
- Child molesters are male in 97 percent of reported cases.

- In 75 percent of child molestation cases, the pedophile is known to the victim.[51]

Other types of extrafamilial child sexual abuse experienced by many teen prostitutes include exhibitionism, voyeurism, bestiality, and ritualistic abuse. Studies show that a high percentage of prostituted girls and boys were victims of these kinds of offenses prior to and after entering the sex trade.[52]

A number of organizations exist that promote sexual relations between children and adults through incest, pedophilia, prostitution, and pornography. The North American Man-Boy Love Association, for example, promotes men engaging in sexual activity with young boys.[53] The same is true for the Childhood Sensuality Circle, which boasts upwards of 10,000 members.[54] Other pro-incest and pedophilia organizations include the Pedophile Alert Network (PAN) and the Pedophile Information Exchange (PIE). The inability to adequately track these groups or legally dissolve them contributes to the sexual abuse and exploitation of children throughout the country and its effects thereof, including juvenile prostitution.

THE EFFECTS OF CHILD SEXUAL ABUSE

Children who are sexually abused face a number of short- and long-term effects that can be detrimental to their physical and emotional well-being and result in such aberrant behaviors as promiscuity, running away, and a prostitution involved lifestyle. According to an expert on the ramifications of child sexual abuse:

> Clinical reports and empirical studies have consistently found that sexual abuse, as well as other forms of maltreatment, may affect children in all areas of development. Victims of sexual abuse, in particular, may be at higher risk for mental health and social functioning problems arising from the powerlessness and stigmatization of the abuse process. The interpersonal problems and coping patterns of young women with a history of sexual abuse are reportedly conditioned by long-term negative effects on sexual self-esteem, self-concept, and sexual adjustment.[55]

Child sexual abuse can interfere with the normal, healthy developing of a child, leading to an inability to "cope emotionally, intellectually, and/or physically with sexual stimulation and responsiveness, regardless of whether the child finds the experience emotionally satisfying, erotically pleasurable, or negative in some fashion."[56]

Researchers have found similarities in the social maturation and psychological effects of incest victims and those sexually exploited by pornography.[57] Most such victims experience feelings of guilt, worthlessness, withdrawal, depression, anxiety, rage and betrayal—all of which can lead to patterns of self-destructive behavior such as prostitution and drug abuse. One study found that the emotional stress and psychological scarring of child sexual abuse often causes the victim to abuse alcohol and drugs as a way to relieve the pain of memories, as well as become numb to the current sexual victimization.[58]

Physical effects of child sexual abuse can be equally devastating, including "lacerations to the genitals, sexually transmitted diseases, pregnancy, internal injuries, broken bones, and even death."[59] Child sexual abuse victims who run from their abusers and into the world of prostitution place themselves at further risk for exposure to the AIDS virus, malnutrition, sleep deprivation, eating disorders, and numerous other physical hazards consistent with the prostitution lifestyle.

Social problems also tend to develop with child sexual abuse victims, including truancy, poor grades, conflicts within the family, irritability around others, and fighting. These often lead to other issues such as substance abuse, sexual problems, running away, prostitution, child pornography, and delinquency.[60]

The type of treatment for child victims of sexual abuse often depends on where they are "situated along the victim continuum in conjunction with such factors as the degree of physical force or violence used by the offender and the intensity of the victim-offender relationship prior to the sex offense."[61]

SUMMARY

Child sexual abuse is a significant correlate of teenage prostitution. Every year many children are being subjected to sexual abuse of different forms. Researchers have found that every type of sexual abuse can affect a child. This can often lead to running away from an abusive environment and turning to a prostitution lifestyle. The vast majority of runaway prostitutes have been victims of child sexual abuse. Intrafamilial child sexual abuse is most commonly associated with teen prostitution. Usually the father or an adult male figure is the aggressor and a young female the victim. But boys are also often child sex abuse victims. Extrafamilial child sexual abuse is also a common occurrence that can lead to or perpetrate teenage prostitution. Child molestation and pedophilia are usually committed by nonfamily members of a victim. Many incest offenders also tend to sexually abuse other children outside the family.

The effects of sexual abuse on the child can be short-and long-term, and include psychological and physical problems. Child sexual abuse affects the victimized child's ability to develop normally, causing many to react through deviant behavior such as running away, promiscuity, prostitution, and involvement in child pornography and substance abuse.

NOTES

1. Public Law 100–294.

2. *Child Abuse and Neglect Reporting and Investigation: Policy Guidelines for Decision-Making* (Washington, D.C.: American Bar Association, 1987), p. 7.

3. Ibid.

4. R. Barri Flowers, *The Victimization and Exploitation of Women and Children: A Study of Physical, Mental and Sexual Maltreatment in the United States* (Jefferson, N.C.: McFarland, 1994), p. 55.

5. Ibid., p. 53.

6. Ibid.

7. Karen McCurdy and Deborah Daro, *Current Trends in Child Abuse Reporting and Fatalities: The Results of the 1992 Annual Fifty State Survey* (Chicago: National Committee for Prevention of Child Abuse, 1993), p. 10.

8. U.S. Department of Health and Human Services, *National Child Abuse and Neglect Data System: Working Paper 2—1991 Summary Data Component* (Washington, D.C.: National Center on Child Abuse and Neglect, 1993), p. 29.

9. Cited in Ann W. Burgess and Christine A. Grant, *Children Traumatized in Sex Rings* (Alexandria, Va.: National Center for Missing & Exploited Children, 1988), p. 2.

10. David Finkelhor, "How Widespread Is Child Sexual Abuse?" in *Perspectives on Child Maltreatment in the Mid '80s* (Washington, D.C.: National Center on Child Abuse and Neglect, 1984).

11. R. Barri Flowers, *Domestic Crimes, Family Violence and Child Abuse: A Study of Contemporary American Society* (Jefferson, N.C.: McFarland, 2000), p. 131.

12. Cited in Carol L. Mithers, "Incest: The Crime That's All in the Family," *Mademoiselle* 96 (June 1984): 18.

13. Heidi Vanderbilt, "Incest: A Chilling Report," *Lear's* (February 1992): 52.

14. Cited in Kathy McCoy, "Incest: The Most Painful Family Problem," *Seventeen* 43 (June 1984): 18.

15. E. P. Sarafino, "An Estimate of the Nationwide Incidence of Sexual Offenses against Children," *Child Welfare* 58, 2 (1979): 127–34.

16. Flowers, *The Victimization and Exploitation of Women and Children*, pp. 71–80, 90–93.

17. Diana Russell, *Intra-family Child Sexual Abuse: Final Report to the National Center on Child Abuse and Neglect* (Washington, D.C.: U.S. Department of Health and Human Services, 1983); L. Berliner and J. R. Wheeler, "Treating the Effects of Sexual Abuse on Children," *Journal of Interpersonal Violence* 2 (1987): 415–24.

18. Flowers, *The Victimization and Exploitation of Women and Children*, p. 56.

19. *American Association for Protecting Children, Highlights of Official Child Neglect and Abuse Reporting 1984* (Denver: American Humane Association, 1985).

20. Cited in Pamela D. Mayhall and Katherine E. Norgard, *Child Abuse and Neglect: Sharing Responsibility* (Toronto: John Wiley & Sons, 1983), p. 100.

21. Peggy Smith and Marvin Bohnstedt, *Child Victimization Study Highlights* (Sacramento, Calif.: Social Research Center of the American Justice Institute, 1981), p. 2.

22. See, for example, Flowers, *Domestic Crimes, Family Violence and Child Abuse*, p. 127; Diana E. Russell, *Intrafamilial Child Sexual Abuse: A San Francisco Survey* (Berkeley, Calif.: Wright Institute, 1983).

23. U.S. Department of Health and Human Services, *Research Symposium on Child Sexual Abuse* (Washington, D.C.: National Center on Child Abuse and Neglect, 1988), pp. 3–4.

24. Ibid., p. 4; B. G. Braun, "The Transgenerational Incidence of Dissociation and Multiple Personality Disorder: A Preliminary Report," in R. P. Kluft, ed., *Childhood Antecedents of Multiple Personality* (Washington, D.C.: American Psychiatric Press, 1985).

25. See, for example, R. Barri Flowers, *The Prostitution of Women and Girls* (Jefferson, N.C.: McFarland, 1998), pp. 82–83; Joseph J. Peters, "Children Who Are Victims of Sexual Assault and the Psychology of Offenders," *American Journal of Psychotherapy* 30 (1976): 398–421.

26. Flowers, *The Victimization and Exploitation of Women and Children*, pp. 39, 43–45; Magnus J. Seng, "Child Sexual Abuse and Adolescent Prostitution: A Comparative Analysis," *Adolescence* 24 (1989): 673; Ronald Simons and Les B. Whitbeck, "Sexual Abuse as a Precursor to Prostitution and Victimization among Adolescent and Adult Homeless Women," *Journal of Family Issues* 12 (1991): 375.

27. Cathy S. Widom and Joseph B. Kuhns, "Childhood Victimization and Subsequent Risk for Promiscuity, Prostitution and Teenage Pregnancy: A Prospective Study," *American Journal of Public Health* 86 (1996): 1607–10.

28. Cited in Patricia Hersch, "Coming of Age on City Streets," *Psychology Today* (January 1988): 31.

29. Cited in Stephanie Abarbanel, "Women Who Make a Difference," *Family Circle* 107 (January 11, 1994): 11.

30. Flowers, *The Victimization and Exploitation of Women and Children*, pp. 81–84.

31. Sparky Harlan, Luanne L. Rodgers, and Brian Slattery, *Male and Female Adolescent Prostitution: Huckleberry House Sexual Minority Youth Services Project* (Washington, D.C.: U.S. Department of Health and Human Services, 1981), p. 21.

32. Mimi H. Silbert, "Delancey Street Study: Prostitution and Sexual Assault," summary of results, Delancey Street Foundation, San Francisco, 1982, p. 3.

33. Quoted in Sheron Boyle, *Working Girls and Their Men* (London: Smith Gryphon, 1994), p. 121.

34. Cited in Flowers, *The Victimization and Exploitation of Women and Children*, p. 86.

35. Flowers, *The Prostitution of Women and Girls*, p. 138.

36. N. Coombs, "Male Prostitution: A Psychosocial View of Behavior," *American Journal of Orthopsychiatry* 44 (1974): 782–89.

37. C. Earls and H. David, "A Psychosocial Study of Male Prostitution," *Archives of Sexual Behavior* 18 (1989): 401–19.

38. Joan J. Johnson, *Teen Prostitution* (Danbury, Conn.: Franklin Watts, 1992), p. 88.

39. Ibid., pp. 88–89.

40. Patricia B. Mrazek, "Definition and Recognition of Child Sexual Abuse: Historical and Cultural Perspectives," in Patricia B. Mrazek and C. Henry Kempe, eds., *Sexually Abused Children and Their Families* (New York: Pergamon Press, 1981), p. 7.

41. R. Barri Flowers, *Women and Criminality: The Woman as Victim, Offender, and Practitioner* (Westport, Conn.: Greenwood Press, 1987), p. 61.

42. S. Kirson Weinberg, *Incest Behavior* (New York: Citadel Press, 1966), pp. 34–40.

43. Herbert L. Packer, *The Limits of the Criminal Sanction* (Stanford, Calif.: Stanford University Press, 1968), pp. 296–316.

44. G. G. Abel, Z. V. Becker, J. Cunningham, M. Mittleman, and J. Rouleau, "Multiple Paraphilic Diagnoses among Sex Offenders," *Bulletin of the American Academy of Psychiatry and the Law* 16, 2 (1988): 153–68.

45. Robert E. Freeman-Longo and Geral T. Blanchard, *Sexual Abuse in America: Epidemic of the 21st Century* (Brandon, Vt.: Safer Society Press, 1998), pp. 42–43.

46. Flowers, *The Victimization and Exploitation of Women and Children*, pp. 63–64.

47. H. Stoenner, *Child Sexual Abuse Seen Growing in the United States* (Denver: American Humane Association, 1972).

48. Flowers, *The Victimization and Exploitation of Women and Children*, p. 63.

49. Johnson, *Teen Prostitution*, pp. 126–27.

50. Flowers, *Domestic Crimes, Family Violence, and Child Abuse*, p. 138.

51. Susan Brownmiller, *Against Our Will: Men, Women and Rape* (New York: Simon & Schuster, 1975), pp. 278–79.

52. Flowers, *The Victimization and Exploitation of Women and Children*, pp. 71–80; Robert H. Morneau and Robert R. Rockwell, *Sex, Motivation and the Criminal Offender* (Springfield, Ill.: Charles C. Thomas, 1980), pp. 73, 87–89.

53. R. Barri Flowers, *Children and Criminality: The Child as Victim and Perpetrator* (Westport, Conn.: Greenwood Press, 1986), p. 77.

54. Ibid.; Freeman-Longo and Blanchard, *Sexual Abuse in America*, pp. 71–73.

55. Quoted in Freeman-Longo and Blanchard, *Sexual Abuse in America*, pp. 134–35.

56. Flowers, *Children and Criminality*, p. 96.

57. Flowers, *The Victimization and Exploitation of Women and Children*, p. 59.

58. Flowers, *Children and Criminality*, p. 97.

59. Flowers, *The Victimization and Exploitation of Women and Children*, p. 59.

60. Burgess and Grant, *Children Traumatized in Sex Rings*, pp. 2–4; M. D. Janus, A. McCormack, A. W. Burgess, and C. R. Hartman, *Adolescent Runaways* (Lexington, Mass.: Lexington Books, 1987).

61. Flowers, *Children and Criminality*, p. 75.

Chapter 14

Child Pornography

Child pornography is another branch of the sexual exploitation of children closely connected with teenage prostitution. In many instances, prostituted youth are simultaneously used by pornographers in the sex trade industry to produce smut in many forms. The lucrative nature of child pornography has made it a global enterprise, though much of its consumption is in the United States. The tremendous reach of the Internet has given participants in the child pornography industry a powerful means to exploit children internationally. This has caused further concern to those who seek to end the sexual misuse and exploitation of children through pornography and prostitution.

DEFINING CHILD PORNOGRAPHY

One expert on child sexual exploitation described child pornography as "the most inhuman of crimes. For pleasure or profit, pornographers have murdered the childhood of a million girls and boys, victims who must live with the dreadful memories of their experience."[1] Child pornography is typically defined as "photographs, videos, books, magazines, and motion pictures that depict children in sexually explicit acts with other children, adults, animals, and/or foreign objects."[2] The federal legal definition of child pornography is "sexually explicit visual depictions of minors;" whereas a minor is "defined as someone who has not yet reached his or her eighteenth birthday."[3] Definitions of child pornography today invariably must include any such images or sounds seen, sent, or heard on the Internet and its endless worldwide web and chat rooms. Furthermore, many juvenile victims of child pornography and child prostitution become young adult participants, thereby continuing the correlation and exploitation into their late teens and beyond.

Often referred to as "kiddie porn," "chicken porn," and "child porn," the modern era of child pornography is generally thought to have begun in China during the mid-1400s with the publication of the sex manual, *The Admirable Discourses of the Plain Child*, which graphically described sexual intercourse and other sexual acts involving children.[4] Today victims of child pornography are exposed to every form of child sexual exploitation, including molestation, rape, sadism, prostitution, bestiality, triolism, exhibitionism, voyeurism, and even murder. Though child pornography is illegal in the United States, there "is a tremendously persistent and widespread underground of child pornographers and an international market for their products."[5]

Many authorities on child sexual exploitation believe that the child porn industry is producing more and more violent, sadistic, and hard core pornography involving children. One magazine, for example, vividly shows adults in different sexual acts with toddlers, while an audio tape, "accompanied by graphic narrative description, records the screams of a young girl being raped."[6] Some pornographic films present children in various forms of torture. "At the end, the unwitting victim is brutally murdered. Although some of the murders are feigned, some officials believe that others are not—that some of the victims never survive their films."[7]

HOW BIG IS THE PROBLEM OF CHILD PORNOGRAPHY?

While no one can be certain just how far and deep the reach of child pornography goes in our society, the indication is that it may be far more severe than most conservative estimates. Child pornography is a thriving multibillion dollar business worldwide. It is estimated that in the United States alone, child porn takes in as much as six billion dollars each year.[8] Child pornography constitutes approximately 7 percent of the total pornography in this country.[9] Eighty-five percent of the worldwide sales of child pornography are made in the United States.[10] In Los Angeles, an estimated 30,000 children are exploited by child pornographers annually.[11]

Much of the kiddie porn magazines and films are imported from such countries as Sweden, Denmark, Germany, and Switzerland. A recent study found that at least 264 different magazines containing pictures and descriptions of children in sexual acts are produced and distributed in the United States every month.[12] Many of these are made quite cheaply. A magazine with sexually explicit depictions of children can be produced for as little as fifty cents and sold for twenty times as much.[13] The profit margin figures to be even greater for child porn when distributed across the Internet.

Despite tough anti-pornography statutes and increased crackdowns on purveyors and consumers, child pornography continues to leave its mark on society and its young victims. Recent examples give rise to the enormity of the problem:

- A woman was suspected of making half a million dollars annually by supplying 80 percent of the child porn market.
- Police in Houston raided a child pornography filled warehouse containing 15,000 color slides, over 1,000 magazines and paperbacks, and more than 1,000 reels of film of children engaged in sexually explicit acts.
- Confiscated from the home of a man arrested for having child pornography was a scrapbook containing articles about the rapes and murders of children.[14]
- A U.S. Postal Service sting operation, "Special Delivery," led to the arrest of a number of respected community members as both distributors and consumers of child porn. They confiscated videos and photographs containing crying, tortured, physically and sexually abused children.[15]
- Another U.S. Postal Service raid, dubbed "Project Looking Glass," used the names and addresses of consumers of child pornography discovered on mailing lists belonging to convicted child pornographers to arrest buyers and confiscate their collections of kiddie porn.[16]

Child pornographers have little trouble finding a steady supply of young participants among runaways, teen prostitutes, and homeless street youth. The children are usually lured into the business with money, drugs, shelter, clothes, trips, and false friendship. Sometimes the pornographers are parents who target their own children. In one such example a nine-year-old girl—already being prostituted by her mother and father—was then introduced into pornography.[17]

Child porn victims are often forced into performing pornographic acts as kidnapped sex slaves. Many are lured into the business under false promises of money, jobs, or other payment. Some victims from overseas become indentured servants to pornographers and pimps as a means to pay off costs associated with smuggling them into the country.[18]

The tragedy of child pornography on its often helpless, tortured victims was described by a member of a sting operation after viewing photographs of a five-year-old boy seized from a collector of kiddie porn:

> He had the blankest expression. It's like he's a dead person that's alive. . . . Many of these children have expressions on their faces of blank silence. They almost look drugged. They're so conditioned that they're robots to this. It's frightening.[19]

WHO ARE THE CONSUMERS OF CHILD PORNOGRAPHY?

The people who support the child pornography industry come from every background and across the social strata. The majority of child porn consumers are male. A high percentage are pedophiles and child molesters.[20] Many are not sex offenders, per se, yet still find satisfaction in viewing pornography depicting children. Some consumers of child porn have been described as "psychopathic or psychologically immature."[21] Others are sexual deviants or were themselves victims of child sexual exploitation. Many are both suppliers and consumers of child porn, and sometimes adult pornography as well.

The FBI's pedophile profile characterizes the typical person who collects child pornography as "intelligent enough to recognize they have a problem," yet somehow justifying that "what they're doing is right."[22] An FBI agent described the mindset of the typical pedophile user of smut: "Pedophilia is a way of life. They believe there's nothing wrong with it, so naturally they're looking for other individuals who support their thinking."[23]

Promoting sexual relations between adults and children through pornography, prostitution, and child molestation are such groups as the North American Man-Boy Love Association, the Pedophile Information Exchange, and the Childhood Sensuality Circle (see Chapter 13). Law enforcement authorities are often powerless to shut down such organizations "without an allegation or a reason to conduct" an investigation.[24]

RUNNING AWAY, TEEN PROSTITUTION, AND CHILD PORNOGRAPHY

The relationship between runaways, prostituted youth, and child pornography is significant. Most authorities on child sexual exploitation believe that the three often go hand in hand. Notes teen prostitution writer Clare Tattersall: "You do not have to be a runaway to be forced into pornography. But because runaways are more likely to become prostitutes, they are also more likely to be forced into pornography."[25] One survey found that around one-third of teenage prostitutes admitted they also participated in pornography.[26]

Similar dynamics exist for teen prostitution and child pornography. Many of the victims are runaways, throwaways, and street kids—and most have been sexually abused. Substance abuse is often a correlate of prostitution and pornography involved youth,[27] as are multiple means of sexual exploitation and child victimization including rape, sexual slavery, and physical assaults, and exposure to sexually and intravenous transmitted diseases.

Girls and boys living on the streets, often as runaways and prostitutes, are frequently targeted by pornographers to be in pornographic films, photographs and magazines. Few desperate and hungry youth can resist the lure of seemingly "easy" money, shelter, drugs, or other temptations that child pornography offers. For many teen prostitutes, pornography serves as a side occupation to supplement their prostitution income. Others are initially sexually exploited through child pornography and become prostitution involved as a consequence.

Many teens engaged in prostitution are manipulated into pornography by pimps as a measure of control. For instance, the pimp may take nude photographs of a girl in his stable, threatening to expose her to family, friends, or even the authorities—thereby breaking any resistance she may have to his authority while at the same time normalizing the participation in prostitution and pornography.[28]

Pimps sometimes use pornographic images of girls to advertise their prostitutes and their bodies to prospective clients. Johns may also photograph young prostitutes for their own collection of porn and personal pleasure. Some men "use pornography to describe the sexual act they want and to rationalize their behavior and their demands of the child."[29]

Child Sex Rings

Child sex rings represent a subcategory of the relationship between child pornography and adolescent prostitution. They typically consist of one or more offenders, usually men, who are involved with multiple children "in sexual abuse with or without commercial gain or exchange of money."[30] Child sex rings often recruit their victims from a pool of runaways, young prostitutes, and other homeless or troubled youth. Most child sex rings create and use pornography in their sexual exploitation of children.

According to child pornography authority Ann Burgess, there are three primary types of child sex rings: (1) solo, (2) transition, and (3) syndicated.[31] In solo child sex rings, the perpetrator often keeps his involvement with children and collection of photographs a secret. Each such ring involves a single perpetrator and multiple child victims. Transition child sex rings involve perpetrators who share their victims, pictures, videos and experience with other child molesters—often through child or child porn swapping. Syndicated child sex rings are the most structured and organized. These sex rings recruit children, produce child pornography, and prostitute their victims through an extensive client base.

A child sex ring, also referred to as a historical child sex ring, most often consists of true pedophiles or preferential child molesters who "have a definite sexual preference for children. Their sexual fantasies and erotic imagery focus on children."[32] The primary characteristics of the preferential child molester are the access to children, multiple victims, and the collecting of child pornography. According to Supervisory Agent Kenneth Lanning of the FBI:

> The preferential child molester who is operating a sex ring is very likely to have sexually explicit and nonsexually explicit visual depictions of the victims. . . . [His] motivations for collecting the material are that it fuels his sexual fantasies, validates his behavior, and is a souvenir of his relationship with the child.[33]

Up to two-thirds of children involved in historical child sex rings are male, typically between ten and sixteen years of age. Whether the victim is a boy or girl, child sex ring offenders tend to lure and control their victims through seduction techniques, bonding, money, gifts, manipulation, and force.

Multidimensional child sex rings also exist.[34] They possess similar characteristics to historical child sex rings and tend to involve multiple victims and offenders, use of fear to control victims, and ritualistic child sexual abuse. Nearly half of the offenders in multidimensional child sex rings are believed to be women, with girls and boys targeted. Most such child sex rings produce and use pornography, as well as exploit their victims through other sexual maltreatment.

THE EFFECTS OF CHILD PORNOGRAPHY

Children who are sexually exploited through involvement in pornography face short-and long-term effects of their victimization. Because many of these children are also prostituted youth and runaways, they experience the same types of effects such as anxiety, withdrawal, hopelessness, low self-esteem, and suicidal behavior. They also experience various physical ordeals such as pregnancy, sexually transmitted diseases, sexual assaults, substance abuse, battering, and death. The psychological devastation of child pornography can be seen in the following victimization:

> Margie, a shy nine year old, was lured into a porn-photo session by a Little League coach who used provocative photographs of Brooke Shields as a child to entice her. Although the coach has been convicted, not all the photos of Margie were found. Presently, she refused to go to her school's open house because she dreamt that her teacher had the missing photographs displayed for everyone to see.[35]

An expert on child sexual exploitation put the harmful effects of child porn into further perspective: "It's not just a physical nakedness; it's an emotional stripping as well. . . . When you see [children] grow up in the photographs, [their] chances for normal development are minimal."[36]

The loss of innocence may be the most damaging aspect of child pornography for the victim. Like teen prostitution, this is something that cannot be adequately measured or put into its proper context.

SUMMARY

Child pornography is a thriving business in the United States and closely associated with runaway youth and the prostitution of girls and boys. Child porn involves the sexual exploitation by adults of children through sexually explicit videos, photographs, magazines, and other avenues including the Internet. Substance abuse is a central component of child porn and teenage pornography. Pimps and pornographers will use every means at their disposal to tempt, charm, blackmail, or force curious or desperate youth into participating in pornography, prostitution, or both.

Consumers of child pornography are typically male pedophiles and child molesters who are particularly fixated on children sexually. Child sex rings exist as an avenue for true pedophiles to collect child porn, trade with other child molesters, and to engage in child prostitution and other sexual services. The three primary types of historical child sex rings are solo, transition, and syndicated. Multidimensional child sex rings often involve multiple victims and offenders, fear tactics, and ritualistic sexual abuse.

The effects of child pornography on the victim include a number of short- and long-term effects similar to prostituted youth including medical and physical trauma, sexual diseases, addiction, and the loss of innocence.

NOTES

1. Rita Rooney, "Children for Sale: Pornography's Dark New World," *Reader's Digest* (July 1983): 53.
2. R. Barri Flowers, *The Victimization and Exploitation of Women and Children: A Study of Physical, Mental and Sexual Maltreatment in the United States* (Jefferson, N.C.: McFarland, 1994), p. 91.
3. U.S. Department of Justice, *Child Sex Rings: A Behavioral Analysis, for Criminal Justice Professionals Handling Cases of Child Sexual Exploitation* (Alexandria, Va.: National Center for Missing & Exploited Children, 1992), p. 7.
4. Cited in Reay Tannahill, *Sex in History* (New York: Stein and Day, 1980), p. 320.
5. Robert E. Freeman-Longo and Geral T. Blanchard, *Sexual Abuse in America: Epidemic of the 21st Century* (Brandon, Vt.: Safer Society Press, 1998), p. 98.
6. Flowers, *The Victimization and Exploitation of Women and Children*, p. 90.
7. Joan J. Johnson, *Teen Prostitution* (Danbury, Conn.: Franklin Watts, 1992), p. 91.
8. R. Barri Flowers, *The Prostitution of Women and Girls* (Jefferson, N.C.: McFarland, 1998), p. 122.
9. Shirley O'Brien, *Child Pornography* (Dubuque, Iowa: Kendall/Hunt, 1983), p. 19; M. Guio, A. Burgess, and R. Kelly, "Child Victimization: Pornography and Prostitution," *Journal of Crime and Justice* 3 (1980): 65–81.
10. Cited in Johnson, *Teen Prostitution*, p. 90.
11. Cited in Flowers, *The Prostitution of Women and Girls*, p. 122.

12. Ibid.

13. R. Barri Flowers, *The Adolescent Criminal: An Examination of Today's Juvenile Offender* (Jefferson, N.C.: McFarland, 1990), p. 64.

14. Johnson, *Teen Prostitution*, p. 90; Flowers, *The Victimization and Exploitation of Women and Children*, p. 91.

15. Freeman-Longo and Blanchard, *Sexual Abuse in America*, p. 99.

16. Johnson, *Teen Prostitution*, p. 90.

17. Ibid., p. 91.

18. Flowers, *The Prostitution of Women and Girls*, pp. 122–23, 182–83.

19. Quoted in Johnson, *Teen Prostitution*, p. 90.

20. Flowers, *The Prostitution of Women and Girls*, p. 123; *Child Sex Rings: A Behavioral Analysis*, pp. 11–12.

21. Johnson, *Teen Prostitution*, p. 91.

22. "Child Pornography on the Rise Despite Tougher Laws," *Sacramento Union* (April 7, 1984), p. E6.

23. Ibid.

24. Ibid.

25. Clare Tattersall, *Drugs, Runaways, and Teen Prostitution* (New York: Rosen, 1999), p. 38.

26. Cited in Johnson, *Teen Prostitution*, p. 91.

27. Flowers, *The Prostitution of Women and Girls*, p. 123; Tattersall, *Drugs, Runaways, and Teen Prostitution*, p. 37.

28. U.S. Department of Justice, *Prostitution of Children and Child-Sex Tourism: An Analysis of Domestic and International Responses* (Alexandria: Va.: National Center for Missing & Exploited Children, 1999), p. 6.

29. Ibid. See also Cathy S. Widom and Joseph B. Kuhns, "Childhood Victimization and Subsequent Risk for Promiscuity, Prostitution and Teenage Pregnancy: A Prospective Study," *American Journal of Public Health* 86 (1996): 1611.

30. Ann W. Burgess and Christine A. Grant, *Children Traumatized in Sex Rings* (Alexandria, Va.: National Center for Missing & Exploited Children, 1988), p. 2.

31. Ibid., pp. 7–12.

32. U.S. Department of Justice, Office of Juvenile Justice and Delinquency Prevention, *Child Molesters: A Behavioral Analysis, for Law Enforcement Officers Investigating Cases of Child Sexual Exploitation* (Alexandria, Va.: National Center for Missing & Exploited Children, 1992), p. 8.

33. *Child Sex Rings: A Behavioral Analysis*, p. 12.

34. Ibid., pp. 17–21.

35. Rooney, "Children for Sale," pp. 54–55.

36. Quoted in Johnson, *Teen Prostitution*, p. 92.

Part IV

The Law and Combating Teenage Prostitution

Chapter 15

Laws and the Prostitution of Teenagers

Child prostitution is considered a crime everywhere in the United States, including laws against prostituted youth, patrons of juvenile prostitutes, pimps, pornographers, and even family members that are involved in the prostitution of minors. Overall, prostitution is prohibited in forty-nine of the fifty states. Only in a few counties in Nevada is adult prostitution allowed.

Most federal and state anti-prostitution laws prohibiting the prostitution of teenagers and preteens tend to focus mostly on those soliciting, procuring, pimping, or profiting from such, rather than the prostituted child—who is often viewed as a victim and not an offender. An example of this can be seen in recently enacted state criminal statutes that "fail to punish adolescent prostitutes either by omitting any mention of sanctions or specifically excluding adolescents involved in prostitution from any liability."[1] This trend is also reflected in civil legislation, "where in many states juvenile participation in prostitution is looked upon as a form of child abuse/sexual exploitation rather than delinquency."[2] In spite of the child prostitution laws on the books, they are not uniformly enforced or adequate for preventing teenage prostitution in this country or dissuading or punishing those who sexually exploit teens.

TEENAGE PROSTITUTION AND THE JUVENILE COURT

With the focus of teenage prostitution more on child sexual exploitation rather than criminality for the prostitution involved teen, most tend to be dealt with informally or within the jurisdiction of the juvenile or family court. According to the U.S. Department of Justice, there were 1,019 arrests of persons under the age of eighteen for prostitution and commercialized vice in 1998.[3] This figure does not include teenage prostitutes who were only detained or referred to the juvenile justice system. In a study examining the response of the criminal justice system to the sexual exploitation of children, while most law enforcement agencies arrested or detained teenagers on prostitution charges, only one in three agencies were concerned with arrest in traditional terms.[4] The majority favored intervention that was non-punitive in nature such as diversion, placement in juvenile detention, or the release of the juvenile to parents.

Although juvenile prostitution generally falls under the same statutes applicable to adult prostitution, sentencing for teen prostitutes is more likely to consist of a state agency commitment. Many habitual teenage prostitutes have extensive backgrounds that include involvement with the juvenile justice system, child welfare agencies, and treatment programs.[5] Law enforcement authorities tend to regard arrest of juvenile prostitutes as a last resort to assist a sexually exploited teen in breaking away from prostitution and controlling, violent pimps, and receiving the services needed.[6] Juvenile or family court jurisdiction is "often invoked to facilitate provision of such services" and get prostituted teens off the streets.[7]

STATE CHILD PROSTITUTION STATUTES

Along with laws that ban the prostitution of juveniles, most states have statutes that apply to adult patrons, pimps, procurers, and promoters of underage prostitutes. The laws vary from state to state but generally cover much of the sexual misuse, exploitation and prostitution of teenagers by others.

Patrons of Teenage Prostitute Laws

Most states have patron laws that prohibit soliciting another for prostitution irrespective of the prostitute's age. However, there are some state statutes that are aimed specifically at patronizing juvenile prostitutes. For example, in Colorado such a statute prohibits involvement in prostitution with a person under the age of eighteen,[8] whereas, three child patronizing statutes exist in New York, varying according to the age of the child.[9] Most state statutes apply to prostituted children under the age of eighteen.[10] In seven states, the applicable age for a child prostitute in patronizing laws is under the age of seventeen,[11] whereas in fourteen states, only juveniles under age sixteen are protected.[12] Some experts in teenage prostitution believe that the age of applicability in protection should be twenty-one, given that even prostitutes age eighteen and older "lack the maturity to extricate themselves from street life" and are significantly challenged in attaining alternative means of employment.[13]

Pimping and Teen Prostitution Laws

There are only four states with statutes that specifically apply to the pimping of prostituted minors: Colorado, California, West Virginia, and Illinois.[14] Colorado's statute outlaws pimping by anyone who knowingly is supported by money earned or received by a person under the age of eighteen.[15] The Illinois statute is applicable to pimps who knowingly prostitute for profit persons under the age of sixteen.[16] Other states address pimping in other prostitution laws.

Pandering and Teen Prostitution Laws

Pandering statutes can include not only pimping but also other prostitution-related charges, including causing an underage person to enter into prostitution. In Iowa, for example, a pandering law applies to anyone who persuades or coerces a juvenile to enter or return to prostitution, or has a place for the express purpose of teenage prostitution, or receives earnings from such a place.[17]

In order for a person to be convicted on pandering charges, they need not receive money or something else of value for the prostituted child's services. In *State v. Steer*,[18] the court ruled that such a provision was limited to the prostituted child and not the one responsible for the child's prostitution. In *People v. Bell*,[19] a broad scope of pandering laws was similarly applied.

Procuring, Inducing, Compelling, Promoting, and Other Teen Prostitution–Related Laws

Various laws exist for offenses related to the prostituting of juveniles for profit or other commercial sexual exploitation. These include laws against procuring, inducing, compelling a child to become a prostitute[20] and the promotion, management, maintenance or earning income through a prostitution business or enterprise.[21] In Oregon, for example, compelling a person under the age of eighteen to participate in prostitution activities is prohibited, even if the juvenile consents to the involvement.[22] Here the child is seen as a victim in need of protection from the destructive effects of a prostituted life.

Statutes regarding promoting prostitution are most commonly used in association with teenage prostitution. These statutes can be both specific in their coverage, such as enticement or compelling, or cover a wide range of charges.[23] Prohibitions that exist under promoting child prostitution laws can include:

- Ownership or management of a place of prostitution.
- Inducing a child to enter into prostitution.
- Procuring a prostitute for a place of prostitution.
- Solicitation of a patron for an underage prostitute.
- Solicitation of a minor to engage in acts of prostitution with a patron.
- Procuring transportation for a juvenile in order to promote the minor's participation in prostitution.

Solicitation of patrons for a teenage prostitute is the most commonly used statutory means of addressing solicitation concerning a minor. Such laws tend to be applied under pimping, promoting, and solicitation of another for purposes of prostitution of a child statutes.[24]

Criminally Liable Parents of Teen Prostitutes Statutes

A few states have prostitution statutes that make the parents of juvenile prostitutes criminally liable for allowing their children to prostitute themselves or not doing enough to prevent such.[25] For example, in Louisiana, parents' criminal liability can apply if they knowingly consent to their child's entrance into prostitution.[26] A similar statute exists in Montana.[27] In other states, parents of prostitution involved youth may be criminally liable through other prostitution laws.

FEDERAL CHILD PROSTITUTION STATUTES

A number of federal statutes also apply to the prostitution and sexual exploitation of children. These require that the violations take place under federal jurisdiction, including interstate or foreign commerce, and offenses occurring in any U.S. territory or possession.

The Mann Act

The issue of child sexual exploitation and juvenile prostitution was first addressed by federal law through the White Slave Traffic Act, now called the Mann Act, enacted in 1910.[28] Its purpose was to combat white slavery, or forced prostitution, and the sale of women and girls into prostitution. The Mann Act made transporting a female across state lines for purposes of prostitution a federal crime. Also included in the statute was persuading, inducing, or coercing a woman or girl into making such a journey while using a "common carrier" or the transportation of a female under the age of eighteen for prostitution or "any immoral practice."

The Mann Act was revised by Congress in 1986 to make it gender neutral and to change "immoral practice" to "any sexual activity" in which any individual can be charged with a crime.[29] The revisions further made it no longer a requirement that transporting a juvenile across state lines need be with a commercial motive. According to Section 2423, with respect to the prostitution of minors, the Act prohibits "transportation with intent to engage in criminal sexual activity [and] travel with intent to engage in sexual acts with [a] juvenile."[30]

Protection of Children from Sexual Predators Act

The Protection of Children from Sexual Predators Act of 1998 further clarified the wording of the Act, included attempt provisions, while increasing penalties for violators.[31] It further added Section 2425 to Title 18 of the U.S. Code, prohibiting use of interstate or foreign commerce for transmitting information about a minor for purposes of enticing, encouraging, or soliciting anyone to participate in criminal sexual conduct.[32] The Act also allows for stiffer sentences to be imposed by the court through enhancements such as for obstruction, coercion, and misrepresentation knowingly.[33]

Racketeer Influenced and Corrupt Organizations Act

Also addressing prostitution and the commercial sexual exploitation of children is the Racketeer Influenced and Corrupt Organizations Act (RICO).[34] It makes it a federal crime to participate in an "enterprise" affecting interstate commerce and constituting an established "pattern" of "racketeering activity." Offenses applicable to the Mann Act are included among crimes defined under such activity. The RICO statute enables prosecutors to file charges against individuals who are only indirectly in control of or participating in an interstate prostitution ring, while allowing victims to seek restitution through civil court action.[35]

Other Federal Laws and Child Prostitution

Sexual exploiters and abusers of children can also be charged with prostitution-related crimes under other federal statutes when the crime is within federal jurisdiction. For instance, federal law on aggravated sexual abuse can be applied to pimps and patrons, particularly when there is violence perpetrated upon the child prostitute. In *United States v. Fulton,*[36] the court held that the statute's requirement that actual force was used on the victim can be fulfilled by the use of such force as necessary to subdue or injure a child. Further, the rape shield law can be applied in prohibiting a defendant from bringing into evidence a prostituted child's sexual history, such as with johns, prior to the occurrence of the alleged rape.[37] In such statutes as *United States v. Yazzie*[38] and *United States v. Ransom*,[39] a mistake-of-age defense in the sexual abuse of a juvenile has been restricted by the courts.

FEDERAL PORNOGRAPHY STATUTES

A number of federal laws address child pornography and the sexual exploitation of children in relating pornography to teenage prostitution. For example, in Sections 2251 and 2252 of Title 18 of the U.S. Code, prohibitions include pimps and procurers photographing underage prostitutes, transportation or shipping in interstate or foreign commerce (this includes by mail or on computer) or receiving or distributing materials that visually depict minors in sexually explicit poses.[40] The statutes do not require proving that a defendant planned to distribute the child pornographic materials.[41]

Prohibitions of Section 2252 were increased in the Child Protection, Restoration and Penalties Enhancement Act of 1990,[42] while a jurisdictional foundation for prosecuting was added with the Protection of Children from Sexual Predators Act of 1998, provided the visual images were produced with materials transported by interstate or foreign commerce, including by mail or computer.[43]

The Child Pornography Prevention Act of 1996 (CPPA) is another federal statute that addresses child sexual exploitation. The CPPA amends Section 2256 in defining circumstances for which visual images are or appear to be minors participating in sexually explicit acts,[44] including through computer imagery. In *United States v. Hilton*[45] and *The Free Speech Coalition v. Reno,*[46] the constitutionality of the Act was upheld. Other federal legislation has also sought to protect children from pornographers, prostitution, and other sexual exploitation.[47]

THE LAW AND TEEN PROSTITUTION ABROAD

In addressing the prostitution and sexual exploitation of minors abroad by pimps, procurers, and patrons, Congress established new protections for foreign minors from prostitution involved sexual misuse in Section 2423 of Title 18 of the U.S. Code. As part of the Mann Act amendments in 1994, the statute made it illegal for a U.S. citizen or permanent resident alien to travel in foreign commerce or conspire to, for purposes of engaging in sexual acts with anyone under the age of eighteen.[48] The law makes it easier to prosecute Americans who sexually exploit prostituted youth in other countries. It is unclear how applicable the statute is to patrons and other sexual exploiters who enter into child sex tourism opportunities to have sexual relations with children, but had not planned to do so prior to entering foreign commerce. Other provisions of Section 2423 cover prohibitions against pimping, procuring, patronizing, and solicitation of teenage prostitutes.[49]

SUMMARY

A number of state and federal statutes are aimed at combating teen prostitution and other sexual exploitation of children, including child pornography. Although teenage prostitutes are in violation of laws prohibiting prostitution, they are generally seen more as victims of sexual exploitation, and attempts are made to divert them to the juvenile justice system, child welfare agencies, treatment programs, or release to parents.

Most state and federal prostitution-related statutes focus on those who sexually exploit minors such as pimps, patrons, procurers, panderers, promoters, pornographers, and others who participate in or profit from the prostitution of children. Prohibitions include transporting minors across state lines or foreign commerce for purposes of prostitution, photographing prostitution involved teens, use of computers or mail for child pornography, and traveling abroad to engage in sexual acts with a minor.

NOTES

1. R. Barri Flowers, *Children and Criminality: The Child as Victim and Perpetrator* (Westport, Conn.: Greenwood Press, 1986), p. 192.
2. Ibid., pp. 192–93; D. Kelly Weisberg, *Children of the Night: A Study of Adolescent Prostitution* (Lexington, Mass.: Lexington Books, 1985), pp. 205–6.
3. U.S. Department of Justice, Federal Bureau of Investigation, *Crime in the United States: Uniform Crime Reports 1998* (Washington, D.C.: Government Printing Office, 1999), p. 220.
4. Cited in U.S. Department of Justice, Office of Juvenile Justice and Delinquency Prevention, *Prostitution of Children and Child-Sex Tourism: An Analysis of Domestic and International Responses* (Alexandria, Va.: National Center for Missing & Exploited Children, 1999), p. 10.
5. Ibid.
6. Ibid.
7. Ibid.
8. Colo. Rev. Stat. Ann. §18–7–406.
9. N.Y. Penal Code §§230.04, 230.05, 230.06.
10. See, for example, Ala. Code §§13A–12–111, 13A–12–112; Or. Rev. Stat. §167.017; Wyo. Stat. §6–4–103.
11. See, for example, Ill. Ann. Stat. ch. 720, para. 150/5.1; N.M. Stat. Ann. §30–6A–4; Tex. Penal Code Ann. §43.05.
12. See, for example, D.C. Code Ann. §22–2704; Mich. Comp. Laws Ann. §750.13; W. Va. Code §61–2–14.
13. *Prostitution of Children and Child-Sex Tourism*, p. 12.

14. Colo. Rev. Stat. Ann. §18–7–405; Cal. Penal Code §266h; W. Va. Code §61–8–8; Ill. Ann. Stat. ch. 720, para. 5/11–19.1.

15. Colo. Rev. Stat. Ann. §18–7–40.

16. Ill. Ann. Stat. ch. 720, para. 5/11–19.1.

17. Iowa Code Ann. §725.3.

18. *State v. Steer*, 517 A, 2d 797 (N.H. 1986).

19. *People v. Bell*, 201 Cal. App. 3d 1396 (1988).

20. *Prostitution of Children and Child-Sex Tourism*, pp. 13–15. See also Ark. Code Ann. §5–70–104; Fla. Stat. Ann. §796.03; Ky. Rev. Stat. Ann. §529.030; Minn. Stat. Ann. §609.322; Or. Rev. Stat. §167.017.

21. See, for example, Haw. Rev. Stat. §712–1202, 1203; N.J. Stat. Ann. §2C: 34–1; Pa. Stat. Ann. tit. 18 §5902.

22. Or. Rev. Stat. §167.017.

23. See, for example, Kan. Stat. Ann. §21–3513; Oh. Rev. Code Ann. §2907.22.

24. See, for example, Cal. Penal Code §266h; Colo. Rev. Stat. Ann. §18–7–402; N.D. Cent. Code §12.1–29–02.

25. See, for example, Nev. Rev. Stat. §201.360; Or. Rev. Stat. §167.017; S.D. Codified Laws Ann. §22–23–2.

26. L.A. Rev. Stat. Ann. §14:82.1.

27. Mont. Code Ann. §45–5–603.

28. Act of June 25, 1910, ch. 395, 36 Stat. 825; codified as amended, 18 U.S.C. §§2421–2424 (1998).

29. P.L. No. 99–628, §5 (1986).

30. 18 U.S.C. §2423, as amended by Protection of Children from Sexual Predators Act, §103, P.L. No. 105–314, 112 Stat. 2974 (1998).

31. Protection of Children from Sexual Predators Act of 1998, P.L. No. 105-314, 101, 112 Stat. 2974 (1998).

32. Ibid.

33. P.L. No. 105–314, §504, 505, 112 Stat. 2974 (1998).

34. 18 U.S.C. §1962 (1982).

35. Ibid.

36. 987 F. 2d 631 (9th Cir. 1993).

37. *United States v. Richards*, 118 F. 3d 622 (8th Cir. 1997).

38. 976 F. 2d 1252 (9th Cir. 1992).

39. 942 F. 2d 775 (10th Cir. 1991), cert. denied, 502 U.S. 1042 (1992).

40. 18 U.S.C. §2251 et seq.

41. *United States v. Smith*, 795 F. 2d 841 (9th Cir. 1986), cert. denied, 481 U.S. 1032 (1987).

42. P.L. No. 101–647, §323, 104 Stat. 4789, 4818 (1990).

43. 18 U.S.C. §2251 (a), as amended by Protection of Children from Sexual Predators Act, §201.

44. P.L. No. 104–208, §121, 110 stat. 3009, 3009–26 (1996).

45. *United States v. Hilton*, No. 98–513, slip op. at 3 (1st Cir. Jan. 27, 1999).

46. 1997 WL 487758 (N.D. Cal.).

47. 33 F. 3d 78 (D.C.C. 1994), rehearing denied, 47 F. 3d 1215 (1995), cert. denied, 515 U.S. 1158 (1995); *Connection Distributing Co. v. Reno*, 154 F. 3d 281 (6th Cir. 1998).

48. 18 U.S.C. §2423 (b), as amended by Protection of Children from Sexual Predators Act, P.L. No. 105–314, §103, 112 Stat. 2974 (1998).

49. *Prostitution of Children and Child-Sex Tourism*, p. 20. See also *United States v. Moore*, 1998 WL 81287 (9th Cir.); *United States v. Childress*, 104 F. 3d 47 (4th Cir. 1996).

Part V

Runaway Youth and Prostituted Teens in Other Countries

Chapter 16

Runaways and Teenage Prostitution Globally

The problem of runaway and prostituted youth is not only a major concern in the United States but throughout the world. The proliferation of the commercial child sex trade industry internationally has seen an increase in the trafficking of children for purposes of prostitution, pornography, sexual slavery, and other child sexploitation. Child sex tourism has become a lucrative business in many countries as the demand for young bodies to sexually appease foreign tourists grows. Millions of victims—often runaways, throwaways, or street kids—are conned, charmed, coerced, or sold into prostitution and other sexual misuse. "Worldwide, prostituted children are exploited by both local and foreign patrons, trafficked across country borders to satisfy demand in the most popular sex-tourism destinations, and often held in virtual slavery or debt bondage by the brothel owners who purchase them."[1]

Victims of the child sex-for-sale industry are not only robbed of innocence "and any semblance of a normal life . . . but also [put] at greater risk for exposure to crime, criminals, unfamiliar foreign countries and languages, and health problems, including the AIDS virus."[2] The laws with respect to child prostitution can vary dramatically from country to country, making it difficult to have international cooperation in controlling the sexual exploitation of children. The result is a global tragedy that shows little sign of abating.

THE SCOPE OF INTERNATIONAL CHILD PROSTITUTION

Just how many children are involved in the international child sex trade as prostitutes? Estimates are often unreliable as governments may, for their own reasons, underestimate their child sex workers—many of whom are hidden in child brothels, massage parlors, or otherwise from authorities and researchers. Even teen prostitutes plying their trade on the street tend to move about or amongst other street youth and adult streetwalkers, making it difficult to ascertain their actual numbers. Most experts on the worldwide sexual exploitation of children concur that tens of millions are being affected by prostitution and related exploitation. According to the U.S. Department of Justice's publication, *Prostitution of Children and Child-Sex Tourism*:

> Child prostitution has emerged in recent years as a global phenomenon of disquieting proportions. It is found in both developing and developed countries. . . . Despite attempts to counter the situation, it remains daunting and intractable. . . . The sexual exploitation of children has become more insidious because of its transfrontier nature. Children are increasingly sold and trafficked across frontiers—between developing and developed countries, among developing countries, and among developed countries. . . . [All] continents of the globe deserve attention.[3]

Various organizations' and researchers' estimates on the extent of prostituted youth in different countries and continents illustrate its magnitude as a global issue. According to the United Nations Children's Education Fund (UNICEF), in Asia alone there are at least 2 million active persons engaged in the sex-for-sale industry as prostitutes. Half of these are believed to be juveniles.[4] End Child Prostitution, Child Pornography and Trafficking of Children for Sexual Purposes (ECPAT) estimated that there are as many as 800,000 child prostitutes in Thailand, 400,000 in India, and 60,000 in the Philippines.[5] Other sources have estimated that up to 500,000 child prostitutes are being sexually exploited in Brazil,[6] with 200,000 teenagers selling sexual favors on the streets of Canada.[7]

ECPAT has reported an increase in recent years in the number of prostitution involved youth in countries in the former Soviet Bloc.[8] Many such teenage children being prostituted by "foreigners and aid workers, and trafficked to Western European brothels are coming from the Czech Republic, Poland, Romania, and Russia."[9] A high rate of adolescent prostitution has been reported in countries in Western Europe, Latin America, and Africa.[10] The worldwide explosion in the prostitution of children has emerged as "a crucial issue for human rights and women's groups and has recently led to a debate in the European Parliament in Strasbourg."[11]

CHILD SEX TOURISM

A major component of the international commercial sexual exploitation of children is the emergence of the child sex tourism industry. In many countries, the prostituting of children is encouraged through government sponsored "packaged sex tours." Child sex tourism is defined by the United Nations as "tourism organized with the primary purpose of facilitating the effecting of a commercial-sexual relationship with a child."[12] It can also consist of "the opportunistic use of prostituted children in regions while traveling on business or for other purposes."[13]

Child sex tourism is most prominent in countries in Southeast Asia such as Thailand and the Philippines, where multibillion dollar industries exist in the sex trade and exploitation of children. In Thailand, "sex-tour promoters feed the stereotype that Asian [females] are submissive and have a strong desire to please men."[14] The Thai government's role as an "international pimp" is reflected in its reliance on the prostitution of young females to bring in a portion of its yearly revenue.[15]

The success of child sex tourism in Southeast Asia has led other countries around the world to follow suit such as Brazil, Cambodia, Sri Lanka, China, Vietnam, Germany, Italy, South Africa, and the Dominican Republic. In the United States, sex tourism involving teenage prostitutes generates millions of dollars for businesses and pimps in cities such as Los Angeles, New York, and Las Vegas. In its *Country Reports*, ECPAT highlights the global nature of child sex tourism:[16]

- According to a 1995 Human Rights Vigilance of Cambodia survey, more than three in ten of the prostitutes in the country were age thirteen to seventeen.
- In a 1994 *Peking People's Daily*, it was reported that in Sichaun alone more than 10,000 females and children were kidnapped and sold into sexual slavery annually.
- In a recent study by the Chamber of Commerce in Bogotá, Columbia, children involved in prostitution had increased five times during a seven year period.
- In Indonesia, boy prostitutes sold sexual favors primarily to tourists, but also to local pedophiles.
- The rise in child prostitution in the Philippines in the 1970s and 1980s was attributed to the country's deepening poverty, tourism development, and an increase in sex tourism, largely due to the presence of American military bases.
- In Sri Lanka, the sexual exploitation of children is related to the rise in the country's sex tourism industry. An estimated 100,000 children age six to fourteen work in child brothels, with another 5,000 age ten to eighteen prostituted in tourist locations.
- An estimated 100,000 child prostitutes work in sex tourism areas of Taiwan.

- It is estimated that as many as two in ten Vietnam sex workers are under the age of eighteen. An increase in child prostitution in the country is attributed mainly to its development of a sex tourism industry.

CANADA

In Canada, hundreds of thousands of teenagers are being recruited as street sex workers in spite of stiff anti-prostitution laws and law enforcement crackdown nationwide on pimps and johns.[17] According to Canadian officials, the Halifax area of North Preston represents the center of Canada's teen sex trade industry. There, as many as fifty pimps actively recruit young females into selling sexual favors.[18] The vast majority of Canadian girls entering prostitution are habitual runaways from home or foster homes. In a study of Winnipeg runaway prostitutes, 87 percent had run away from home five times or more.[19] Most had been victims of sexual or physical abuse.

The business of pimping in Canada and, as a consequence, the prostituting of Canadian girls is blamed at least in part on the racial inequality for blacks spanning decades, "bad schools and ostracism by the white community."[20] Today in virtually every major Canadian city, "men from North Preston and three black communities adjacent to it own the rights to most corners on the hookers' strolls—and own the mostly white teenage girls working them."[21] In an exposé on girl prostitution and pimps in Canada, the author reported:

> No one knows how many teenage girls have been coerced into a life of prostitution by men from the Halifax area . . . [or] how many thousands of Nova Scotia girls have been pimped throughout Canada and as far away as New York, Los Angeles and even, in one case, Naples, Italy. . . . Dozens of pimps have been jailed; scores of young women have given evidence of torture and confinement in cities across the country. . . . No one knows how many girls have died at the hands of pimps. Until recently, no one seemed to care.[22]

Most of the prostitution involved youth in Canada are substance abusers. In a Toronto study of teenage prostitutes, nearly 90 percent abused alcohol or drugs.[23] Some had alcohol or drug problems before entering the trade. Others were introduced to drugs on the job.

BRAZIL

In Brazil, where prostitution is legal, it is estimated that anywhere from 500,000 to as many as 10 million children are involved in the country's commercial sex trade industry.[24] Hundreds of thousands, perhaps millions, of Brazilian girl and boy prostitutes are runaways, throwaways, or homeless youth who are enticed by the earnings they can make and "access to luxuries and their desire to escape a life that offers few opportunities."[25]

Many of Brazil's juvenile prostitutes are forced into the business due to impoverishment, lack of education, or false promises. Rio investigators have reported "girls as young as nine being rented by destitute parents to neighborhood men. Poverty-stricken northeastern cities . . . are drawing organized sex tours from Europe. Everywhere in Brazil . . . there are reports of children being kidnapped and forced into prostitution or sold to pimps by their parents."[26] An estimated 25,000 girls from poor families in remote Amazon villages and gold mining camps have been lured into prostitution by recruiters promising high paying jobs only to end up as indentured sex slaves forced to prostitute themselves to "work off their 'debt' for their transport, upkeep, food, and malaria medicine."[27]

Because it is not against the law to be a prostitute in Brazil, the authorities are nearly powerless to halt the prostituting of children. Customers can be charged with rape, but only if the prostitute is under the age of fourteen. This is often difficult to prove with children living on the streets, stripped of any attachment to family or other means of identification.

THAILAND

There are nearly 1 million child sex workers in Thailand, one of the world's leading traffickers of girls for prostitution and sexual exploitation.[28] Between 62 and 87 percent of the country's female population are estimated to be active participants in the sex trade industry.[29] Thai girl prostitutes can make relatively high earnings compared to non-prostitute workers. In a study of Thailand prostituted girls, their income was estimated to be twenty-five times higher than that of other professions.[30] Many of these girls become prisoners of indentured sexual servitude, "typically recruited from rural families; the sum given to the parents representing several months' advance salary, with the rest to be remitted after a ten-month or one year term. . . . This form of contract binds the sex worker to her job, the sense of family obligation overwhelming [her] negative feelings about the work itself."[31]

Very young brothel and girl sex workers are often chosen by men in Thailand for sexual favors because of beliefs that they are either free of HIV infection or the cure for the disease. Unfortunately, this is not the case. With weaker immune systems, young girl prostitutes are more vulnerable to contracting AIDS. It is estimated that half the prostituted girls in Thailand are infected with HIV.[32] The following is a tragic example of a typical Thai girl prostitute:

> Armine Sae Li, 14 . . . was spirited away from northern Chiang Rai province at age 12 when child traffickers convinced her parents they would give her a good job in a beach resort restaurant. When she reached Phuket, a center for sex tourism, she was forced into prostitution in conditions of virtual slavery until she was released last December by Thai police. But they arrived too late. Armine has tested HIV positive and will die of AIDS.[33]

INDIA

Child prostitution is rampant in India as girls are the object of trafficking for sexual exploitation and religious prostitution. As many as 400,000 minors are prostitution involved in the country's sex bazaar.[34] Ninety percent of these are indentured sex servants.[35] Of the estimated 100,000 female prostitutes in Bombay, at least 20 percent are believed to be younger than eighteen.[36] Prostituted girls as young as nine "can fetch up to 600,000 rupees, or $2,000, at auctions where Arabs from the Persian Gulf bid against Indian men who believe sleeping with a virgin cures gonorrhea and syphilis."[37]

Indian girl prostitutes have a high rate of sexually transmitted diseases, including AIDS. The Human Rights Watch reported that "India's red-light districts are the primary vector of [the] spread [of] AIDS into the general population."[38] Bombay is seen as the epicenter for the AIDS epidemic in India, with girl prostitutes most susceptible to HIV infection.[39]

Prostitution itself is legal in India; however, the prostituting of children is strictly prohibited. Political and police corruption, along with organized criminals, make it relatively easy for sexual exploiters in India's lucrative child sex trade to circumvent the law and turn children into prostitutes and sex slaves. An investigative report illustrates the horrible, degrading conditions common for many young female Indian prostitutes in sexual bondage:

> Dozens of sari-clad prostitutes sat on wooden benches that overlooked a half-moon shaped interior courtyard. There were twenty-five metal cubicles, each with a pallet. The cubicles, where the girls perform their tricks and otherwise live, were no more than 3 feet by 6. In one of them, decorated with a montage of Hindu elephant gods and movie stars, a prostitute dozed while a toddler scooted across the floor sucking on a used condom.[40]

Some sexual misuse of Indian children occurs through religious prostitution. The most common form is known as *devadasi* and is described as follows:

> *Devadasi* cults are found in Southern India and . . . other parts of the country. . . . They derive customary sanction from oppressive upper-caste temple traditions. Pre-pubertal girls, aged between five and nine years, from poor, low-caste homes, are dedicated by an initiation rite to the deity in the local temple during full moon. After a girl is married to the deity by the *tali* rite, she is branded with a hot iron on both shoulders and her breasts. She is then employed by the temple priest. . . . She is auctioned for her virginity; the deflowering ceremony . . . becomes the privilege of the highest bidder. The market value of a girl falls after she attains puberty, when she is said to have no recourse other than prostitution.[41]

RUSSIA

The dismantling of the Soviet Union has led to the creation of a "new population of impoverished girls and women . . . and is grist for the mill of international organized prostitution."[42] Deregulation and privatization in Russia, along with other countries in the former Soviet bloc, have led to severe social and economic hardships. Tens of thousands of females have been forced into street prostitution in Moscow and other cities as a necessity or a way to better their lives. Others have entered the sex trade as a result of the emergence of organized crime and the trafficking of Russian girls to brothels in Western societies.[43]

Many are trained in licensed striptease schools to become prostitutes before being shipped to countries such as Germany, Sweden, Singapore, and the United States, "where they can earn up to $120 a night for up to a six-month tour of duty, with 15 percent of their earnings going to the school's director."[44] The fact that a high percentage of these "graduates" remain abroad beyond the six months working as prostitutes supports the belief that such schools are nothing more than fronts for "international organized prostitution."[45]

Many young Russian prostitutes are lured abroad with promises of high paying jobs or marriage—ending up instead as indentured sex slaves. For some, the temptations of the foreign sex trade can be overwhelming, given the bleak conditions back home. In a *Time* article titled "The Skin Trade," Margot Hornblower describes the sexual exploitation of Russian females by international interests:

> In the puritanical Middle East, charter flights full of Russian [prostitutes] disembark weekly at Dubai's airport, ply their trade on 14-day visas and head home. . . . Scores of ads for "entertainment services," many boasting "hot new Russians" riddle the Israeli papers. . . . In Tokyo, Russian girls are the latest addition to the menu in

> fancy "hostess" bars. . . . Major Chinese cities now offer blond, blue-eyed Russian "hostesses."[46]

AFRICA

Africa has the highest rate of HIV infection among females in the world. Of particular concern is the transmission of AIDS through prostituted African females, primarily through unprotected sexual relations.[47] Underage females in many depressed and politically unstable African countries are especially at risk for becoming prostitution involved and exposed to the HIV virus. African boys are also prone to being prostituted and sexually exploited by child molesters. The enormity of the problem of juvenile prostitution in Africa was illustrated in a report by ECPAT:

> In Africa many countries are faced with a rising child prostitution problem, partly due to poverty, migration from rural to urban areas, and with the advent of [sex] tourism. The linkage with tourism is exemplified by the situation in Senegal. In Zimbabwe, the problem is related to the sex trade near the border. The Sudan, Kenya, and Libya are all on the list of countries facing the challenge. Algeria has been reported as a place of transit for traffickers. In Mauritania there are reports of foreign paedophiles at work and an increase in boy prostitutes. In Ghana, young girls are tricked into prostitution in the belief they will be housemaids. Visible increases in sexual exploitation are noted in Cote d'Ivoire and Burkina Faso.[48]

Studies conducted in West and East Africa on the relationship between prostitution and the deadly AIDS virus have concluded that intervention through AIDS education and providing condoms to prostitutes can be significant in reducing the rapid spread of AIDS in Africa.[49]

OTHER COUNTRIES AND THE PROSTITUTION OF CHILDREN

Young females and males are being prostituted and sexually exploited in virtually every part of the world. Examples are plentiful. In England, tens of thousands of British runaways and homeless youth in London and other cities work the streets as prostitutes for pimps, drugs, and survival.[50] In Japan, where it is legal for adults to have sex with children over the age of twelve, thousands of school girls are involved in prostitution or "financially supported dating."[51] In the Czech Republic, girls are routinely battered or tortured into becoming sex workers.[52] In the United Arab Emirates and Oman, reports have been made of girls being trafficked in for sexual slavery.[53] It is estimated that in Bangladesh, 5,000 girls starting at the age of ten are prostitution involved in one area of Dacca alone,[54] whereas in Costa Rica children are commonly sold to pedophiles from abroad as part of packaged sex tours.[55] These and similar examples of children used as prostitutes in other countries worldwide illustrate the severity of the problem of child sexual exploitation and the need to address it.

RESPONDING TO THE GLOBAL PROSTITUTION OF GIRLS AND BOYS

Government corruption or indifference, weak or non-uniform laws, inadequate law enforcement, and lack of comprehensive global cooperation in fighting the commercial sexual exploitation of children all contribute to the problem. Various organizations have responded to child prostitution and sexploitation with varying degrees of success. ECPAT was one of the first organizations to seek an end to the prostituting of children. Originating in response to child sexual exploitation in the Asian sex tourism industry, ECPAT now has offices all over the world and maintains an extensive network of connections with social, religious, and women's groups. It has been influential in the passage or strengthening of laws in many countries, including New Zealand, Germany, Australia, and the United States.[56]

One of the most important responses in combating child prostitution was the 1989 United Nations Convention on the Rights of the Child (UNCRC), which condemned the sexual exploitation of children. Under Article 34, signatory nations must work toward preventing the "inducement or coercion of a child to engage in any unlawful sexual activity, the exploitative use of children in prostitution, or other unlawful sexual practices; the exploitative use of children in pornographic performances and materials."[57] The UNCRC has been ratified by 191 countries, including the United States.

In 1996, the first World Congress Against Commercial Sexual Exploitation of Children was held in Stockholm, Sweden, as a means to create strategies and solutions in the fight against child sexploitation. The Congress called upon governments worldwide to end child prostitution and child pornography, increase penalties against sexual exploiters of children, and better assist child victims of prostitution and sexual exploitation.[58]

These and more efforts are needed to continue to respond to the worldwide crisis of runaways, throwaways, homeless and abused kids, and their sexual exploitation through prostitution, pornography, and other sexual offenses.

SUMMARY

Prostituted and sexually exploited children are problems of global proportions. Millions of girl and boy runaways, throwaways, and otherwise vulnerable youth are lured, coerced, sold, and enslaved as prostitutes in countries around the world. The child sex tourism industry is fueling much of the prostituting of children as nations sexually exploit and traffic young victims to spur local economies and generate revenue. Inconsistent and lax laws, political corruption, organized crime, and lack of cooperation between nations are primarily responsible for the proliferation of the international child sex trade. Efforts by ECPAT, UNCRC, and UNICEF are leading the way in the fight against child sex tourism and the commercial sexual misuse and exploitation of children. More effort is needed to combat the problem of worldwide child prostitution and its implications.

NOTES

1. U.S. Department of Justice, Office of Juvenile Justice and Delinquency Prevention, *Prostitution of Children and Child-Sex Tourism: An Analysis of Domestic and International Responses* (Alexandria, Va.: National Center for Missing & Exploited Children, 1999), p. 32.

2. R. Barri Flowers, *The Prostitution of Women and Girls* (Jefferson, N.C.: McFarland, 1998), p. 176.

3. *Prostitution of Children and Child-Sex Tourism*, p. 32.

4. Cited in "Conference Urges Action Ending Child Sexual Exploitation," *Oregonian* (August 29, 1996), p. A3.

5. Cited in Flowers, *The Prostitution of Women and Girls*, p. 177. See also Carol Smolenski, "Sex Tourism and the Sexual Exploitation of Children," *Christian Century* 112 (1995): 1079.

6. Cited in "Legal and Pervasive Prostitution Draws Young Brazilians," *Oregonian* (June 12, 1996), p. A12.

7. Cited in Myrna Kostash, "Surviving the Streets," *Chatelaine* 67 (October 1994): 104.

8. *Prostitution of Children and Child-Sex Tourism*, p. 35.

9. Ibid. See also Helena Karlen and Christina Hagner, *Commercial Sexual Exploitation of Children in Some Eastern European Countries* (Bangkok: End Child Prostitution, Child Pornography and Trafficking of Children for Sexual Purposes, 1996).

10. Flowers, *The Prostitution of Women and Girls*, p. 177; *Prostitution of Children and Child-Sex Tourism*, pp. 33–34; I. Rizzini, "Street Children: An Excluded Generation in Latin America," *Childhood* 3, 2 (1996): 215–34.

11. Marlise Simons, "Child Abuse Growing Trend in Sex Market," *Oregonian* (April 30, 1993), p. A4.

12. Report of the Special Rapporteur on the Sale of Children, Child Prostitution and Child Pornography, United Nations Economic and Social Council, Commission on Human Rights, 1996.

13. *Prostitution of Children and Child-Sex Tourism*, p. 32.

14. Smolenski, "Sex Tourism and the Sexual Exploitation of Children," p. 1080.

15. Alice Leuchtag, "Merchants of Flesh: International Prostitution and the War on Women's Rights," *The Humanist* 55, 2 (1995): 13.

16. "End Child Prostitution, Child Pornography and Trafficking of Children for Sexual Purposes," *Country Reports*, http://www.rb.se/ecpat/country.htm, August 21, 1996.
17. Deborah Jones, "Pimped," *Chatelaine* 67 (November 1994): 109–13.
18. Ibid.
19. Kostash, "Surviving the Streets," p. 104.
20. Jones, "Pimped," p. 110.
21. Ibid.
22. Ibid., pp. 109–10.
23. Cited in Kostash, "Surviving the Streets," p. 104.
24. Cited in "Legal and Persuasive Prostitution Draws Young Brazilians," p. A12.
25. Ibid.
26. Ibid.
27. *The Prostitution of Children and Child-Sex Tourism*, p. 33. See also Dorianne Beyer, "Child Prostitution in Latin America," in U.S. Department of Labor, *Forced Labor: The Prostitution of Children* (Washington, D.C.: International Child Labor Program, 1996).
28. Michael S. Serrill, "Defiling the Children," *Time* 141 (June 21, 1993): 52.
29. Lillian S. Robinson, "Touring Thailand's Sex Industry," *The Nation* 257 (1993): 494.
30. Ibid., p. 495.
31. Ibid., p. 496.
32. Ibid.
33. Serrill, "Defiling the Children," p. 54.
34. Ibid., p. 52.
35. Robert I. Friedman, "India's Shame: Sexual Slavery and Political Corruption Are Leading to an AIDS Catastrophe," *The Nation* 262 (1996): 12.
36. Ibid.
37. Ibid.
38. Ibid.
39. Ibid.
40. Ibid., pp. 14–15.
41. Judith Ennew, Kusum Gopal, Janet Heeran, and Heather Montgomery, *Children and Prostitution: How Can We Measure and Monitor the Commercial Sexual Exploitation of Children?* (New York: UNICEF, 1996), pp. 4–5.
42. Leuchtag, "Merchants of Flesh," p. 16.
43. Karlen and Hagner, *Commercial Sexual Exploitation of Children in Some Eastern European Countries*.
44. Leuchtag, "Merchants of Flesh," p. 16.
45. Ibid.
46. Margot Hornblower, "The Skin Trade," *Time* 141 (June 21, 1993): 45–47.
47. Flowers, *The Prostitution of Women and Girls*, pp. 188–89.
48. As quoted in *Country Reports*.
49. Flowers, *The Prostitution of Women and Girls*, pp. 188–89; Alfred Neequaye, "Prostitution in Accra," in Martin M. Plant, ed., *AIDS, Drugs, and Prostitution* (London: Routledge, 1990), pp. 175–81.

50. Sheron Boyle, *Working Girls and Their Men* (London: Smith Gryphon, 1994), pp. 122–27.

51. Valerie Reitman, "Tokyo's Latest Fad: Teen Prostitution," *Wall Street Journal* (October 2, 1996), p. A8.

52. Hornblower, "The Skin Trade," p. 46.

53. Simons, "Child Abuse Growing Trend in Sex Market," p. A4.

54. Audrey Magee and Philip Sherwell, "For Girls, Few Choices—All Bad: Seamstress, Servant, or Prostitute?" *World Press Review* 43 (1996): 12.

55. *Prostitution of Children and Child-Sex Tourism*, p. 34.

56. Flowers, *The Prostitution of Women and Girls*, pp. 193–94.

57. Smolenski, "Sex Tourism and the Sexual Exploitation of Children," p. 1081; http://www.oneworld.org/child-rights/child_rights.html.

58. Draft Declaration and Agenda for Action, World Congress Against Commercial Sexual Exploitation of Children, Stockholm, Sweden, August 27–31, 1996.

Bibliography

Abarbanel, Stephanie. "Women Who Make a Difference." *Family Circle* 107 (January 11, 1994): 11.

Abel, G. G., Z. V. Becker, J. Cunningham, M. Mittleman, and J. Rouleau. "Multiple Paraphilic Diagnoses among Sex Offenders." *Bulletin of the American Academy of Psychiatry and the Law* 16, 2 (1988): 153–68.

Abramson, Hilary. "Sociologists Try to Reach Young Hustlers." *Sacramento Bee* (September 3, 1984), p. A8.

Adams, G. R., T. Gulotta, and M. A. Clancy. "Homeless Adolescents: A Descriptive Study of Similarities and Differences between Runaways and Throwaways." *Adolescence* 79 (1985): 715–24.

Adler, Freda. *The Incidence of Female Criminology in the Contemporary World.* New York: New York University Press, 1981.

Akers, Ronald L. *Deviant Behavior: A Social Learning Approach.* 3rd ed. Belmont, Calif.: Wadsworth, 1985.

———, Marvin D. Krohn, Lonn Lanza-Kaduce, and Marcia Radosevich. "Social Learning and Deviant Behavior: A Specific Test of a General Theory." In Dean G. Rojek and Gary F. Jensen, eds., *Exploring Delinquency: Causes and Control.* Los Angeles: Roxbury, 1996.

Allen, Donald M. "Young Male Prostitutes: A Psychosocial Study." *Archives of Sexual Behavior* 9 (1980): 399–426.

American Association for Protecting Children, Highlights of Official Child Neglect and Abuse Reporting 1984. Denver: American Humane Association, 1985.

Barry, Kathleen. *The Prostitution of Sexuality.* New York: New York University Press, 1995.

Bartollas, Clemens. *Juvenile Delinquency.* New York: John Wiley & Sons, 1985.

Becker, Howard. *Outsiders, Studies in the Sociology of Deviance.* New York: Macmillan, 1964.

Benjamin, Harry, and R.E.L. Masters. *Prostitution and Morality*. New York: Julian Press, 1964.

Berliner, L., and J. R. Wheeler. "Treating the Effects of Sexual Abuse on Children." *Journal of Interpersonal Violence* 2 (1987): 415–24.

Betchel, J. A. "Statement before the Senate Subcommittee to Investigate Juvenile Delinquency." Washington, D.C., January 14, 1973.

Beyer, Dorianne. "Child Prostitution in Latin America." In U.S. Department of Labor, *Forced Labor: The Prostitution of Children*. Washington, D.C.: International Child Labor Program, 1996.

Bowker, Lee H. *Women, Crime, and the Criminal Justice System*. Lexington, Mass.: Lexington Books, 1978.

Boyle, Sheron. *Working Girls and Their Men*. London: Smith Gryphon, 1994.

Bracey, Dorothy H. *"Baby-Pros": Preliminary Profiles of Juvenile Prostitutes*. New York: John Jay Press, 1979.

Brannigan, A., and Erin Gibbs Van Brunschott. "Youthful Prostitution and Child Sexual Trauma." *International Journal of Law and Psychiatry* 20 (1997): 344.

Braun, B. G. "The Transgenerational Incidence of Dissociation and Multiple Personality Disorder: A Preliminary Report." In R. P. Kluft, ed., *Childhood Antecedents of Multiple Personality*. Washington, D.C.: American Psychiatric Press, 1985.

Brennan, Tim. *The Social Psychology of Runaways*. Toronto: Lexington Books, 1978.

Brownmiller, Susan. *Against Our Will: Men, Women and Rape*. New York: Simon & Schuster, 1975.

Burgess, Ann W., and Christine A. Grant. *Children Traumatized in Sex Rings*. Alexandria, Va.: National Center for Missing & Exploited Children, 1988.

Burgess, Robert L., and Ronald L. Akers. "A Differential Association-Reinforcement Theory of Criminal Behavior." *Social Problems* 14 (1966): 128–47.

Burt, Cyril. *The Young Delinquent*. London: University of London Press, 1938.

Butler, D. *Runaway House: A Youth-Run Project*. Washington, D.C.: Government Printing Office, 1974.

Callahan, Bill. "Pimp's 'Boss Hooker' Gets Five Years in Prison." *San Diego Union-Tribune* (July 30, 1998), p. B2.

———. "Prisoners without Chains: For Teen-agers like Peaches, Coming Back Is an Uphill Battle." *San Diego Union-Tribune* (June 21, 1998), p. A19.

Caukins, S., and N. Coombs. "The Psychodynamics of Male Prostitution." *American Journal of Psychotherapy* 30 (1976): 441–51.

Chiasson, M. A., A. R. Lifson, R. L. Stoneburner, W. Ewing, D. Hilderbrandt, and H. W. Jaffe. "HIV-1 Seroprevalence in Male and Female Prostitutes in New York City." Abstracts from the Sixth International Conference on AIDS, Stockholm, Sweden, June 1988.

Child Abuse and Neglect Reporting and Investigation: Policy Guidelines for Decision-Making. Washington, D.C.: American Bar Association, 1987.

"Child Pornography on the Rise Despite Tougher Laws." *Sacramento Union* (April 7, 1984), p. E6.

Commonwealth Fund, The. "First Comprehensive National Health Survey of American Women Finds Them at Significant Risk." News release, New York, July 14, 1993.

"Conference Urges Action Ending Child Sexual Exploitation." *Oregonian* (August 29, 1996), p. A3.

Coombs, N. "Male Prostitution: A Psychosocial View of Behavior." *American Journal of Orthopsychiatry* 44 (1974): 782–89.

"Crack: A Cheap and Deadly Cocaine Is a Spreading Menace." *Time* 127 (June 2, 1986): 18.

Crawford, Lindsay. "Troubled Teens Take to the Streets: Rebellious Youths with Nowhere to Run Away from Their Problems and Their Homes." *Silver Chips Online* (April 13, 2000), pp. 1–18.

Crowley, Maura G. "Female Runaway Behavior and Its Relationship to Prostitution." Master's thesis, Sam Houston State University, Institute of Contemporary Corrections and Behavioral Sciences, 1977.

Dalgaard, Odd S., and Einar Kringlen. "A Norwegian Twin Study of Criminality." *British Journal of Criminology* 16 (1976): 213–33.

Danna, Alfred. "Juvenile Male Prostitution: How Can We Reduce the Problem?" *USA Today* 113 (May 1988): 87.

"Daughter Forced into Prostitution." *Associated Press* (December 5, 1993).

Davis, Kingsley. "The Sociology of Prostitution." *American Sociological Review* 2 (1937): 744–55.

Densen-Gerber, Judianne, and S. F. Hutchinson. "Medical-Legal and Societal Problems Involving Children-Child Prostitution, Child Pornography, and Drug-Related Abuse: Recommended Legislation." In Selwyn M. Smith, ed., *The Maltreatment of Children*. Baltimore: University Park Press, 1978.

Dorfman, Andrea. "The Criminal Mind: Body Chemistry and Nutrition May Lie at the Roots of Crime." *Science Digest* 92 (1984): 44.

Draft Declaration and Agenda for Action. World Congress Against Commercial Sexual Exploitation of Children, Stockholm, Sweden, August 27–31, 1996.

Earls, C., and H. David. "A Psychosocial Study of Male Prostitution." *Archives of Sexual Behavior* 18 (1989): 401–19.

"Enablers, The." *Juvenile Prostitution in Minnesota: The Report of a Research Project*. St. Paul: The Enablers, 1978.

"End Child Prostitution, Child Pornography and Trafficking of Children for Sexual Purposes." *Country Reports*, August 21, 1996. http://www.rb.se/ecpat/country.htm.

English, C. J. "Leaving Home: A Typology of Runaways." *Society* 10 (1973): 22–24.

Ennew, Judith, Kusum Gopal, Janet Heeran, and Heather Montgomery. *Children and Prostitution: How Can We Measure and Monitor the Commercial Sexual Exploitation of Children?* New York: UNICEF, 1996.

Eysench, Hans J. *The Inequality of Man*. San Diego: Edits Publishers, 1973.

Faris, Robert E. *Social Disorganization*. New York: Ronald Press, 1955.

Felsman, J. K. "Abandoned Children: A Reconsideration." *Children Today* (1984): 13–18.

Finkelhor, David. "How Widespread Is Child Sexual Abuse?" In *Perspectives on Child Maltreatment in the Mid '80s*. Washington, D.C.: National Center on Child Abuse and Neglect, 1984.

———. *Sexually Victimized Children*. New York: Free Press, 1979.

Fishbein, Diana H. "Biological Perspectives in Criminology." In Dean G. Rojek and Gary F. Jensen, eds., *Exploring Delinquency: Causes and Control*. Los Angeles: Roxbury, 1996.

Flowers, R. Barri. *The Adolescent Criminal: An Examination of Today's Juvenile Offender*. Jefferson, N.C.: McFarland, 1990.

———. *Children and Criminality: The Child as Victim and Perpetrator*. Westport, Conn.: Greenwood Press, 1986.

———. *Domestic Crimes, Family Violence and Child Abuse: A Study of Contemporary American Society*. Jefferson, N.C.: McFarland, 2000.

———. *Drugs, Alcohol and Criminality in American Society*. Jefferson, N.C.: McFarland, 1999.

———. *Female Crime, Criminals and Cellmates: An Exploration of Female Criminality and Delinquency*. Jefferson, N.C.: McFarland, 1995.

———. *The Prostitution of Women and Girls*. Jefferson, N.C.: McFarland, 1998.

———. *Sex Crimes, Predators, Perpetrators, Prostitutes, and Victims: An Examination of Sexual Criminality and Victimization*. Springfield, Ill.: Charles C. Thomas, 2000.

———. *The Victimization and Exploitation of Women and Children: A Study of Physical, Mental, and Sexual Maltreatment in the United States*. Jefferson, N.C.: McFarland, 1994.

———. *Women and Criminality: The Woman as Victim, Offender, and Practitioner*. Westport, Conn.: Greenwood Press, 1987.

Freeman-Longo, Robert E., and Geral T. Blanchard. *Sexual Abuse in America: Epidemic of the 21st Century*. Brandon, Vt.: Safer Society Press, 1998.

Freud, Sigmund. *New Introductory Lectures in Psychoanalysis*. New York: W. W. Norton, 1933.

Friedman, Robert I. "India's Shame: Sexual Slavery and Political Corruption Are Leading to an AIDS Catastrophe." *The Nation* 262 (1996): 12–15.

Gable, Jenny. "Problems Faced by Homosexual Youth." http://www.lmsa.edu/jgable/lbg/paper.html, 1995.

Gibsonainyette, I., D. I. Templer, R. Brown, and L. Veaco. "Adolescent Female Prostitutes." *Archives of Sexual Behavior* 17, 5 (1988): 431–38.

Giobbe, Evelina. "An Analysis of Individual, Institutional and Cultural Pimping." *Michigan Journal of Gender and Law* 1 (1983): 33–48.

———. "Juvenile Prostitution: Profile of Recruitment." In Ann W. Burgess, ed., *Child Trauma I: Issues and Research*. New York: Garland, 1992.

Goldsmith, Barbara. "Women on the Edge: A Reporter at Large." *New Yorker* 69 (April 26, 1993): 65–66.

Goldstein, J. Paul. *Prostitution and Drugs*. Lexington, Mass.: Lexington Books, 1979.

Goodall, Richard. *The Comfort of Sin: Prostitutes and Prostitution in the 1990s*. Kent, England: Renaissance Books, 1995.

Gray, Diana. "Turning Out: A Study of Teenage Prostitution." Master's thesis, University of Washington, 1971.

Green, Richard. *Sexual Science and the Law*. Cambridge, Mass.: Harvard University Press, 1992.

Griffin, Gil. "Running on Empty: Kids Take to the Streets When They Don't Feel Loved at Home." *San Diego Union-Tribune* (July 26, 1997), pp. E1–E2.

Guio, M., A. Burgess, and R. Kelly. "Child Victimization: Pornography and Prostitution." *Journal of Crime and Justice* 3 (1980): 65–81.

Haberman, Paul W., and Michael M. Baden. *Alcohol, Other Drugs, and Violent Death*. New York: Oxford University Press, 1978.

Haft, Marilyn G. "Hustling for Rights." In Laura Crites, ed., *The Female Offender*. Lexington, Mass.: Lexington Books, 1976.

Hale, Ellen. "Center Studies Causes of Juvenile Prostitution." *Gannet News Service* (May 21, 1981).

Harlan, Sparky, Luanne L. Rodgers, and Brian Slattery. *Male and Female Adolescent Prostitution: Huckleberry House Sexual Minority Youth Services Project*. Washington, D.C.: U.S. Department of Health and Human Services, 1981.

Healy, William, and Augusta F. Bronner. *New Light on Delinquency and Its Treatment*. New Haven, Conn.: Yale University Press, 1936.

Hersch, Patricia. "Coming of Age on City Streets." *Psychology Today* (January 1988): 31–37.

Hildebrand, James A. "Why Runaways Leave Home." *Police Science* 54 (1963): 211–16.

Hirschi, Travis. *Causes of Delinquency*. Berkeley: University of California Press, 1969.

———. "Labeling Theory and Juvenile Delinquency: An Assessment of the Evidence." In W. R. Gove, ed., *The Labeling of Deviance: Evaluating a Perspective*. New York: John Wiley, 1975.

———, and Michael J. Hindelang. "Intelligence and Delinquency: A Revisionist Review." *American Sociological Review* 42 (1977): 571–86.

Homer, Louise. "Criminality Based Resource for Runaway Girls." *Social Casework* 10 (1973): 474.

Honig, Werner. *Operant Behavior: Areas of Research and Application*. New York: Appleton-Century-Crofts, 1966.

Hooton, Ernest A. *Crime and the Man*. Cambridge, Mass.: Harvard University Press, 1939.

Hornblower, Margot. "The Skin Trade." *Time* 141 (June 21, 1993): 45–47.

Hubbell, John G. "Child Prostitution: How It Can Be Stopped." *Reader's Digest* (June 1984): 202, 205.

Hughes, Joe. "Five Arrested in Teen Prostitution Case." *San Diego Union-Tribune* (November 28, 1996), p. B3.

Hutchings, Bernard, and Sarnoff A. Mednick. "Registered Criminality in the Adoptive and Biological Parents of Registered Male Criminal Adoptees." In R. R. Fiene, D. Rosenthal, and H. Brill, eds., *Genetic Research in Psychiatry*. Baltimore: Johns Hopkins University Press, 1975.

Jackson, Norman, Richard O'Toole, and Gilbert Geis. "The Self-Image of the Prostitute." In John H. Gagnon and William Simon, eds., *Sexual Deviance*. New York: Harper & Row, 1967.

James, Jennifer. *Entrance into Juvenile Prostitution*. Washington, D.C.: National Institute of Mental Health, 1980.

———. *Entrance into Juvenile Prostitution: Progress Report, June 1978*. Washington, D.C.: National Institute of Mental Health, 1978.

———. "Motivations for Entrance into Prostitution." In Laura Crites, ed., *The Female Offender*. Lexington, Mass.: Lexington Books, 1976.

———. "Prostitute-Pimp Relationships." *Medical Aspects of Human Sexuality* 7 (1973): 147–63.

———. "Two Domains of Streetwalker Argot." *Anthropological Linguistics* 14 (1972): 174–75.

Janus, M. D., A. McCormack, A. W. Burgess, and C. R. Hartman. *Adolescent Runaways*. Lexington, Mass.: Lexington Books, 1987.

Johnson, Joan J. *Teen Prostitution*. Danbury, Conn.: Franklin Watts, 1992.

Johnson, Ray. "Dealing with Domestic Violence and Teen-age Runaways." *San Diego Union-Tribune* (October 22, 1997), p. B5.

Jones, Deborah. "Pimped." *Chatelaine* 67 (November 1994): 109–13.

Jorgenson, S., H. Thornburg, and J. Williams. "The Experience of Running Away: Perceptions of Adolescents Seeking Help in a Shelter Case Facility." *High School Journal* 12 (1980): 87–96.

Kandel, Minouche. "Whores in Court: Judicial Processing of Prostitutes in the Boston Municipal Court in 1990." *Yale Journal of Law & Feminism* 4 (1992): 329.

Karlen, Helena, and Christina Hagner. *Commercial Sexual Exploitation of Children in Some Eastern European Countries*. Bangkok: End Child Prostitution, Child Pornography and Trafficking of Children for Sexual Purposes, 1996.

Kessler, R. C., R. L. Brown, and C. L. Broman. "Sex Differences in Psychiatric Help-Seeking: Evidence from Four Large-Scale Surveys." *Journal of Health and Social Behavior* 22 (1981): 49–64.

Kostash, Myrna. "Surviving the Streets." *Chatelaine* 67 (October 1994): 103–4.

Kuehl, S. "Legal Remedies for Teen Dating Violence." In Barbara Levy, ed., *Dating Violence: Young Women in Danger*. Seattle: Seal Press, 1998.

Lane, Brian, and Wilfred Gregg. *The Encyclopedia of Serial Killers*. New York: Berkley, 1995.

LeBlanc, Adrian W. "I'm a Shadow." *Seventeen* 52 (March 1993): 216.

"Legal and Pervasive Prostitution Draws Young Brazilians." *Oregonian* (June 12, 1996), p. A12.

Lemert, Edwin M. *Social Pathology*. New York: McGraw-Hill, 1951.

Lester, David. *Serial Killers: The Insatiable Passion*. Philadelphia: The Charles Press, 1995.

Leuchtag, Alice. "Merchants of Flesh: International Prostitution and the War on Women's Rights." *The Humanist* 55, 2 (1995): 13–16.

Levine, R. S., D. Metzendorf, and K. A. Van Boskirk. "Runaway and Throwaway Youth: A Case for Early Intervention with Truants." *Social Work in Education* 8 (1986): 93–106.

Lloyd, Robin. *For Money or Love: Boy Prostitution in America*. New York: Ballantine, 1976.

Loeber, R., and T. Dishion. "Early Predictors of Male Delinquency: A Review." *Psychological Bulletin* 94 (1983): 68–99.

Loken, Gregory A. "Child Prostitution." In U.S. Department of Justice, *Child Por-*

nography and Prostitution: Background and Legal Analysis. Alexandria, Va.: National Center for Missing & Exploited Children, 1987.

Lombroso, Cesare. *Crime, Its Causes and Remedies.* Boston: Little, Brown, 1918.

———, and William Ferrero. *Criminal Man.* Montclair, N.J.: Patterson Smith, 1972.

MacNamara, D. "Male Prostitution in American Cities: A Socioeconomic or Pathological Phenomenon?" *American Journal of Orthopsychiatry* 35 (1965): 204.

Magee, Audrey, and Philip Sherwell. "For Girls, Few Choices—All Bad: Seamstress, Servant, or Prostitute?" *World Press Review* 43 (1996): 12.

Males, Carolyn, and Julie Raskin. "The Children Nobody Wants." *Reader's Digest* (January 1984): 63.

Mayhall, Pamela D., and Katherine E. Norgard. *Child Abuse and Neglect: Sharing Responsibility.* Toronto: John Wiley & Sons, 1983.

McCord, J. "Myths and Realities about Criminal Sanctions." Paper presented at the American Society of Criminology Convention, San Francisco, November 1980.

McCord, William, and Joan McCord. *The Psychopath.* Princeton, N.J.: Van Nostrand, 1964.

McCormack, A., M. D. Janus, and A. W. Burgess. "Runaway Youths and Sexual Victimization: Gender Differences in an Adolescent Runaway Population." *Child Abuse and Neglect* 10 (1986): 387–95.

McCoy, Kathy. "Incest: The Most Painful Family Problem." *Seventeen* 43 (June 1984): 18.

McCurdy, Karen, and Deborah Daro. *Current Trends in Child Abuse Reporting and Fatalities: The Results of the 1992 Annual Fifty State Survey.* Chicago: National Committee for Prevention of Child Abuse, 1993.

McLaughlin, Barry. *Learning and Social Behavior.* New York: Free Press, 1971.

Meddis, Sam. "Teen Prostitution Rising, Study Says." *USA Today* (April 23, 1984), p. 3A.

Mednick, Sarnoff A., W. F. Gabrielli, and Bernard Hutchings. "Genetic Influences in Criminal Convictions: Evidence from an Adoption Cohort." *Science* 234 (1984): 891–94.

Minnesota Attorney General's Office. *The Hofstede Committee Report: Juvenile Prostitution in Minnesota.* http://www.ag.state.mn.us/home/files/news/hofstede.htm, August 23, 2000.

Mithers, Carol L. "Incest: The Crime That's All in the Family." *Mademoiselle* 96 (June 1984): 18.

Modeen, Martha. "Four Years after the Becca Bill Became Law, There Are Troubling Questions about How Well It Is Working." *HeraldNet* (June 27, 1999): 1.

Moran, Susan. "New World Havens of Oldest Profession." *Insight on the News* 9 (1993): 12–16.

Morneau, Robert H., and Robert R. Rockwell. *Sex, Motivation and the Criminal Offender.* Springfield, Ill.: Charles C. Thomas, 1980.

Mrazek, Patricia B. "Definition and Recognition of Child Sexual Abuse: Historical and Cultural Perspectives." In Patricia B. Mrazek and C. Henry Kempe, eds.,

Sexually Abused Children and Their Families. New York: Pergamon Press, 1981.

Neequaye, Alfred. "Prostitution in Accra." In Martin M. Plant, ed., *AIDS, Drugs, and Prostitution*. London: Routledge, 1990.

O'Brien, Shirley. *Child Pornography*. Dubuque, Iowa: Kendall/Hunt, 1983.

Packer, Herbert L. *The Limits of the Criminal Sanction*. Stanford, Calif.: Stanford University Press, 1968.

Peters, Joseph J. "Children Who Are Victims of Sexual Assault and the Psychology of Offenders." *American Journal of Psychotherapy* 30 (1976): 398–421.

Plant, Martin A. "Sex Work, Alcohol, Drugs, and AIDS." In Martin A. Plant, ed., *AIDS, Drugs, and Prostitution*. London: Routledge, 1990.

Pollak, Otto. *The Criminality of Women*. Philadelphia: University of Philadelphia Press, 1950.

Pollock, Joy. "Early Theories of Female Criminality." In Lee H. Bowker, ed., *Women, Crime, and the Criminal Justice System*. Lexington, Mass.: Lexington Books, 1978.

Powers, J. L., B. Jaklitsch, and J. Eckenrode. "Behavioral Indicators of Maltreatment among Runaway and Homeless Youth." Paper presented at the National Symposium on Child Victimization, Anaheim, Calif., April 1988.

Quay, Herbert C. "Crime Causation: Psychological Theories." In S. H. Kadish, ed., *Encyclopedia of Crime and Justice*. Vol. 1. New York: Free Press, 1983.

———. "Patterns of Delinquent Behavior." In Herbert C. Quay, ed., *Handbook of Juvenile Delinquency*. New York: Wiley-Interscience, 1987.

Rader, Dotson. "I Want to Die So I Won't Hurt No More." *Parade Magazine* (August 18, 1985): 4–6.

" 'Rat Pack' Youth: Teenage Rebels in Suburbia." *U.S. News & World Report* (March 11, 1985): 51.

Rausch, Sharla. "Court Processing versus Diversion of Status Offenders: A Test of Deterrence and Labeling Theories." In Dean G. Rojek and Gary F. Jensen, eds., *Exploring Delinquency: Causes and Control*. Los Angeles: Roxbury, 1996.

Reckless, Walter C. *The Crime Problem*. 5th ed. Santa Monica, Calif.: Goodyear, 1973.

———, Simon Dinitz, and Ellen Murray. "Self-Concept as an Insulator against Delinquency." In James E. Teele, ed., *Juvenile Delinquency: A Reader*. Itasca, Ill.: Peacock, 1970.

Reitman. Valerie. "Tokyo's Latest Fad: Teen Prostitution." *Wall Street Journal* (October 2, 1996), p. A8.

Report of the Special Rapporteur on the Sale of Children, Child Prostitution and Child Pornography. United Nations Economic and Social Council. Commission on Human Rights, 1996.

Rizzini, I. "Street Children: An Excluded Generation in Latin America." *Childhood* 3, 2 (1996): 215–34.

Robins, Lee W. *Deviant Children Grown Up*. Baltimore: Williams and Wilkins, 1966.

Robinson, Lillian S. "Touring Thailand's Sex Industry." *The Nation* 257 (1993): 494–96.

Rooney, Rita. "Children for Sale: Pornography's Dark New World." *Reader's Digest* (July 1983): 53–55.

Rosenbleet, Charles, and Barbara J. Pariente. "The Prostitution of the Criminal Law." *American Criminal Law Review* 11 (1973): 373.

Rother, Caitlin. "7 More Youths Flee from County Children's Centre." *San Diego Union-Tribune* (February 18, 1998), p. B1.

" 'Runaways,' 'Throwaways,' 'Bag Kids'—An Army of Drifter Teens." *U.S. News & World Report* (March 11, 1985): 53.

Russell, Diana E. *Intrafamilial Child Sexual Abuse: A San Francisco Survey*. Berkeley, Calif.: Wright Institute, 1983.

———. *Intra-family Child Sexual Abuse: Final Report to the National Center on Child Abuse and Neglect*. Washington, D.C.: U.S. Department of Health and Human Services, 1983.

Sarafino, E. P. "An Estimate of the Nationwide Incidence of Sexual Offenses against Children." *Child Welfare* 58, 2 (1979): 127–34.

Satchel, Michael. "Kids for Sale: A Shocking Report on Child Prostitution across America." *Parade Magazine* (July 20, 1986): 4.

Schiraldi, Vincent, and Jason Zeidenberg. *Runaway Juvenile Crime? The Context of Juvenile Crime Arrests*. Washington, D.C.: Justice Policy Institute, 1998.

Schur, Edwin. *Labeling Deviant Behavior*. New York: Harper & Row, 1972.

Seng, Magnus J. "Child Sexual Abuse and Adolescent Prostitution: A Comparative Analysis." *Adolescence* 24 (1989): 671–73.

Serrill, Michael S. "Defiling the Children." *Time* 141 (June 21, 1993): 52–54.

Sheldon, William H. *Varieties of Temperament*. New York: Harper & Row, 1956.

Shellow, Robert. "Suburban Runaways of the 1960s." *Monographs of the Society for Research in Child Development* 32 (1967): 17.

Silbert, Mimi H. "Delancey Street Study: Prostitution and Sexual Assault." Summary of results. Delancey Street Foundation, San Francisco, 1982, p. 3.

———. *Sexual Assault of Prostitutes: Phase One*. Washington, D.C.: National Institute of Mental Health, 1980.

———, and Ayala M. Pines. "Entrance into Prostitution." *Youth and Society* 13 (1982): 479–80.

———, and Ayala M. Pines. "Occupational Hazards of Street Prostitutes." *Criminal Justice and Behavior* 8 (1981): 397.

Simons, Marlise. "Child Abuse Growing Trend in Sex Market." *Oregonian* (April 30, 1993), p. A4.

Simons, Ronald, and Les B. Whitbeck. "Sexual Abuse as a Precursor to Prostitution and Victimization among Adolescent and Adult Homeless Women." *Journal of Family Issues* 12 (1991): 370–75.

Smith, Peggy, and Marvin Bohnstedt. *Child Victimization Study Highlights*. Sacramento, Calif.: Social Research Center of the American Justice Institute, 1981.

Smolenski, Carol. "Sex Tourism and the Sexual Exploitation of Children." *Christian Century* 112 (1995): 1079–81. http://www.oneworld.org/child-rights/child_rights.html.

Staats, Arthur. *Social Behaviorism*. Homewood, Ill.: Dorsey Press, 1975.

Stieber, Tamara. "The Boys Who Sell Sex to Men in San Francisco." *Sacramento Bee* (March 4, 1984), p. A22.

Stoenner, H. *Child Sexual Abuse Seen Growing in the United States*. Denver: American Humane Association, 1972.

Sullivan, Clyde, Marguerite Q. Grant, and J. Douglas Grant. "The Development of Interpersonal Maturity: Applications to Delinquency." *Psychiatry* 20 (1957): 373–85.

Sutherland, Edwin H. *Criminology*. 4th ed. Philadelphia: Lippincott, 1947.

———. *Principles of Criminology*. Philadelphia: Lippincott, 1939.

Tannahill, Reay. *Sex in History*. New York: Stein and Day, 1980.

Tattersall, Clare. *Drugs, Runaways, and Teen Prostitution*. New York: Rosen, 1999.

Thomas, William I. *Sex and Society: Studies in the Social Psychology of Sex*. Boston: Little, Brown, 1907.

———. *The Unadjusted Girl: With Cases and Standpoint for Behavior Analysis*. New York: Harper & Row, 1923.

Thornton, Kelly. "Girl, 14, Finds Her Life on the Streets Has an Abrupt, Deadly Ending." *San Diego Union-Tribune* (February 5, 1994), p. B2.

Thorsell, B., and L. Klemke. "The Labeling Process: Reinforcement or Deterrent." *Law & Society Review* 6 (1972): 393–403.

Tirelli, U., D. Erranto, and D. Serraino. "HIV-1 Seroprevalence in Male Prostitutes in Northeastern Italy." *Journal of Acquired Immune Deficiency Syndrome* 1 (1988): 414–15.

Tittle, C. "Deterrents or Labeling?" *Social Forces* 53, 3 (1975): 399–410.

Trujillo, Laura. "Escort Services Thriving Industry in Portland Area." *Oregonian* (June 7, 1996), p. B1.

U.S. Department of Health and Human Services. *National Child Abuse and Neglect Data System: Working Paper 2–1991 Summary Data Component*. Washington, D.C.: National Center on Child Abuse and Neglect, 1993.

———. *Research Symposium on Child Sexual Abuse*. Washington, D.C.: National Center on Child Abuse and Neglect, 1988.

U.S. Department of Health and Human Services. Administration on Children, Youth and Families. *Child Maltreatment 1997: Reports from the States to the National Child Abuse and Neglect Data System*. Washington, D.C.: Government Printing Office, 1999.

U.S. Department of Health and Human Services. Family Youth and Services Bureau. "FYSB Update." Silver Springs, Md.: National Clearinghouse on Families & Youth, October 1995.

———. *Youth with Runaway, Throwaway, and Homeless Experiences: Prevalence, Drug Use, and Other At-Risk Behaviors*. Silver Springs, Md.: National Clearinghouse on Families & Youth, October 1995.

U.S. Department of Justice. *Child Abuse and Neglect: A Shared Community Concern*. Washington, D.C.: National Center on Child Abuse and Neglect, 1992.

———. *Child Sex Rings: A Behavioral Analysis, for Criminal Justice Professionals Handling Cases of Child Sexual Exploitation*. Alexandria, Va.: National Center for Missing & Exploited Children, 1992.

U.S. Department of Justice. Federal Bureau of Investigation. *Crime in the United States: Uniform Crime Reports 1998*. Washington, D.C.: Government Printing Office, 1999.

U.S. Department of Justice. Office of Justice Programs. *Juvenile Offenders and Vic-*

tims: 1999 National Report. Washington, D.C.: Office of Juvenile Justice and Delinquency Prevention, 1999.

U.S. Department of Justice. Office of Juvenile Justice and Delinquency Prevention. *Child Molesters: A Behavioral Analysis, for Law Enforcement Officers Investigating Cases of Child Sexual Exploitation*. Alexandria, Va.: National Center for Missing & Exploited Children, 1992.

———. *Juvenile Offenders and Victims: 1999 National Report*. Washington, D.C.: Government Printing Office, 1999.

———. *Law Enforcement Policies and Practices Regarding Missing Children and Homeless Youth: Research Project*. Washington, D.C.: Government Printing Office, 1993.

———. *Missing, Abducted, Runaway, and Thrownaway Children in America, First Report: Numbers and Characteristics, National Incidence Studies*. Washington, D.C.: Government Printing Office, 1990.

———. *Prostitution of Children and Child-Sex Tourism: An Analysis of Domestic and International Responses*. Alexandria, Va.: National Center for Missing & Exploited Children, 1999.

Vanderbilt, Heidi. "Incest: A Chilling Report." *Lear's* (February 1992): 52.

Volkonsky, Anastasia. "Legalizing the 'Profession' Would Sanction the Abuse." *Insight on the News* 11 (1995): 20–21.

Waldorf, Dan, and Sheigla Murphy. "Intravenous Drug Use and Syringe-Sharing Practices of Call Men and Hustlers." In Martin A. Plant, ed., *AIDS, Drugs, and Prostitution*. London: Routledge, 1990.

Warr, E. Mark. "Age, Peers, and Delinquency." In Dean G. Rojek and Gary F. Jensen, eds., *Exploring Delinquency: Causes and Control*. Los Angeles: Roxbury, 1996.

Weinberg, S. Kirson. *Incest Behavior*. New York: Citadel Press, 1966.

Weisberg, D. Kelly. *Children of the Night: A Study of Adolescent Prostitution*. Lexington, Mass.: Lexington Books, 1985.

Whitbeck, Les B., and Ronald L. Simons. "Life on the Streets: The Victimization of Runaway and Homeless Adolescents." *Youth and Society* 22 (1990): 113–19.

Whitcomb, Debra, Edward De Vos, and Barbara E. Smith. *Program to Increase Understanding of Child Sexual Exploitation, Final Report*. Washington, D.C.: Education Development Center, Inc., and ABA Center on Children and the Law, 1998.

Widom, Cathy S., and Joseph B. Kuhns. "Childhood Victimization and Subsequent Risk for Promiscuity, Prostitution and Teenage Pregnancy: A Prospective Study." *American Journal of Public Health* 86 (1996): 1607–11.

———, and M. A. Ames. "Criminal Consequences of Childhood Sexual Victimization." *Child Abuse & Neglect* 18, 4 (1994): 303–18.

Winick, Charles, and Paul M. Kinsie. *The Lively Commerce: Prostitution in the United States*. Chicago: Quadrangle Books, 1971.

Yates, Gary L. et al. "A Risk Profile Comparison of Homeless Youth Involved in Prostitution and Homeless Youth Not Involved." *Adolescent Health* 12 (1991): 547.

Yi, Matthew. "Police Say Sex-Slave Ring Is Broken Up." *Associated Press* (November 14, 1998).

York, Frank, and Robert H. Knight. "Reality Check on Homeless Gay Teens." *Family Policy*. http://www.frc.org/fampol/fp98fcv.htm, 1998.

Zaccaro, John, Jr. "Children of the Night." *Woman's Day* (March 29, 1988): 137–38.

Index

About the Author

R. BARRI FLOWERS is an independent criminologist and crime writer. He is the author of 22 published books, including *Children and Criminality* (Greenwood Press, 1986), *Women and Criminality* (Greenwood Press, 1987), *Minorities and Criminality* (Greenwood Press, 1988), *Demographics and Criminality* (Greenwood Press, 1989), *The Victimization and Exploitation of Women and Children* (1994), and *The Sex Slave Murders* (1995), among others.